Freedom from Advertising

THE HISTORY OF COMMUNICATION

Robert W. McChesney and John C. Nerone, editors

Freedom from Advertising

E. W. Scripps's Chicago Experiment

DUANE C. S. STOLTZFUS

UNIVERSITY OF ILLINOIS PRESS
URBANA AND CHICAGO

© 2007 by Duane C. S. Stoltzfus
All rights reserved
Manufactured in the United States of America
C 5 4 3 2 1
∞ This book is printed on acid-free paper.

Library of Congress Cataloging-in-Publication Data

Stoltzfus, Duane C. S., 1959–
Freedom from advertising : E.W. Scripps's Chicago experiment /
Duane C.S. Stoltzfus.
p. cm. — (The history of communication)
Revision of the author's dissertation (Ph. D.)—Rutgers
University, 2001.
Includes bibliographical references and index.
ISBN-13: 978-0-252-03115-1 (cloth : alk. paper)
ISBN-10: 0-252-03115-6 (cloth : alk. paper)
1. Day book (Chicago, Ill.)
2. Advertising, Newspaper.
3. Journalism—Objectivity.
4. Scripps, E. W. (Edward Willis), 1854–1926.
I. Title. II. Series.
PN4899.C375D398   2007
071 .7311—dc22   2005035177

To Karen, Kate, and Emily, with love

Contents

Acknowledgments

I was on vacation from graduate school, with a stack of books, trolling for a dissertation topic. That's how I happened to reread Ben H. Bagdikian's *The Media Monopoly,* a sobering critique of the emergence of a communications cartel with far-reaching powers to control the flow of news and to shape national political agendas. Bagdikian finds advertisers emboldened as they seek to influence the news in this new media landscape. In a chapter on the economic and political consequences of advertising, Bagdikian laments that a very different approach, "the success of E. W. Scripps with adless papers," had been "relegated to brief mention in books of journalism history." That comment in passing prompted my search for a success story overlooked, which eventually led to the *Day Book,* Scripps's adless paper in Chicago.

William S. Solomon, my dissertation director at Rutgers University, encouraged my pursuit of the subject from the start and provided the best of counsel during both research and writing stages. He has the ability to spot a misplaced modifier and a misshapen chapter with equal ease. I'm also indebted to the other members of my committee, Gerald J. Baldasty, Linda Steiner, and Christopher Vaughan, whose thoughtful criticism and insights improved the work with each succeeding draft.

Thanks must also be extended to staff members at the Chicago Historical Society, the nearby Newberry Library, Rutgers University Libraries, the Toledo-Lucas County Public Library in Ohio, and the University of Illinois at Urbana-Champaign Library. At Ohio University, which houses the E. W. Scripps Correspondence, George W. Bain, Janet M. Carleton, and Karen Jones provided generous support. Given its possession of nearly all issues of the *Day Book* in hard copy form, and solicitude in sharing them, the Center for Research Libraries in Chicago deserves special mention.

As the project evolved from a dissertation into a book manuscript, Goshen College provided additional support through several research grants, issued through the good graces of Dean Anita Stalter's office. One of those grants made possible the assistance of J. Landon Yoder, an undergraduate student with graduate facilities. Two other students deserve mention. Joel Fath lent his considerable photographic skills, as did Brian Schlabach, who assisted with the index.

I also thank Kerry P. Callahan, Richard Martin, and other members of the staff of the University of Illinois Press, as well as their anonymous reviewers, for helping to shape a dissertation into a book.

Versions of this work, especially Chapter 6, were published as articles in *American Journalism* and *The Common Review,* and I'm grateful to editors at both publications, Karla K. Gower and Daniel Born, respectively, for their careful critiques.

My parents, Dale and Doris Stoltzfus, and my parents-in-law, Lon and Kathryn Sherer, deserve special thanks for their child-care support (and faith in my work) when research time was at a premium. My daughters, Kate and Emily, grew up alongside this book and provided a constant reminder that much of the joy in life is to be found in pulling a wagon or pushing a swing, even when the research indoors is most compelling. My wife, Karen, remains my first and best editor.

FREEDOM FROM ADVERTISING

Introduction

Even as he enjoyed the comforts of his Southern California estate in the fall of 1911, surrounded by servants and eucalyptus trees, the publisher E. W. Scripps had his mind on the bold slugger of cities, Chicago. He had dispatched one of his lieutenants to the city to carry out what Scripps regarded as the most important experiment that the press could ever hope to conduct, and one that he believed needed to be executed with utmost secrecy. Rejecting conventional wisdom, Scripps wanted to prove that a newspaper could be profitable without so much as a single column inch of advertising. It was a radical notion, given that advertising had supplanted subscriptions and street sales as the main source of newspaper revenue a decade earlier, and that department stores and other large advertisers appeared to be gaining more influence over newspapers' content with each passing year. The trends troubled Scripps, who had long had an antagonistic relationship with advertisers, even as they had helped to finance the building of his newspaper chain, the largest in the country, and of his estate, one of the grandest. Journalism, Scripps believed, had greedily sold its soul to a commercial devil. In his view, publishers and editors were unwilling to print some of the most important news stories for fear of offending advertisers, and colored much of what they did publish to stay in the good graces of these financial investors. "The whole editorial staff of every modern newspaper," he said, "is little more than an auxiliary of the advertising department."[1] As a result, news was ignored or presented in a dishonest way. Citing an example from his own chain, he said the *Cincinnati Post* had battled that city's political machine but found that when it aggressively exposed corruption, businesses linked with the political powers would withdraw advertising. So the *Post* had been "compelled to a course of persistent compromise" and had "kept its hands off of enough to still enjoy a large amount of advertising."[2] This kind of subservient press acted as a drag on democracy, he said, and it was only by having newspapers become "as independent of the bankers and merchants as most of our newspapers are now independent of the politicians and office holders" that readers would be well served.[3]

In starting an ad-free newspaper in Chicago, called the *Day Book,* Scripps was intent on setting the highest standards for honest and independent reporting. He wanted to create an inexpensive paper that would appeal to the working class in an entertaining way and would at the same time crusade for higher wages, more unions, safer working conditions, and other causes dear to the hearts of the many Americans who aspired to better their lot. To reach its goal, the *Day Book* would not be above catering to what Scripps called a taste for the common—a delectable mix of lowbrow cartoons, boiled-down news briefs, courtroom drama, and sensational crimes. But Scripps was determined to start a publication that would not only entertain, but would also take up the cause of the working class without compromise. The primary obstacle to honest reporting, from his point of view, was advertising. As long as newspapers (or magazines, for that matter) relied on advertising, he reasoned, they would remain beholden to the captains of department stores and other industries whose interests often ran counter to the people they employed, the workers for whom the *Day Book* was intended. Scripps wanted to be able to have a newspaper forcefully campaign for higher wages for store clerks, for example, without fearing that a Marshall Field's could pull its advertising and put the newspaper out of business. For years, Scripps had limited advertising in his other newspapers, decreeing that the "news hole" should never be smaller than the space devoted to advertising and that only relatively small ads should be accepted, the better to exclude department stores. Beginning in 1904, he began earnestly planning for a breed of newspaper that would be fully independent of advertisers and would rely solely on readers for its revenue. In a memorandum that Scripps titled the "Non-Advertising Newspaper Scheme," he said that he first came upon the idea nearly thirty years earlier in learning about the editor Charles A. Dana's unrealized plans to reduce and then eliminate advertising in the *New York Sun*.[4] Scripps envisioned his Chicago newspaper as the beginning of a chain of adless papers, based in large cities across the country—Baltimore, Boston, Chicago, New York, Philadelphia, St. Louis, and Washington topped the list. He also saw himself creating a model for other publishers, large and small. He wanted to prove that an ad-free newspaper could be started with only a modest investment of capital, so that anyone who shared his vision could follow his lead, even if they did not enjoy his level of wealth, and "build up another class of newspapers which would serve the public and the readers alone."[5] The potential for altering the course of journalism, as he envisioned it, was great, if not revolutionary. Scripps entertained the notion that adless journalism might one day supplant commercial journalism altogether, putting out of business those papers that blindly insisted on publishing ads.

A Reformer Leads a Small Staff

The experiment in Chicago depended upon the success of a small staff led by Negley D. Cochran, who was regarded as one of the most reform-minded and crusading editors in the Scripps organization and who was the longtime editor of the *News-Bee* in Toledo, Ohio. Assisting Cochran were a managing editor, a business manager, several reporters, and a corps of young canvassers hired to line up subscribers by going door-to-door in neighborhoods near the office. The reporters included Carl Sandburg, who emerged as a national poet while reporting on politics and social issues for the *Day Book,* and Don MacGregor, a firebrand who left to cover the miners' strikes in Colorado, and the violence that ensued, and later went to Mexico hoping to fight alongside Francisco "Pancho" Villa. To turn a profit—and Scripps was adamant that the ad-free paper would eventually show an annual profit of 15 percent, the standard for all of his papers—Scripps calculated that the *Day Book* needed to attract about 30,000 subscribers. But testing the profitability and effectiveness of an ad-free paper was only part of the experiment in Chicago. Scripps also wanted to try out a small-sized paper as the best vehicle for adless journalism. He reasoned that a reduced tabloid form would make the most economical use of paper— keeping costs low was a priority in any Scripps venture—and that it would appeal to readers, who could easily hold it and turn the pages, even when standing on a crowded train. The *Day Book,* while using no more newsprint than a standard four-page paper, relied on a rebuilt press with a special folder to create a mini-newspaper of thirty-two pages, each page eight and seven-eighths inches long by six and one-eighth inches wide. Cochran referred to the paper as the first true tabloid; in Chicago, at the time, the other dailies were usually about eighteen inches by twenty-four inches.

The business model was fairly simple. Scripps agreed to set aside $30,000 a year for, as he put it, "pure unadulterated public service."[6] He and Cochran both understood that at one level "the whole foundation of this adless newspaper idea is that sufficient profit can be made on white paper to run a newspaper."[7] The *Day Book* was to get by on a modest budget of $2,500 a month, not including the cost of newsprint. It took a pound of paper to produce fifteen copies of the *Day Book*. The cost of newsprint, at the start, was about forty dollars a ton, or two cents a pound; with delivery and related costs added, it came to just about two-and-a-half cents a pound. The *Day Book* was sold to newsboys for fifty cents per hundred, or a half cent for each paper; the newsboys in turn sold the paper for a penny a piece, earning for themselves a half cent per paper. So for every pound of newsprint that yielded fifteen papers, proceeds were divided accordingly: two-and-a-half cents for the white paper; seven-and-a-half cents for the carriers; and five cents for the *Day Book*. When the paper reached a circulation of 30,000, Cochran figured, it would be self-sustaining. That circulation would require 2,000 pounds of paper daily, and a profit of five cents a pound on the paper meant revenue of one hundred dollars per day, or $2,600 a month, based on twenty-six publishing days (there was no paper on Sundays). If the *Day Book* kept to its $2,500 monthly budget, it would become a moneymaker, albeit a modest one.

An Adless Experiment Becomes a Footnote

Did the *Day Book* ever turn a profit? Did it provide a viable ad-free model for other newspapers? Even close readers of journalism history would be hard-pressed to know exactly how the experiment turned out. By and large historians have treated the *Day Book* as little more than a footnote—"relegated to brief mention" is how Ben Bagdikian put it—if they refer to the little paper at all.[8] Frank L. Mott's *American Journalism: A History of Newspapers,* for example, includes numerous citations for Scripps and his newspaper organization.[9] Mott's primary interest, however, is tracing the development of the innovative Scripps newspaper chain, with a smattering of details on E. W. himself, notably his poor health and heavy drinking. Willard G. Bleyer's *Main Currents in the History of American Journalism* does not mention the *Day Book* at all.[10] Other contributors to the core literature on the history of the press, including recent works, do little to fill in the gaps surrounding this adless experiment.[11] Much more attention has been paid to *PM,* a more recent, and, in its own day, better publicized, effort at ad-free publishing. *PM,* a daily based in New York whose fortunes were widely watched in the 1940s, has been the subject of a book and several articles and received significant mention in journalism histories.[12]

Neither publication, as it turned out, proved to be financially sound. With only one profitable month to its run between 1911 and 1917, the *Day Book* certainly did not make a convincing case for its viability as a business. But a comparative analysis of the *Day Book* and competing dailies suggests that its content, rather than its financial troubles and short lifespan, may be the best measure of its contribution to the practice of journalism. The *Day Book* redefined news in Chicago, and it did so in part because of freedom from commercial pressures. In response to Upton Sinclair's questioning in 1919 whether a newspaper existed that would print unfavorable news about a department store, the staff of the *Day Book* could answer that such a newspaper had indeed existed until two years earlier.[13] As an example, they could point to a series of articles in January 1917 in which the *Day Book* used the front page to juxtapose record profits at Marshall Field's with workers' futile demands for year-end bonuses. While the Chicago press raved about the quality of goods for sale at Marshall Field's and other department stores, the *Day Book* focused on the employees who did the unpacking, stacking, sorting, and selling, and urged the stores to worry less about profits and more about raising the standard of living for their employees. The paper also campaigned for safer working and shopping conditions, publishing accounts of accidents that other papers ignored. Regardless of its modest circulation, which peaked at 22,839 in October 1916, well short of the 30,000 goal, the *Day Book* remained a steadfast ally of the working class and the dispossessed, and a primary, and sometimes only, source of news about their struggles. In so doing, the *Day Book* stands as an example of a newspaper that treated readers more as citizens, with rights to be respected and safeguarded, than as consumers, with buying impulses to be stoked.

Rise of Commercial Influence

With advertising dollars forming the financial foundation of the newspaper industry, press historians certainly have some justification for giving any ad-less ventures only a passing mention. U.S. Census data from roughly the same time as the formation of the Scripps newspaper chain show advertising supplanting subscriptions and sales as the primary source of financing for newspapers and other periodicals by 1899 and then surging far ahead, never again to play second fiddle to subscription revenue.[14] In 1879, a year after Scripps and his associates established the *Cleveland Press,* the first paper in what would become the Scripps chain, subscriptions and sales accounted for $49.9 million, or 56 percent of revenue, for the industry; that compared with advertising's contribution of $39 million, or 44 percent. Advertising rapidly gained ground in the 1890s, and by 1899 contributed $95.9 million, or 54.5 percent, outdistancing the $80 million, or 45.5 percent, from subscriptions and sales. By the time Scripps acquired his last newspaper, the *New Mexico State Tribune,* in 1923, the ratio was better than two-to-one in favor of advertising, 68.7 percent to 31.3 percent.

Looking at the period from 1833, with the founding of the *New York Sun,* through the Civil War, William E. Huntzicker traces the evolution of American newspapers from partisan and mercantile journalism to the commercial penny press. The period marked a growing independence of newspapers from political elites, longtime providers of content and financial support. This independence came about in part because papers sent reporters into the field to gather facts and information—and also because local advertising increasingly accompanied local news. "By taking advertising money instead of political subsidies and dependable subscriptions," Huntzicker writes, "penny editors traded subsidies from a few influential readers for large volumes of small ads carrying people's wants and needs."[15] Ads appeared to announce marriages and deaths, promote museums, proffer violin lessons, sell potatoes, or find nurses. And with those ads came a different kind of risk. John C. Nerone has forcefully punctured one of the abiding myths of the press: that advertising came as a liberator, freeing newspapers from servitude to powerful political parties and interests.[16] In so doing, newspapers, as the myth would have it, became "a social instrument of popular democracy"[17]—politically and editorially independent. As Nerone and others note, this myth ignores the well-documented ways in which advertising came to exercise a controlling influence over the press.[18]

Challenging the "Church-State" Wall

The *Day Book* presents an alternative model—if not in business terms, certainly in philosophical ones—for a U.S. press that is more dependent than ever on advertisers. Perhaps the most egregious recent example of commercial influence run amok in the newsroom came during the reign of a California publisher who was no E. W. Scripps. The publisher, Mark H. Willes, will be remembered as something of a corporate cowboy who strode into the newsroom of the *Los Angeles Times* determined to bust down the wall separating news and advertising. Willes pledged to "use a bazooka, if necessary," to remove the wall, which he saw as hindering business growth.[19] A former vice chairman at the cereal maker General Mills, Willes became chief executive of the Times Mirror Company in 1995 and chairman in 1996, responsible for a national media company whose flagship property was the *Times*.[20] The newspaper's economic fortunes had been flagging, and Willes was brought in to ensure profitable returns there, and across the company. His vision for success, however, called for shattering a wall that had long been compared to the divide between church and state, a wall, however porous, that was intended to ensure that business interests would not overly compromise editorial integrity and unduly influence the coverage of news. Under the Willes regime, representatives from news, advertising, marketing, and operations worked in teams to create new sections and devise strategies to increase circulation and profits.[21] Reporters and editors considered ways to sell more ads, even as the advertising staff suggested articles to boost revenues. Willes made no secret of his first order of business: "The fundamental challenge is to be successful on the business side, because that's also the way we're going to be successful on the journalism side."[22] Leo Wolinsky, who was the managing editor, phrased it more bluntly: "Money is always the first thing we talk about. The readers are always the last thing we talk about."[23] The push for innovative partnerships in advertising and news led to a highly unusual venture in which the paper agreed to share the profits of a Sunday magazine issue (October 10, 1999) with the very subject of that issue, a new downtown sports arena. For its part, the arena urged its contractors and patrons to take out ads in the magazine, suggestive of "a kickback scheme."[24] When word of the hidden profit-sharing arrangement leaked out later that month, the news staff revolted, senior editors apologized, and the paper's media critic printed a 30,000–word report on the debacle. Faced with widespread criticism, the publisher of the *Times,* Kathryn M. Downing, promised to take steps to insulate the newsroom from business operations, in effect signaling a retreat from the all-out assault on the wall between news and commerce. Several months later, in an acquisition driven by a desire to create media hubs across the country, the Tribune Company bought the Times Mirror Company, ending the Willes reign. But the effects of advertising on news gathering remain in Los Angeles, and elsewhere, even if they take a more oblique form. Weeks after the *Los Angeles Times* won five Pulitzer Prizes in spring 2004, company executives announced that the newsroom staff would be reduced because of a shortfall in advertising revenue. As one research analyst observed, "Although journalism is important, at the end of the day, investors care more about the number of newspapers you sell and the ad rate increases you get, rather than the number of Pulitzer Prizes."[25]

But the *Los Angeles Times,* even under the reign of Willes, may not have been so much an anomaly as a bellwether, an indicator of the extent of commercial influence. Tom Wicker, a former associate editor of the *New York Times,* speaks for most journalists in his conviction that "absolute separation" should be maintained between news and advertising.[26] Journalists regard this divide as a kind of sacred barrier, and point to times when the public was well served—Wicker recalls how the *New York Times* rose in stature during World War II when, faced with newsprint rationing, the paper chose to cut back on advertising rather than reduce space devoted to news—as evidence of a healthy separation. Such stories too easily feed into a romanticized view of the journalism culture, in the words of an *American Journalism Review* critique, a tendency to "view the newsroom an oasis separate from the messy details of money and business."[27] Scripps's dire warnings made it clear that he found plenty of breaches in the wall during his time, and there are ample indicators, post-Willes, that the news and business sides remain at least as cozy, if not more so. In papers across the country, Sharyn Vane writes in *American Journalism Review,* "what was once verboten now looks to some like good business practice," as the news staff is expected to keep their counterparts in advertising updated on planned news coverage so that sales representatives can pursue clients more effectively.[28] Such teamwork can also make it possible to start new sections—focusing on, for example, real estate, food, or education—or to reinvigorate languishing sections. Ben Bagdikian describes a growing trend to "turn over sections of the 'news' to the advertising department" to produce what amounts to "promotional material under the guise of news."[29] Along with this growing level of "fluff" in support of advertisers, as papers become properties of large media conglomerates, pressures remain to screen out news that would offend advertisers. With newspapers getting 80 percent of their revenue from ads and magazines receiving about half of theirs from ads, Bagdikian says, "nineteenth-century money changers of advertisers have not been invited into the temple, they have been given the deed to the temple."[30] The risks of such cooperation, as Scripps pointed out, also include self-censorship, in which reporters know better than to offend important advertisers who help to make possible paychecks at the end of the week.

Meaning and Measure of News

The *Day Book*'s rejection of advertising is not the only challenge to modern sensibilities. The paper's crusading brand of journalism would appear to run completely afoul of standards of objectivity that largely govern newsrooms. For more than a century, objectivity has reigned as "the supreme deity" for journalists, recognized by its parts: detachment, nonpartisanship, the inverted pyramid style, facticity, and balance.[31] While individual journalists may be less comfortable ascribing "objectivity" to their work (the Society of Professional Journalists' Code of Ethics now favors terms like *truth* and *accuracy* over *objectivity*), "objective journalism" remains a dominant news strategy. But in *Just the Facts: How "Objectivity" Came to Define American Journalism,* David Mindich makes clear how elusive this central tenant is and how early its flaws were visible. In the coverage of lynching in the late 1800s, for example, "objectivity" failed to tell the truth about the evil being visited on African-Americans. As an independent investigator of lynchings in the South, Ida B. Wells, at great risk, revealed the flaws and biased assumptions of the mainstream press. As Mindich notes, "Wells was not 'objective,' but perhaps some journalists ought not be."[32]

Brent Cunningham, the managing editor of *Columbia Journalism Review,* offers more recent examples of how the pursuit of objectivity can turn reporters into stenographers for presidents and other official sources, accepting at face value claims about evidence of an Iraq-al Qaeda connection or the wisdom of a $726 billion tax cut. Writing in *Columbia Journalism Review,* he identifies "a particular failure of the press: allowing the principle of objectivity to make us passive recipients of news, rather than aggressive analyzers and explainers of it."[33] Among his proposals: acknowledge that reporting is more subjective and less detached than is often suggested, and develop the expertise necessary to make sense of competing claims and underlying assumptions. Bryan Keefer, the assistant managing editor of *Columbia Journalism Review's* Campaign Desk, seconded Cunningham's recommendation in an analysis of political spin in the 2004 American presidential campaign: "Striving for fairness and balance does not mean we can't adjudicate the facts. When the truth is knowable, the press should not hesitate to point it out."[34]

Sandburg, the senior reporter on the *Day Book* staff, would have concurred. He repeatedly offered a counterpoint to those who would advocate a passive approach in reporting and to those who would let entertaining chatter and diversionary gossip masquerade as worthy content. He reflected on the meaning of news in an article in 1915 after the Hearst newspapers in Chicago had published accounts of a love affair between a sculptor and an architect, but declined to write about Rose Goodman, who was arrested four times for picketing in front of a garment shop and who suffered a fractured breastbone during one such arrest.[35] Goodman had quit her job, which paid sixteen dollars a week, to join the strikers, whom she described as "girls who don't get enough pay to buy what they want to eat." Sandburg wrote: "It seems to be a Hearst rule that what happens in a bedroom is news and should be published to the wide, wide world. But what goes on in the streets, a contest of significant social forces, isn't news at all and can't get in."

Chapter 1 places the *Day Book* in the context of the Progressive Era, when a crusading spirit flourished in the press and many Americans were engaged in efforts for reforms in business and politics and for improvements in social conditions. As Chapter 2 makes clear, Scripps had long embraced working-class concerns as a newspaper publisher, using his corporate editorial voice to fight for pure food legislation, lower streetcar fares, workers' freedom to organize, higher wages, women's right to vote, and safer factory conditions. This chapter tells of shaping the Scripps chain into a model business organization, focused on untapped markets for the working class. Chapter 3 recounts the years of secretive planning that preceded the *Day Book,* as Scripps sought the best person to supervise the experiment and the best place in which to carry it out. By 1908, Scripps had picked Negley Cochran, one of his Ohio editors, to lead the adless enterprise, and they soon focused on the Chicago market. With publication underway, Scripps and Cochran struggled to find a successful blend of news and features for the newspaper (for a time, they even favored removing virtually all news and treating the *Day Book* as a magazine). This editorial tinkering, as well as the ever-present financial and circulation struggles, including the divergent business strategies favored by Scripps and Cochran, are described in Chapter 4. Chapter 5 documents the paper's coverage of the competing press in Chicago, especially the violent circulation battles that had been ignored by most dailies as well as the labor troubles that shook the city in 1912. The staff of the paper is introduced in Chapter 6, led by Carl Sandburg, who emerged as a national poet while reporting on politics and social issues for the *Day Book*. The *Day Book* also served as a watchdog on State Street, where Marshall Field's and other retailers held sway. The paper, as Chapter 7 details, urged the retailers to worry less about profits and more about raising the standard of living among their employees. The effort to hold stores accountable was also apparent in the thorough reporting of elevator accidents. The *Day Book* was often the only paper to track down the details, which in Cochran's view, confirmed that other papers were suppressing the news so as not to alarm shoppers or alienate advertisers. Chapter 8 presents the *Day Book* as a champion of labor through and through, demonstrated by an unfailing sympathetic coverage of events in Chicago and across the nation. As the coverage of World War I intensified, Chapter 9 recounts, Scripps and Cochran increasingly turned their attention from Chicago to the nation's command central, in Washington, and matters of state security. The Conclusion presents various reasons for the paper's demise, including Cochran's detached style of leadership and the wartime hike in the cost of newsprint. A brief history of the adless newspaper *PM,* including its ironic ties to the *Day Book,* is found in the Epilogue. In the end, though it failed to turn a profit, the *Day Book* succeeded in redefining news and pointing the way toward a more expansive and democratic press. Therein lies its legacy.

ONE

A Time for Dissent and Reform

In January 1912, three months after the *Day Book* first went to press, the Procter and Gamble Company introduced "An Absolutely New Product, A Scientific Discovery Which Will Affect Every Kitchen in America."[1] The product was Crisco, a solid vegetable shortening that Procter and Gamble anticipated would eclipse what were then the standard shortenings in most American kitchens, pork lard and beef tallow. Crisco was made from cottonseed oil, which Procter and Gamble also used in its best-known product, Ivory Soap. In the company's view, Crisco would join its lineup of valuable consumer products and also help to expand control of the cottonseed oil market. To get Crisco on shelves everywhere, Procter and Gamble executed "the most elaborate and expensive marketing campaign ever seen,"[2] sending free samples to grocers across the country and taking out ads in newspapers and magazines. Crisco symbolized, in many respects, the far-reaching changes at the turn of the century both in the national economy and in everyday life, with "science" and "progressive reform" as the watchwords of the emerging consumer culture.[3] For Americans, it was a time to aspire to a better standard of living, with a home filled with labor-saving appliances and packaged goods.[4] In order to supply a mass market with products like Crisco, Procter and Gamble and other corporations relied on mass production. They retooled factories in search of maximum efficiency and a smooth-running operation, ready to work around the clock to make packaged foods, clothing, furniture, automobiles, cigarettes, and household products. The goal of mass production was to have materials "flow through the workplace in a continuous process,"[5] with raw materials at one end and finished products at the other. To complete the process, corporations refined their distribution methods, creating brand names and assembling national sales forces to ensure that what was made would sell.

A New Corporate Order

Stretching from city to city, these factories reflected a new corporate order. By the start of the twentieth century, as Alan Trachtenberg noted, the nation "seemed to belong to its entrepreneurs,"[6] a cast of youthful private corporations. In the 1850s, incorporation began in the railroad industry, and in the decades that followed it spread to other industries, becoming the primary form of business organization. Railroads formed the foundation of the new economy, making it possible to develop steel, iron, and coal.[7] Across industries, a flurry of mergers further shifted the economic landscape, giving rise to ever larger corporations. By 1904, about 300 industrial corporations in the nation controlled more than two-fifths of all manufacturing.[8] In 1909, less than 5 percent of manufacturing firms employed 62 percent of all workers in manufacturing.[9] Trusts dominated in steel, oil, copper, sugar, tobacco, and shipping. Hundreds of railroad lines had been consolidated into six huge systems, four of which were controlled by John Pierpont Morgan. The pattern of corporate domination extended well beyond those industries. A handful of Americans exercised great power, and held great wealth, as they dominated their respective regional markets. In the Midwest, for example, the McCormicks and Deerings controlled the manufacturing of farm machinery. Then there were the meat-packers—the Armours, Cudahys, Morrises, and Swifts. And Marshall Field, the retailer and wholesaler, provided clothing, housewares, and other goods.

The nation's industrial giants required a large labor force, more than a third of the population by the turn of the century, reflecting what Trachtenberg called "a massive movement of rural peoples into factories and cities."[10] But the workers who poured into those factories often found unsafe conditions and low wages, in addition to repetitive and unrelenting tasks. They encountered what many regarded as dehumanizing systems of control, like time clocks, to mark their arrival and departure, and stopwatches, recommended by the management guru Frederick Winslow Taylor, who argued that production steps could be scientifically calculated, with each task assigned an optimal length of time. Workers, including those at Marshall Field's, often could not afford the very products they made or sold: while the per capita gross national product (GNP) had increased by almost 50 percent between 1896 and 1914, the prosperity was spread unevenly. The princes of industry enjoyed electricity, telephones, and indoor plumbing; their workers lived in tenements, dependent on kerosene lamps and water drawn from hydrants.[11] An unskilled worker earned an average of ten dollars a week, making it a stretch to rent a dilapidated two-room apartment with no running water.[12] Still, workers returned each day to the factory floor, back to the conveyor systems and rollers that never tired.

A Surge in Organizing

Businesses steadily strengthened their control of industry and sought lower labor costs. At the same time, machinists, miners, printers, garment workers, and others responded by organizing, seeking not only economic security but also greater independence in their work. Steven J. Diner found that "most workers continually feared unemployment," as heavy demand for products alternated with slack times, and the ever-present risk of an accident that could strike down a family's primary wage earner loomed overhead.[13] Union membership in the American Federation of Labor rose from 447,000 at the end of the 1890s—less than 5 percent of American wage earners—to 2,073,000 in 1904.[14] Most union workers, especially skilled laborers, belonged to the American Federation of Labor, which had formed in 1881 and was an early advocate of the eight–hour day (as opposed to a ten-, twelve-, or fourteen-hour day). Others joined the Industrial Workers of the World, which formed in Chicago in 1905 as a more militant alternative to the AFL. Big Bill Haywood and other leaders of the IWW thought that the American Federation had made too many concessions to the capitalist system. The IWW drew socialists, anarchists, and radical unionists committed to one powerful union of the entire working class, regardless of skills, gender, or race. While the AFL had Chicago's stockyard workers belonging to fifty-six different union groups, the IWW wanted the rank-and-file directly united without separate craft groupings.[15] The primary impetus driving workers, whether they signed up with the AFL or the IWW, was to secure a better standard of living. Two-thirds of male adult workers earned less than $600 a year, a benchmark set by sociologists as the minimum needed to maintain a decent living.[16]

In Chicago, many spent their days working ten to twelve hours in dark, confined sweatshops and then returned to substandard tenement housing in the evening. These workers, many of them immigrants, "did not passively accept their lot,"[17] Jon Bekken observed. They were involved in a wide array of organizations besides unions, including independent mutual aid societies that served as a kind of insurance in the event of illness, unemployment, or death. The surge in association building served to improve social connectedness, as well as economic security. Mutual aid in various forms was a core feature of what the sociologist Robert D. Putnam called "several decades of exceptional social creativity."[18] In the closing decades of the nineteenth century and the start of the twentieth, Putnam found, Americans created and joined "an unprecedented number of voluntary associations," like the Knights of Columbus (1882), Hull-House (1889), United Mine Workers (1890), Sierra Club (1892), 4-H (1901), Rotary (1905), Boy Scouts (1910), and Girl Scouts (1912).[19]

Flocking to the City

Factories and cities were replacing farms and towns as the engines of the economy, and mass-production industries hired tens of thousands of workers, often unskilled. Urban growth was a gradual, if vital, part of the nation's economic development: the total population living in cities increased from 5.1 percent in 1790 to 15.3 percent in 1850, 28.2 percent in 1880, 39.7 percent in 1900, and 51.2 percent in 1920.[20] Urban populations expanded as immigrants swept into the nation, especially from Europe. Four million came in the 1890s and eight million more in the first decade of the twentieth century. The immigration to the United States took place in three waves: during the first two waves, 1815–1860 and 1860–1890, the majority came from northern and western Europe—Britain, Germany, Holland, Ireland, Scandinavia, and Switzerland; during the third wave, from 1890–1914, most immigrants arrived from southern and eastern Europe—Austria-Hungary, Greece, Italy, Romania, Russia, and Turkey.[21]

Chicago benefited from being, as Carl H. Smith said, "in the right place at the right time" as the nineteenth century unfolded.[22] At the southwestern tip of the Great Lakes, Chicago was accessible from the Atlantic Ocean after the Erie Canal opened in 1825 between the Hudson River and Lake Erie; and when the Illinois and Michigan Canal was added in 1848, Chicago enjoyed a link to the Mississippi River. With the entrance of railroads to the city in the 1850s, Chicago became the hub joining manufacturers in the East and growers in the West. In addition to the advantages that came with being a major port and rail nexus, the city was a leading financial center. Workers flocked to Chicago to enter one of the nation's most promising job markets. The population more than tripled from 1880 to 1900, going from 503,298 to 1,698,575, a population second only to that of New York; by 1910, the city's count stood at 2,185,283.[23] At the turn of the century, the population was diverse, with most Chicago residents either having been born in another country or being the children of immigrants, including many Czechs, Germans, Lithuanians, Poles, and Russians. Of the city's residents, 43 percent were immigrants, and an additional 34 percent were born to immigrant parents.[24] By 1919, Bekken noted, 90 percent of the city's wage earners worked for businesses, often large factories, rather than for individuals.

Progressive Banner

To many journalists at the turn of the century, corporate power had overreached.[25] The United States was the foremost industrial power in the world, but that rise to prominence had come with significant costs. The corporations that put Crisco on shelves and Model T's on roadways had also introduced what many journalists, and other Americans, came to see as unacceptably harsh labor conditions. A crusading spirit flourished in the press, reflective of broad efforts around the country for reforms in business and politics and for improvements in social conditions. Journalists and other writers described the plight of Americans who worked long hours for low wages, and under conditions that put many in harm's way; they reported on a rising concentration of businesses across industries; they detailed political corruption in city after city. Writing in the news media of the day, in books, newspapers, and magazines, these reformer-journalists added their voices to the widespread campaigns for change that became known as progressivism. Many diverse and even conflicting groups "marched under the progressive banner"[26] in the period from about 1900 to 1915, which became known as the Progressive Era. They included workers seeking better pay, urban reformers advocating improvements in housing, politicians wanting stricter controls on corporations, women demanding the right to vote, and others who wanted immigrants to shed the ways of their home countries. Demands for a more just society echoed those of earlier periods, but what set the Progressive generation apart was its wide-ranging and pragmatic approach to remedying problems. During the presidencies of Theodore Roosevelt (1901–1909), William Howard Taft (1909–1913), and Woodrow Wilson (1913–1921), reformers were heavily engaged in politics, with practical results to show for their work.[27] Laws were enacted like the Pure Food and Drug Act, the Hepburn Act to regulate railroads, and the Mann-Elkins Act to regulate telephone and telegraph systems. The Federal Trade Commission was created to control the growth of monopolies, and the Federal Reserve system to oversee banking and finance. At the heart of the reform effort was the conviction that the growth and merging of businesses had led to untenable economic monopolies. Aside from corporate controls, the immense personal holdings of the captains of industry pointed to a skewed distribution of wealth. Two New York newspapers, the *World* and the *Tribune,* competed in a search to uncover American millionaires, with the *Tribune* (4,047) besting the *World* (3,045).[28] The so-called robber barons included John D. Rockefeller in oil, Andrew Carnegie in steel, and J. P. Morgan in railroads and finance. Despite overall gains in national income, the reformers said, a handful of Americans plundered the country's resources and grew wealthy, while the majority of workers struggled just to make a living.

For many, the best way to ensure appropriate reforms was to empower people with information. David Paul Nord describes an emerging information function played by the press in the 1890s, with an emphasis on "facts, facts, and more facts."[29] With city life increasingly fragmented, newspapers provided the means for people of all walks of life to construct a shared social reality. The problems of urban life were seen in part as "information problems, problems that could be solved through the scientific gathering, ordering, and application of facts."[30] Journalists and urban reformers shared this confidence that information was power, and that if people were given the necessary facts, they would make good choices and chart the best course.

A Turn to Muckraking

Americans welcomed a new breed of magazine that emerged at the turn of the century, publications with a radical and investigative bent. These muckraking magazines exposed corrupt politicians, uncovered child exploitation, described sordid sweatshop conditions, defended women's right to vote, and revealed companies consumed by greed. Before the turn to muckraking, magazines with mass appeal generally avoided controversy. With the exception of B. O. Flower's more radical *Arena,* they followed a formula that called for entertaining articles and an avoidance of provocative social issues.[31] For the conservative reader, muckraking appeared as a destroyer of magazine standards; critics dismissed the writing as "literature of exposure."[32] President Theodore Roosevelt derisively coined the term "muckraker" to describe those writers whom he regarded as fixated on society's worst aspects. Some blamed the "yellow" journalism of Pulitzer and Hearst for the rise of this advocacy writing; others viewed it as an outgrowth of socialist theory, or a result of Roosevelt's own reform agenda. But whatever lay behind it, muckraking, for millions of Americans, was a welcome alternative to the staid publications of the past. The leading muckraker magazine was *McClure's,* which published articles by some of the foremost crusaders of the day. The issue of January 1903 set the standard, with three long articles that pointed to a widespread disregard for the law: Ida Tarbell's ongoing exposé on Standard Oil, Lincoln Steffens's account of a corrupt administration in Minneapolis, and Ray S. Baker's examination of how unions kept nonunion men from working. With this issue of *McClure's*, Louis Filler noted in his study of the period, the magazine had ushered in "a new, moral, radical type of writing" that "savagely exposed grafting politicians, criminal police, tenement eyesores."[33] The overall intent was not revolution, but rather an effort to rein in the excesses of capitalism and to ensure that democracy flowered.

The muckraking style extended into books as well. One of the most influential works was Upton Sinclair's *The Jungle*, which first appeared serially in a socialist newspaper, *Appeal to Reason*, with a circulation of half a million. Sinclair was twenty-seven when he left his home in New Jersey to spend seven weeks living amid the slums and stockyards of Chicago. The resulting novel was a harsh indictment of conditions in the stockyards, as seen through the eyes of Jurgis Rudkus, a Lithuanian immigrant. The book, published in 1906, portrayed the hardships of factory life, of children who earned five cents an hour and their parents who died young and penniless from backbreaking labor. With its images of rotting meat headed to the canner and workers falling into vats to become part of Durham's Pure Leaf Lard, the book gave Americans cause for alarm and helped to advance the campaign for pure food laws. One of the earliest readers of the book was President Roosevelt, who had told a Senate investigating committee several years earlier that he would rather have eaten his hat than the canned meat the U.S. military served up in Cuba during the Spanish-American War. After looking over his advance copy of the book, Roosevelt wired Sinclair to set up a meeting to discuss the stockyards. The public, the president included, focused on the gruesome details of meat production, which to Sinclair's mind was a secondary theme of the book. Sinclair had wanted foremost to build a case for socialism, envisioning a nation in which wealth and resources would be distributed more equally.[34]

This kind of investigative work was apparent in newspapers across the country; indeed, *McClure's, Everybody's,* and other reform-minded magazines of the period sprang in part from "the cultural soil of a mass newspaper press."[35] A strong cross-fertilization linked newspapers and magazines in the crusade for changes. Some magazine writers, like Steffens and Baker, were former newspaper reporters, and the expansive exposés that ran in magazines were sometimes inspired by earlier articles in newspapers. In cities like New York, Chicago, and San Francisco, William Randolph Hearst sought the support of the working class in his newspapers (and his political races), railing against monopolies in coal and gas and urging higher wages for employees. During coal strikes in 1900 and 1902, for example, Hearst papers harshly attacked mine owners. The newspapers of E. W. Scripps's organization were also published for the working class, though generally in smaller industrial cities where he rarely had to compete with Hearst for readership.[36] The Scripps papers provided sympathetic coverage of workers' demands for higher wages and safer working conditions, as well as the right to collective bargaining and to strike, and urged political reforms that would give voters a stronger voice through initiative, referendum, and recall.

Conditions for Newsworkers

The pressures for improved working conditions extended to the ranks of newspaper employees as well, especially with regard to the treatment of newsboys. In the early part of the century, children played a crucial role in the distribution of afternoon newspapers, fanning out by streetcar stops, department stores, and other heavily trafficked areas to sell papers to workers for the commute home. These newsboys, or newsies, were "the last and most vital link in the business chain."[37] By and large they were part of the working class, sons of laborers, peddlers, and factory hands. They bought papers at a discounted rate from circulation managers and then sold them on the street, although not without risks. As described by one writer in *Everybody's Magazine,* the newsboy is not an employee with protections such a position would bring: "He is a merchant. He buys his papers and then resells them. He occupies the same legal position as Marshall Field & Co. Therefore he does not fall within the scope of the child-labor law."[38] The children, many between the ages of eleven and fifteen, applied their best business acumen in calculating how many papers to buy, knowing that if they had papers left at the end of the day they were stuck with the bill for the unsold extras, and that if they ran short on papers, customers would lose patience.[39] Labor reform groups railed against the risks and meager pay that went with these jobs. The *Day Book* competed with the other Chicago dailies for child workers, both to deliver papers and to sell them on the street, and the papers often raided one another's distribution crews. Negley Cochran complained about losing his newsboys because of financial incentives offered by the *Chicago Daily News* and the *Press* after the Chicago newspaper strike ended in the fall of 1912.[40] Publishers organized baseball leagues, furnished clubhouses, and gave away Thanksgiving turkeys and theater tickets in an effort to build up employee loyalty.[41] The work proved especially hazardous during the circulation wars in Chicago around the time of the *Day Book*'s startup, when newsboys and newsstand operators were forced to buy more papers than they could hope to sell, as in the case of Benjamin Meyer. He had a stand at the corner of Division and Western streets. In May 1913, two drivers for the *Journal* told Meyer that he was going to have to take another ten papers or so every day, whether or not he could sell them. The newsboys called this "eating" papers, a reference to sluggers who dismissed any protests on the part of newsboys wondering what they would do with the extra papers by saying they could just as well "take them home and eat 'em for supper."[42] When Meyer refused to "eat" any extra copies of the *Journal*, the paper stationed two newsboys on either side of his stand to sell the paper. The situation grew tense, and one of the newsboys hit Meyer in the head with a horseshoe, sending Meyer to the hospital for four days. By the time he was released and returned to the stand, the *Journal* had withdrawn its two newsboys and the order for extra copies. But no sooner had Meyer gained a reprieve than Hearst's *American* raised its ante. A driver for the *American,* Martin Cusack, told Meyer that he would have to carry twenty additional copies of the *American* every night. Meyer refused to pay for the extra papers. When Cusack threatened to force Meyer to pay, Meyer threw a horseshoe and hit Cusack on the head, a rare instance, the *Day Book* said, of a newsboy getting the better of a slugger.

Seeking an Independent Press

Reformers also sought changes in the financing of newspapers, especially with regard to advertising. Marion Tuttle Marzolf has described "the quest for an ideal newspaper"[43] that consumed journalists at the turn of the century. Press reformers in this period railed against the growing commercialism of newspapers and magazines, as well as the sensationalism of yellow journalism. An anonymous New York editor, writing in the *Atlantic Monthly* in 1908, described how department stores influenced the editorial policies of at least three daily papers. In one case, a daily with "the utmost expressed deference to labor unions" tilted its coverage in the other direction to ensure steady profits; the paper ended its attacks on traction companies during a subway strike after stores threatened to withdraw advertising.[44]

In one of the most ambitious examinations of the press, Will Irwin, a newspaper reporter and magazine writer, published a fifteen-part series in 1911 in *Collier's* magazine entitled "The American Newspaper: A Study of Journalism in Its Relation to the Public."[45] He argued that democracy depended on a healthy press, but advertising too often corrupted this fourth estate, leading to the suppression of news. In exchange for financing newspapers, Irwin said, advertisers expected several favors in return: "Sometimes a whole change of editorial policy—as when the Pittsburgh newspapers were forced to support a candidate for the bench chosen by the department stores; more often the insertion of personal matter of no news value in itself; most often the suppression of news harmful to himself, his family, or his business associates."[46] Citing an example that would be echoed by Cochran and Sandburg at the *Day Book,* Irwin said that newspapers invariably printed stories about shoplifting without mentioning the name of the store; to keep from worrying customers, newspapers would say only that an item was stolen at "an uptown department store" or "a Fourteenth Street emporium." In a lukewarm tribute to Chicago journalists, Irwin said that some are "fairly free" of advertising control and would even name a store in a shoplifting case.[47] But there remain "ugly spots" in Chicago journalism, notably the failure to link slum conditions to the low wages paid by department stores: "A feeder of the dive and brothel is the cheap department stores." "In this respect," he said, "Chicago is perhaps a little worse than the average." Though an "adless newspaper" might be the best remedy, Irwin held out little hope that readers would be willing to pay the three to five cents per issue that he estimated would be required to finance a paper without ads. In what may have been a nod to E. W. Scripps, who was interviewed by Irwin, he said an editorial genius may yet come up with a plan to make an adless paper pay at one or two cents an issue.

Despite the surge of muckraking in publications like *McClure's,* some reformers thought that the press as a whole would remain too much a product of the political and economic system unless the relationship changed. They wanted newspapers and magazines to achieve real independence from advertisers as well as from political parties, so that the press would be freer to expose wrongdoing and could better carry out its moral responsibility to educate and serve the public. The concept of endowed newspapers was put forward as a viable alternative to a press dependent on advertising. Edward Alsworth Ross, a sociologist at the University of Wisconsin, was a leading advocate of an endowed publication, which he believed would "be a corrective newspaper, giving a wholesome leverage for lifting up the commercial press."[48] In a 1910 article in *Atlantic Monthly,* he said that newspapers too often suppressed important news to protect their profits and their owners' sacred cows. An endowed newspaper, financed by public-spirited individuals and managed by an independent foundation, could print a more honest version of the day's news, he said. Such a newspaper, he wrote, would be "free to ignore the threats of big advertisers or powerful interests, one not to be bought, bullied, or bludgeoned, one that might at any moment blurt out the damning truth about police protection to vice, corporate tax-dodging, the grabbing of water frontage by railroads, or the non-enforcement of the factory laws."[49] The notion of an endowed newspaper had appeared as early as 1890 in an article by W. H. H. Murray in *Arena*.[50] An editorial in *Dial* in 1893, written to catch the attention of philanthropists, argued that a greater good could be accomplished by endowing a newspaper than by underwriting a church, college, or hospital. "We can hardly conceive of a more civilizing influence," the editorial said, than a daily newspaper "dependent for support upon no political organization, no special group of commercial and industrial interests, no popular favor of any kind."[51] Such a newspaper would stand as an alternative to the papers of the days, which catered to "the tastes of the vulgar, and vicious, and unlettered," as publishers became caught up in the "modern scramble for wealth."[52] But an endowed newspaper, by its financial independence, the editorial said, would be in a position to "keep its readers in touch with the best thought of the world" and stand for "honest government and the purity of private morals." While the idea of such a newspaper gained adherents in the decades that followed, it failed to materialize as a serious undertaking beyond, perhaps, university classrooms. Scripps, meanwhile, was developing his own model of an independent press. He too wanted a press free of the influence of advertisers; but the best approach, he believed, would be a publication dependent on a loyal base of readers rather than his own generosity.

TWO

Chain-Builder for the Common People

On the eve of becoming the editor of a new Scripps paper in Houston, Paul C. Edwards visited E. W. Scripps at his Miramar estate, on a windswept mesa about sixteen miles outside of San Diego.[1] Scripps, who was fifty-six, had gone into semiretirement at the remote estate three years earlier, in 1908, but he kept up a regular correspondence with his editors, and from time to time summoned them for tutorials and marching orders. On the first night, following dinner, Scripps grilled Edwards with a spate of questions on the history and workings of Houston. Edwards, twenty-nine, who was about to publish his first issue of the new paper, the *Press,* with a castoff press and two reporters, knew Texas well. He had spent the past three years as managing editor of another Scripps paper, the *Dallas Dispatch,* and had read up on Houston before the visit, anticipating just such an examination. The next morning, Scripps talked for three hours about his philosophy of journalism and the strengths and weaknesses he observed in himself and in those who worked for him. Edwards barely got in more than a few words. The tutorial continued the following morning; at nine o'clock Scripps began talking, and he went on without a break until noon. By this time, Edwards felt reasonably well informed on the organization's state of affairs and business methods. On the third morning, Scripps again sent for him. This time, however, instead of lecturing, Scripps called for his secretary and, with Edwards present, started dictating a letter that began: "My dear Mr. Edwards."[2]

Scripps used the opportunity to convey in the strongest terms his distrust of advertising in the newspaper business. The May 20 letter, a copy of which Edwards took back to Houston, began by informing the young editor that he would enjoy an initial grace period in which he would have latitude to set news policy to his liking and to experiment with journalistic conventions. But the time would come when the paper would increasingly be regarded as an investment property, Scripps said, and the stockholders, Edwards among them, would be tempted to increase its value at the expense of editorial independence. To guard against this, Scripps told Edwards to prevent the advertising business from growing too quickly. He urged him to "so conduct your paper that never at any one time will you be tempted to color in the least possible particular your editorial policy for the purpose of maintaining the patronage of advertisers."[3] It is easier, he continued, to "resist the temptation to do cowardly and crooked work for the purpose of getting a new patron than it is to resist the temptation of doing the same thing for the purpose of maintaining patronage." The right approach from the outset, therefore, would be to regard potential advertisers as "your enemies" and "men of extremely sordid minds" whose only interest is in making money.[4]

Scripps acknowledged in the letter that he wanted all of his papers to be profitable, but he maintained that his overriding purpose was always to develop papers with a growing circulation and a vital role in the community. He advised Edwards to start without soliciting any advertisements, and indeed, not to print any commercial notices at all, even if retailers came calling. Instead, Edwards might run an editor's note informing potential advertisers and other readers that when circulation reached a certain level, the paper would begin accepting ads. Following this course, Scripps wrote, "you would have created a personality for your paper and established all of its principles so that every advertiser whose patronage you should thereafter obtain would come to you with his business well knowing that you were independent and resourceful and that he would have no possible reason for hoping or expecting to influence your editorial course by his patronage."[5] Publish not for advertisers, Scripps exhorted, but for "that class of people and only that class of people from whom you cannot even hope to derive any other income than the one cent a day they pay you for your paper."[6]

Flowering of a California Estate

On his return trip to Texas, Edwards later wrote, he could not help reflecting on the striking incongruities between the advice he had just received and the man from whom he had received it. For while Scripps continually spoke of using his financial and journalism resources to improve the lot of the working class, or "the 95 percent,"[7] as he often called them, he lived on his ranch "like a potentate, master of all he surveyed, seeing only those he wanted to see."[8] On the barren mesa where Miramar began to flower in 1891, Scripps built a house with some forty rooms, planted orchards of lemons, oranges, and grapefruit, as well as seven hundred acres of eucalyptus trees, and constructed dams to catch rainfall and fountains to display his water. As was true in publishing, he sometimes let his contrary nature dictate his estate planning. Having been told that he would never get oranges to grow at Miramar, Scripps used dynamite to carve out a basin and hauled in topsoil suitable for an orange grove. As Edwards recalled it, Scripps lost interest after the first crop, his point having been made. Scripps also served as his own architect, inspired by a North African style that he remembered from a castle he had seen on the Adriatic Sea. Three one-story wings angled out from a paved courtyard. He could climb to the flat roof of a wing, and from there glimpse the Pacific Ocean, inspiring the name Miramar, which he translated as "view of the sea."[9] As Scripps walked the grounds of his year-round home, the only immediate reminder of the masses who struggled for a living was to be found in the corps of servants who toiled for him. He employed large crews of Japanese house servants as well as men who worked the ranch grounds, and he could be heard barking orders across the courtyard.[10] Though Edwards acknowledged feeling somewhat troubled by Scripps's retreat to this baronial estate, he went on to note that "the more I thought upon it the more convinced I became that he was sound and sincere in his principles, that he believed in the rightness of his purpose and that he was, indeed, a friend of the people, a democrat in the true sense of the word."[11]

"A Man of Many Contradictions"

Edwards was not alone in this struggle to reconcile Scripps's life and thought. As Oliver Knight graciously noted in a biographical essay, Scripps was "a complex man of many contradictions" who could "sometimes be read in a number of ways."[12] In some respects, he was truly a champion of the people, a reformer driven by his idealism. Scripps had long embraced working-class concerns as a newspaper publisher, using his corporate editorial voice to fight for pure food legislation, lower streetcar fares, workers' freedom to organize, higher wages, women's right to vote, and safer factory conditions. He wanted to close the divide between the rich and the poor, or, failing that, at least keep the gap from growing any wider. He made this point forcefully in a letter

Scripps standing in the courtyard of Miramar, his ranch in California, probably between 1914 and 1916. (E. W. Scripps Archive, Mahn Center for Archives and Special Collections, Ohio University Libraries)

to two of his senior executives in 1910: "I have only one principle, and that is represented by an effort to make it harder for the rich to grow richer and easier for the poor to keep from growing poorer."[13] By 1911, when he started the *Day Book,* he had succeeded in creating a chain of penny papers that flourished in working-class markets in smaller cities like Cleveland, Cincinnati, Toledo, Spokane, and Tacoma.

Scripps regarded most of the U.S. press as elitist and controlled by business and advertising interests, all of which he railed against as harmful to the common good. He believed that most publishers tried to enrich themselves by running as much advertising as possible, and that in the process they gave up their freedom to publish anything that might run counter to the interests of the advertisers, who were typically large employers and not predisposed to advocating higher wages and other measures that would cut into profits. In order to serve as an effective advocate of the workers, Scripps sought to limit what he saw as this corrupting influence of advertising. Moreover, he thought that the well-being of the nation's democratic system depended on a press that would stand up to the privileged elites, the economically and politically powerful, while advocating on behalf of the majority of Americans.

Drive for Financial Success

But Scripps's decision to publish for the masses—referred to throughout his organization as the 95 percent or the C.P., for the common people—represented more than an effort at staking out a moral high ground. The decision also made sound business sense: there was money to be made among the working class because that circulation market was largely untapped in the smaller industrial cities where Scripps started newspapers.[14] However democratic his vision, Scripps was certainly a shrewd and exacting businessman. In studying Scripps's business practices, Gerald Baldasty found E. W. unwavering in his drive for financial success: "Had the working-class newspaper not been profitable, Scripps would not have been its prophet. He had come to journalism first with a desire to make money."[15] Scripps demanded that every one of his papers hold down expenses and strive for a 15 percent profit. And while Scripps urged higher wages for American workers, he often paid his own nonunion staff members—reporters, editors, and business managers—bottom-barrel salaries. His chain of papers flourished on penny-pinching budgets, and Scripps's personal fortune grew. As Edwards was made keenly aware on his trip to Miramar, Scripps himself was clearly of the ruling class. Scripps's commitment to the common people extended only so far, and that was largely on philosophical grounds. He had little interest in rubbing shoulders with the hoi polloi. This had become vividly clear to Scripps in 1877, at age twenty-four, when he joined his brother George on a visit to Europe. One day E. W. leisurely watched carriages roll up to a grand house on Brook Street in London, and the footmen scurried to help the lords and ladies as they disembarked. At that moment, Scripps recalled, he saw the world starkly divided into "two classes of people, masters and slaves; drivers and driven; employers and employed."[16] And Scripps resolved that he would belong to the master class, and that he would not be subject to the orders of someone who paid him his wages. Beyond the independence that money made possible, there were material comforts, and Scripps wanted them too. Knight said Scripps was "fond of quoting an unnamed author who had said he would die for the common man but not live with him."[17] Indeed, his views of the masses conveyed in private correspondence could be startling. In a letter to a close professor friend in California, Scripps said, "I have an idea that your scientific friends are only lice after all and that like the people of Chicago, they stand more in need of being put out of existence than of being aroused to greater energy."[18] At Miramar, Scripps kept his distance from the common people and nearly everyone else, as he did with consummate effectiveness in later years when he took to sea on his yacht, the "Ohio."

Born into a Publishing Family

From his earliest years, Scripps was aware of the accounts of both stunning financial success and failure in his family's past. Scripps was born on a farm in Schuyler County, Illinois, on June 18, 1854, the youngest of thirteen children. Publishing genes ran in the family. His grandfather William Armiger Scripps was a successful journalist in London, editor of the *True Briton* and publisher of the *Daily Sun*. A cousin, John Locke Scripps, was a founder of the *Chicago Tribune,* and there were other cousins who were involved with local papers in Illinois. But E. W. Scripps's father, James Mogg Scripps, was not cut out for journalistic or publishing success: he had twice failed to succeed as a bookbinder in London. Grandfather William Armiger Scripps purchased a tract of land in Illinois for his son, and it was there that James Mogg Scripps took his family in 1844; by then, he was a widower with six children. During a stopover in Cleveland on the way to Illinois, he married his third wife, Julia Osborn, a schoolteacher, and they would have seven children of their own, with E. W. the last in line. As a child, E. W. Scripps worked on the family farm, but his interests lay elsewhere. His half-sister Ellen Browning Scripps, who was eighteen years older, became his protector and teacher. She introduced him to the books in the family's enviable library, brought from England, and he learned to read before he was five. He was drawn to journalism as a young man and had his sights fixed on becoming a newspaperman. His best chance lay with his brother James E., who had become an owner and editor of the *Detroit Tribune*. Though James was not particularly fond of his strong-willed youngest brother, E. W. talked his way into a job there in 1873. He started as an office boy in the counting room. Later that year a fire consumed the *Tribune* building one night. In collecting the insurance money, James saw an opportunity to start afresh, and to create a different kind of newspaper. He had long dreamed of tapping into an underserved working-class market by publishing a highly condensed inexpensive paper, boiling down stories to their essentials and printing them on small pages. James used the insurance money to start just such a venture, the *Detroit Evening News,* a four-page paper, on pages about eighteen inches long. The paper sold for ten cents a week, compared with the twenty-five or thirty cents that other papers cost, and it soon gained a following among the working class. In the office, expenses were kept to a bare minimum; writing paper, for example, was discarded only after both sides had been used. James's views on journalism and business would have a strong influence on E. W., which became apparent when the younger brother had his own newspapers to manage. Like James, E. W. would demand strict economy in the office and condensed news for the working class, the better to make the paper affordable, the quicker to make it profitable.

A Foot in the Newsroom Door

E. W. Scripps started as a circulation manager at the *News,* and showed his business acumen and sure managerial touch by building up routes in the city and then the country, hiring young boys (he thought the most industrious and dependable were the sons of widows) to be his carriers. The income from the city routes alone eventually reached fifty dollars a week, making him the highest-paid person on staff, and letting him save the additional earnings from the country routes. But he was restless with his sinecure: Scripps wanted above all else to write. James had ridiculed E. W.'s early efforts at writing, which only served to make Scripps more determined. E. W. hung out in the city room of the paper, practiced rewriting items from the competition, and volunteered to run errands for the city editor or to help in any way. By default, E. W. became the early rewrite man because he arrived at the office before everyone else. After about a year, in 1875, the city editor, Michael J. Dee, was promoted to write editorials, and Scripps, at twenty-one, became the city editor, earning fifteen dollars a week, less than a third of what he had earned in circulation. To Scripps, though, it was the moment of his arrival in journalism, and he celebrated by getting drunk, betraying a fondness for alcohol that would in time damage his health. As city editor, Scripps largely gave up writing to manage the staff of three to five reporters. He encouraged crusading journalism, relying on the tools of investigative reporting. The exposés that followed sometimes resulted in libel suits, and it was a sense of vulnerability to a legal onslaught that led James to incorporate the paper as the Detroit Evening News Association, removing personal liability. At the time of the incorporation, in 1877, James E. held thirty of the fifty shares; his brother George had sixteen; Ellen, two; a cousin, John Sweeney, and Scripps, one each. Scripps's single share came about because he had plowed the earnings from his country circulation routes back into the paper. As Oliver Knight pointed out, that share, valued at $1,000, "laid the foundation of his later fortune and the extensive E. W. Scripps newspaper properties," which would be valued at roughly $40 million when he died in 1926.[19] In 1878, he used that share of *News* stock as collateral for a 20 percent stake in the family's new venture in Cleveland, the *Penny Press*. Scripps went to Cleveland as the editor, with John Sweeney as business manager, and their stewardship soon proved a profitable one. The family business continued to expand, and papers were added in St. Louis, and then Cincinnati, giving the Scrippses four newspaper companies. Even as business thrived, James and E. W. clashed as always over management methods and authority. Their battle for leadership took a significant turn in 1887, when James had to give up control of the family business because of illness. E. W. maneuvered his way to become the supreme commander of all four papers, and, in 1888, merged them into the Scripps League, the beginning of the first modern newspaper chain. The two brothers continued to struggle, with E. W. committed to expanding the papers and James wanting them to remain small and reliable payers of dividends. In 1890, the brothers separated for good, with James retaining control of the Detroit and Cleveland papers, and E. W. holding onto the southern papers, in Cincinnati and St. Louis. E. W. folded his two papers into a new organization that he founded with his chief lieutenant, Milton A. McRae, calling it the Scripps–McRae League. Within two years, E. W.'s brother George would shift his allegiance from James to E. W. and add the Cleveland paper to the Scripps–McRae League. The chain grew quickly. In the 1890s alone, papers would be acquired in Kansas City, San Diego, and San Francisco, and others would be started in Akron, Ohio, Kentucky, Los Angeles, and Seattle.

E. W. Scripps as a young newspaper publisher, around the 1880s. (E. W. Scripps Archive, Mahn Center for Archives and Special Collections, Ohio University Libraries)

"Prototype of the Modern Publisher"

In his authoritative study of the Scripps newspaper chain, Baldasty credited Scripps with creating "a modern newspaper organization."[20] While two other newspaper entrepreneurs of the era, William Randolph Hearst and Joseph Pulitzer, were experimenting with news content and entertainment fare, Scripps brought innovation to the news business. Baldasty described Scripps as "the prototype of the modern publisher, concentrating on long-range planning, performance goals, budgets, circulation methods, revenue sources, and a broad range of other business concerns."[21] His efforts were directed at creating a chain of papers that were both centrally managed and economically efficient. To be sure, Scripps was not the first publisher to assemble a chain of newspapers. There were eight chains founded before the Scripps–McRae League, but none were as extensive.[22] Pulitzer, for example, owned two newspapers, but he never developed a centralized business system along the lines of the Scripps concern. And Hearst put together a chain, but only after Scripps did, and it was at least in some measure a product of his political ambitions (starting a Chicago paper, for example, to advance his presidential prospects). For his part, Scripps thought that having newspapers affiliated would allow them to better withstand the rigors of competition and rising prices, by drawing on shared resources like newsprint purchased in bulk. Moreover, all of the newspapers in the chain had access to affordable features and editorials from the Newspaper Enterprise Association, a syndicate started by Scripps, and to foreign and national news from the United Press Associations, Scripps's answer to The Associated Press. And as papers were bought or founded, used type and presses could be handed down to them from the established papers in the chain. When the *Day Book* was preparing to publish, for example, Scripps donated an idled press.

One of the hallmarks of the Scripps chain was cost control, which sometimes meant using old presses that had to be coaxed into service and letting talented staff members move on to better-paying jobs in other newsrooms. When Scripps started the *Star* in Seattle in 1899, Baldasty noted, the paper was limited by executive fiat to the minimal four pages and printed on the thinnest and cheapest of newsprint.[23] The first issue was even delayed by a day because the used press failed to run, not unlike the stubborn press that had Negley Cochran cussing a blue streak in trying to get the first *Day Book* printed. The reporting staff in Seattle consisted of three inexperienced writers who were hired at low pay. And since the newspaper office was situated in a dilapidated building outside the central business district, the editor, E. H. Wells, and the business manager, E. F. Chase, had trouble hiring newsboys to sell the paper. It was a typical Scripps operation, reflecting what Baldasty called "the penny-pinching methods of the *Star's* chief stockholder."[24] Scripps was keenly aware of the advantages to holding down expenses, especially when a newspaper was getting started. For one thing, many new ventures failed, regardless of the publisher, and Scripps wanted to limit his losses; moreover, by preserving as much of his capital as possible, he was in a position to expand into new cities. Scripps was always on guard against what he regarded as a human tendency toward wasteful spending, like outfitting a fancy newsroom, which he thought only distracted employees from their journalistic mission and cut into profits. Most of the offices were in low-rent districts; warehouses were a popular choice (like the harness maker's building in which the *Day Book* set up shop). As part of the effort to hold down expenses, Scripps tried to get by with as few reporters as possible, often just three or four, at a time when rival papers employed three times that number.[25] Salaries for the news staff were comparatively low as well, and Scripps papers at times found their editors and reporters bolting for higher pay elsewhere. On the West Coast at the turn of the century, for example, Scripps wanted editors to work for fifteen or twenty dollars a week when lower-ranking reporters at rival papers were earning that much or more.[26]

Sharing the Cost of News

Scripps was also able to reduce expenses by means of vertical integration. As early as the 1870s, the Scripps family was taking advantage of the cost savings in having common content for its papers, with Ellen Browning Scripps writing short articles for the papers in Detroit and Cleveland. When E. W. Scripps was managing the Scripps League of four papers in the 1880s, he required them to exchange news items, and opened bureaus in New York and Washington to furnish news for all four papers. The effort to share short stories and news features was formalized in 1900 with the Scripps Editorial Alliance; two years later the effort expanded with the formation of the Newspaper Enterprise Association, which specialized in photographs, cartoons, features, and editorials. By eventually spreading the production costs across the chain of two dozen Scripps papers, with the older, more established papers paying at a higher rate on a sliding scale, the savings, especially for fledgling papers, was significant. In 1907, the average cost for a full column of NEA items was about fifty-one cents, compared with the $4.38 that one Scripps paper, the *Cincin-*

nati Post, was spending several years earlier for a column of its own local news. As a rule of thumb, Scripps suggested that NEA content fill at least a fourth to a third of each paper's news hole, though in fact it often accounted for half. The reliance on common content was especially pronounced among newer papers in the chain. Baldasty found that Scripps newspapers generally had "far less local news" than their competitors.[27]

While the NEA was supplying the chain with features and editorials, the United Press Associations was providing national and foreign news. United Press grew out of the Scripps League's New York wire service and other regional wire services that Scripps combined into a national unit in 1907. Cochran notes that of Scripps's accomplishments, the one that Scripps regarded as among his greatest contributions to press freedom and the country was the formation of a national news service to compete with The Associated Press.[28] The old United Press had gone bankrupt in 1897, leaving AP with a powerful monopolistic grip on the collection and distribution of news. Linking his Scripps–McRae Press Association in New York, the Scripps News Association on the West Coast, and the newly purchased Publishers Press Association on the East Coast, Scripps assembled a national rival to the AP. (In 1958, United Press Associations merged with Hearst's International News Service to form United Press International.) Scripps's portrayal of the making of the press association gives the impression of an altruistic public servant: "Perhaps my greatest reason, however, for my objecting to becoming an integral part of the [AP] press association in the crisis was that I knew at least 90 per cent of my fellows in American journalism were capitalists and conservatives. I knew, at that time at least, that unless I came into the field with a news service it would be impossible for the people of the United States to get correct news through the medium of The Associated Press."[29] But in his disquisitions (specifically, "Driftwood" and "Founding of the United Press")[30] Scripps also acknowledges clear economic motivations. He said he knew that it would be profitable for him to start the press service and share content, and that controlling the flow of news would guarantee timely access for all of his papers, which were largely published in the afternoon and could be disadvantaged if AP catered to morning papers, as it sometimes did. Of even more concern, some Scripps papers had been denied AP contracts when they entered markets where the wire service already had clients.[31] Scripps also envisioned UP evolving into a national newspaper, which figured in his journalistic master plan. To top it off, Scripps was by then estranged from his brother James, who was a major player in AP, and E. W. relished the prospect of showing him up with a rival news service.

Secrecy as a Business Method

While E. W. Scripps displayed a competitive streak in bucking The Associated Press, his business instincts led him to avoid competition whenever possible. In establishing a daily, Scripps sought to limit any attention given the new venture. Baldasty describes the "cloak-and-dagger secrecy" surrounding a new Scripps paper in Portland, Oregon, in 1906.[32] Only three employees were involved in the planning, and they used a code name, Columbia, in discussing the undertaking. The press and Linotype for the new venture were stored in another city until just before they were needed, the better to keep the focus away from Portland. Meanwhile, closeted away in Seattle, the editor and business manager for the new paper were kept in the dark about where they were being assigned until minutes before they left for Portland. Such stealth was typical of the Scripps approach. Eight months before starting the *Day Book,* Scripps wrote to Cochran at the *News-Bee* in Ohio and urged him to secrecy: "I think you will agree that as a matter of policy it will be better that no one else but you and I should have any knowledge of anything we are doing."[33] Scripps saw his newspapers serving largely untapped markets for the working class, part of what Baldasty calls the chain's strategy of market segmentation.[34] Scripps reasoned that if others knew of the money to be made in such markets in smaller cities, they would try to beat him to it, perhaps by shifting an established paper into the working-class neighborhoods and offering price discounts (Scripps papers generally sold for a penny a piece, while others sold for two to five cents), premiums for new readers, and special content. That in turn would force Scripps to invest more time and money to sign up readers, and might delay profitability. Scripps thought secrecy would give him time to stake out the territory first and thereby avoid any costly battles for circulation and advertising. He emphasized that his staff should look for new readers as opposed to raiding subscribers from existing papers, which would invite retaliation. The same cautionary word applied to advertisers. Scripps papers were explicitly directed not to lure advertisers from the competition. In several cities, including Dallas, Denver, and San Francisco, Scripps papers declined to take any advertising at all until a circulation base of 2,000 had been established; with other startups, advertising was accepted immediately, but little effort was expended in soliciting it. And once advertising was welcomed, business managers were under orders to seek out smaller merchants, especially those who were not already running ads elsewhere, and to steer away from department stores. While Scripps certainly regarded the big stores as a threat to editorial control, he also knew that they were among the most lucrative advertisers and that rival publishers would not look kindly on losing their patronage.

Though historians are often inclined to highlight the public service ideals of the Scripps organization, as Baldasty and Myron Jordan point out, Scripps would sometimes stoop to questionable measures in his effort to corner a market.[35] Scripps papers entered into joint ventures with their competitors, reaching agreements to set uniform advertising and subscription rates; at times, these agreements even specified publication size and exclusive zones of delivery that divided the market into segments.[36] As of 1900, all of the Scripps dailies had some kind of a "combination," the term used for these joint ventures. These secret antitrust activities were subject to the Sherman Act, under which such anti-competitive action was a misdemeanor, but the newspaper executives making these decisions apparently paid no attention to the antitrust law and paid no price for their misdeeds.[37] These somewhat shadowy arrangements bear striking similarities to contemporary joint operating agreements between competing newspapers, partnerships that are now federally sanctioned; the first of these agreements began in Albuquerque, New Mexico, in 1933 and involved a Scripps paper. After the courts in the 1960s found the cozy arrangements of fixing prices and sharing profits to be illegal, the newspaper industry lobbied in Washington, pushing for the passage of a special exemption from the antitrust law, in a bill called the Newspaper Preservation Act. The Nixon administration initially opposed the bill as harmful to the public interest, but then reversed itself in 1969. (Richard Nixon's endorsement of the Newspaper Preservation Act ensured crucial support from the press, including the Scripps–Howard papers, in his 1972 campaign for re-election.[38]) In 1970, Congress passed an antitrust exemption, allowing separately owned papers in the same market to share business costs and operations while keeping their newsrooms separate.

Keeping Advertisers in Check

Scripps's efforts to strike business deals with competitors around the turn of the century meant lower costs and better odds for profitability, and the arrangements paid other dividends as well. A newspaper with lower production costs had less need for advertising revenue, of no small matter to Scripps. Baldasty has pointed out that Scripps's concerns about the role of advertising grew more pronounced in the 1890s, when he "became convinced that advertising had become the proverbial tail wagging the dog."[39] Scripps was especially wary of big advertisers, like the department store Bon Marche in

Seattle. In 1903, Bon Marche withdrew its advertising from Scripps's *Star* after the newspaper refused to allow the store to censor articles that cast it in a bad light. Scripps congratulated the *Star's* business manager for standing firm against retail encroachment, though the business manager regretted the turn of events and felt consolation was more in order. For the industry as a whole, and business managers in particular, advertisers were deserving of special treatment; the percentage of revenue from advertising had risen from half in 1880 to 64 percent in 1910, eclipsing circulation income. But Scripps believed that advertisers would make more and more demands for control, such as advertisements disguised as news articles and the outright suppression of important stories. The result would be news content shaped to please a minority, big business, rather than a majority, the working class, which irked Scripps to no end. The press would become a timid purveyor of news, in his view, little more than a propaganda tool of the elites. "Advertising galled him so much that his dislike was almost obsessive,"[40] according to Knight. Scripps told Lemuel T. Atwood, the treasurer of the Scripps organization, that he wanted newspapers that were "the servant of the common people and not of the money class and especially not of the advertising public."[41]

Scripps took several steps to limit the influence of advertisers, including a commitment to small newspapers. The standard size for a Scripps paper was four pages. His reasoning was that smaller papers would have lower production costs and would be able to pay the bills, for the most part, with circulation revenue. Larger papers (and some Scripps papers did grow to eight pages) required more money for news content, printing, and paper. Scripps also limited the amount of space that could be devoted to advertising. The general rule was that advertising should not fill more than half of a newspaper's space, and that 40 percent would be better than 50 percent.[42] The size of individual advertisements was also limited: forty inches in Pueblo, New Mexico; twenty inches in Denver; and twenty inches in Terre Haute, Indiana. Baldasty noted that limiting the number of pages and the size of ads effectively excluded advertising by department stores.[43] Scripps wanted to keep department stores at bay not only to prevent their having an influence over content, but also to avoid hidden costs. Because of their high-volume advertising, stores often sought special rates, lower than that paid by small businesses. And the department stores frequently wanted daily changes in their display ads, which added to composition costs. When the editor of the *Tacoma Times,* E. H. Wells, wanted to buy a new press to accommodate the demand for more advertising space, Atwood, as company treasurer, told him that smaller was better. Atwood said that a four-page paper would actually be more profitable than an eight-page one because of the additional costs for paper, personnel, and a new press.[44] To further limit the influence of advertisers, Scripps sought to distance the operations of the newsroom from business managers and publishers.[45] The Scripps editor, rather than the business manager, oversaw the composing room and the final handling of every line of type that was published, whether news or advertising. The editor held the final say over whether to accept or reject an advertisement.

After being deeply involved in developing Miramar in the 1890s, Scripps returned to a more active management of the organization around 1900 and became angry at the growth of advertising that had occurred in his relative absence. He had yet another reason for holding advertisers as suspect. At the turn of the past century, many of the leading advertisers were patent medicine makers who promoted products like Pape's Cold Compound and Lydia Pinkham's Vegetable Compound. Patent medicines, promising benefits like a cure for gonorrhea or relief from constipation, represented the largest source of national advertising. Some of the medicines were harmless at best, but others contained sizable doses of morphine or alcohol laced with herbs. Newspapers and magazines received handsome payments to run such ads. But in 1900, Scripps ordered a reduction in department store advertising and banned the lucrative patent-medicine advertising, becoming the first newspaper publisher to do so.[46] In a letter to one of his top executives, Robert F. Paine, on January 19, 1900, Scripps complained that advertising had grown far too powerful and corrupting, and that he was committed to "cure this evil."[47] To Scripps, patent medicine represented "dirty advertising,"[48] and he specifically railed against medicines that were billed as cures for venereal disease. Three years later, he appointed Paine to censor all national advertising copy before it appeared in Scripps papers. It is estimated that his organization lost $500,000 in potential revenue in one year because of that censorship.[49]

But clearly Scripps was not wholly opposed to advertising, as long as it was on his terms. Revenue from advertisers was essential in building the Scripps newspaper empire, and advertising played a more prominent role in the papers started or bought after 1906, many of which had more than four pages. And Scripps indirectly encouraged a reliance on some advertising by demanding that his papers return a profit of 15 percent. Years after editing the *Day Book,* Negley Cochran observed, "Scripps believed in advertising as a good thing, in its place."[50] For example, Cochran said, Scripps appreciated the role of advertising in stimulating trade and creating more jobs, and even in fostering a desire in people to better their lives in material ways. What he would not brook was having advertisers shape the coverage of news and

E. W. Scripps, who wore a velvet skullcap to keep from catching colds, reading a newspaper on board a leased yacht while cruising off Florida, around 1918. (E. W. Scripps Archive, Mahn Center for Archives and Special Collections, Ohio University Libraries)

newspaper policy. In laying out his principles on journalism in 1910, Scripps wrote: "A newspaper fairly and honestly conducted in the interest of the great masses of the public must at all times antagonize the selfish interests of that very class which furnishes the larger part of a newspaper's income, and occasionally so antagonize this class as to cause it not only to cease patronage, to a greater or lesser extent, but to make actually offensive warfare against the newspaper."[51]

THREE

The Secret Plan Takes Shape

For Scripps, journalism in its purest form came without advertising. The challenge was finding a way to eliminate ads and still publish a profitable paper. Over the years, in letters and in conversations, he nurtured his dream of publishing such a paper, and to do so with an investment of capital so small that others who shared his vision could follow his lead, regardless of their financial means. Such a newspaper, he believed, would be as free as it was possible to be in publishing the news. Not only did Scripps envision such a newspaper as the beginning of his own chain of adless papers, based in large cities across the country—Baltimore, Boston, Chicago, New York, Philadelphia, St. Louis, and Washington were at the top of his list—but he regarded it as creating a mold. Other publishers could start similar ventures with relatively modest financing, "to build up another class of newspapers which would serve the public and the readers alone."[1] The potential for altering the course of journalism, as he envisioned it, was revolutionary. Scripps entertained the notion that adless journalism might one day supplant commercial journalism altogether, putting out of business those papers that insisted on publishing ads. Even if his efforts on behalf of adless journalism fell short of that mark, at the least, Scripps reasoned, he could provide an alternative kind of newspaper for the discriminating reader in many cities.

In a 1904 memorandum that Scripps titled the "Non-Advertising Newspaper Scheme," he said that he first came upon the idea of adless journalism nearly thirty years earlier in hearing or reading—he could not remember which—about the editor Charles A. Dana and his unrealized plans to reduce and then eliminate advertising in the *New York Sun*.[2] Like Scripps, Dana was committed to separating the news and business operations of a newspaper, and to finding an audience among the working class. When Dana was serving his apprenticeship in journalism in the early 1850s, working as a deputy to Horace Greeley, editor of the influential *New York Tribune,* Dana "pioneered in journalism's move to delineate between news and advertisements."[3] At the time, the *Tribune* received most of its revenue from advertisements rather than subscriptions, and like its competitors, routinely larded its news columns with items discreetly intended to promote its advertisers. Dana introduced a policy in 1852 that banned such "puffs and announcements" from news pages unless they were clearly marked as advertisements.[4] When Dana took over as editor of the *Chicago Republican* in 1865, one of his first actions was to eliminate ads on page one and to serve notice that the editorial and news pages were not for sale.[5] When he purchased the *Sun* in 1868, Dana continued his campaign for separating advertisements from news and editorial material. In his first editorial in the *Sun,* Dana pledged that the newspaper would be independent of political parties as well and would present news in a lively and economical manner. The approach found a receptive audience among the working class, as the *Sun* doubled its fifty-thousand circulation within three years. The *Sun* also benefited by selling a four-page paper for two cents, compared with most of its rivals, which sold eight-page papers for four cents. Despite reserving one-quarter of the newspaper for ads, Dana spoke of "the desirability of discouraging advertising and depending on circulation for profits";[6] he envisioned a day when the paper would decline all advertising. He pointedly accused the other profitable New York papers—the *Tribune, Times,* and *Herald*—of viewing circulation only as a means to secure advertising. In 1875, Dana declared in an editorial that with its circulation at 120,000, the *Sun* had a readership base that permitted it to have sufficient revenues to ease its dependence on advertisers; in fact, he said, the paper already restricted the space allotted for advertisements. By doing so and by excising windy news coverage, the paper was able to present readers with "all the real news of the day" at a more affordable price.[7] He suggested that the paper was near to being able to sustain itself on sales and subscriptions alone, and toward that end, anticipated in the near future turning away more advertisements than it took in. According to Dana's plans, the *Sun* would be the first to earn the title "Journal of the Future," taking "'a long stride in the progress of intellectual as distinguished from commercial journalism.'"[8] Though Dana expressed a vision of a newspaper that would be independent of advertisers and politicians alike, he never realized his ideal of an adless newspaper. Moreover, his interest in championing workers, so apparent in the 1870s, came to seem increasingly strained, and faced with a progressive challenger in Joseph Pulitzer's *New York World,* he "beat a conservative retreat into the middle class."[9] By the late 1880s, the *Sun* had become a voice of business interests rather than that of labor.

A Model of Adless Journalism

Scripps credited Dana with promoting the virtues of adless journalism, but he praised the Salvation Army for having proved its practicability. On March 26, 1904, he wrote to Robert F. Paine, who was the former editor of a Scripps paper in Cleveland and became one of Scripps's closest advisers, to tell him that Frederick Booth-Tucker, a leader of the Salvation Army who would spend several decades serving in India, had visited Scripps at his Miramar estate and had described how the Salvation Army's adless newspaper, the *War Cry,* was turning a sixty-thousand-dollar annual profit through subscription sales alone.[10] Scripps was duly impressed with the religious organization's weekly newspaper and wrote, "Those fellows have succeeded in doing just what I have always had a hankering to do. They are running a great and successful business without being assisted or trammeled by advertisers. . . . Some day or another I am going to try this non-advertising newspaper business myself."[11] Seven years later, Scripps kept his word when he started the *Day Book.* But in his enthusiasm over the Salvation Army's experience with adless journalism, Scripps neglected to consider its limitations as a viable model. The *Day Book,* as a general circulation daily newspaper in Chicago, confronted markedly different challenges than those faced by the *War Cry,* a religious weekly published by an international organization for a readership committed to the cause.

Still, to Scripps, adless journalism was an idea with the force of democracy on its side, and he believed it would succeed on its merits in a secular form as well. It was no longer possible to reach the masses of Americans through oratory, he wrote in the adless memorandum. Newspapers, he continued, furnished virtually all the information with which voters based their judgments when they went to the polls. He wrote, "Doubted, and even reviled, as the daily press may be, on account of its shortcomings, still the government of the United States depends entirely upon judgments formed as a result of the contents of the daily newspapers."[12] But publishers and editors were unwilling to publish a great deal of news, and colored much of what they did publish, to stay in the good graces of advertisers, Scripps maintained. "The whole editorial staff of every modern newspaper," he said, "is little more than an auxiliary of the advertising department."[13] As a result, vital news was suppressed or distorted. He found a compelling example in his experiences at the *Cincinnati Post.* He said the paper had battled with a political machine in that city and found that when the paper aggressively exposed corruption businesses linked with the political powers would withdraw advertising. So the *Post* had been "compelled to a course of persistent compromise" and had "kept its hands off of enough to still enjoy a large amount of advertising."[14] A press so beholden to advertisers undermined its pretensions as an agent of democracy, he said, and it was only by becoming "as independent of the bankers and merchants as most of our newspapers are now independent of the politicians and office holders" that readers would be well served.[15]

At the same time, Scripps implicitly acknowledged a certain oversimplification to his argument that jettisoning ads alone would guarantee impartiality. Reporters, editors, and publishers would still bring their own biases to the tasks at hand; this would be reflected in the subjects covered, the questions asked, the photographs selected, and so forth. He recalled a time when he worked on the staff of a daily newspaper (which he did not identify) that was covering local elections. The publisher and owner of the paper wanted one slate of candidates to win the elections; the staff wanted another set of candidates, and conspired to support them covertly. So while the paper's editorial page urged voters to support one side, the reporters did their best to provide more favorable coverage of the other side. The newspaper staff writers, or at least the candidates whom they supported, won the election, bolstered by slanted coverage, Scripps said. In that case, advertisers had little if anything to do with the outcome. In addition to these internal influences on the content of the paper, he allowed, there would be external ones as well, even barring advertising and government controls. An adless paper would be dependent on a sufficient base of paying subscribers and, in some measure, would have to give them what they wanted to read. "I cannot proclaim truth too loudly and too persistently," Scripps wrote, "and especially those truths which are distasteful to the popular prejudice."[16] In effect, such a paper must be partisan, and champion the interests of the targeted audience of working-class readers, by pushing for higher wages or supporting employees on strike. Even with merchants and politicians at arm's length, he said, "final independence, however, is impossible."

Planning for Content and Costs

The content of the adless paper, as Scripps conceived of it in 1904, would be comprehensive, so that the readers would have as complete a record as possible of events in the city, nation, and world. Curiously, though Scripps emphasized the high-minded role of newspapers in keeping voters informed on issues and on the workings of government, he was at least as interested in providing entertainment as he was in providing political instruction and empowerment. He envisioned the tone of the paper as "light, humorous, and flippant," with two or more pages devoted to a short story every issue and about half of the paper given over to features, including fashion tips, jokes, cartoons, and profiles. The staff members involved in editing and rewrite, especially, should bring to the job a humorist's touch, he said. The features would be complemented by a full digest of local, national, and foreign news, tightly written.[17] The news hole would be filled accordingly: one-quarter with local coverage (including items culled from competing dailies, rewritten and shortened), one-quarter with national and foreign news from the Scripps organization's United Press, and one-half with features from the organization's Newspaper Enterprise Association. Despite its predesignated role as an innovative force in journalism, the ad-free paper would hew to the standard Scripps approach in relying on inexpensive, shared content and limiting the run of local news.[18]

As to other details of the adless experiment, as envisioned in 1904, Scripps proposed to situate the paper in Chicago, with its broad working-class base on which to build circulation. He wanted to be outside the business center, to take advantage of cheaper rents (the cost should not exceed one hundred dollars per month), but in a thickly populated area. He planned to have an office spacious enough to handle an initial circulation of 100,000. The ground floor would have room for five presses; upstairs, a room of about twenty feet by thirty feet would accommodate editors, composers, and telegraph equipment. The publication he foresaw would have sixteen pages, each about six inches by nine inches. The circulation strategy would be to get one hundred subscribers as near to the office as possible, and gradually fan out from there; a second route of one hundred subscribers would be added, and then a third; only when the reliable base of residential subscribers reached 40,000 should street sales be permitted. The adless proposal reflected the standard Scripps method of concentrating in working-class neighborhoods and building up circulation through home delivery.[19]

The financing for the adless experiment was to come from a $500,000 inheritance from Scripps's older half-brother George, who had died in 1900. Scripps said that on several occasions he and George had talked about starting an independent paper in Chicago; George had in mind forming a string of local newspapers across the city and then merging them into one formidable citywide paper. Using some of George's money for an adless paper would, in effect, Scripps said, "build a monument to his memory."[20] Scripps was willing to suffer early financial losses with such a venture, but not to subsidize it indefinitely; he expected his papers, all of them, to eventually show 15 percent profit each year. In a memorandum dated November 2, 1904, Scripps projected that the regular expenses of the paper would be five hundred dollars weekly, or two thousand dollars monthly, including salaries and the cost of paper; three weeks later, he had revised the estimates, and put the monthly expenses at $2,400 to $2,500.[21] Scripps even anticipated the salary costs for his adless newsroom workers: one (editor in chief, presumably) at thirty-five dollars a week, one (managing editor or senior reporter) at twenty-five dollars a week, two (reporters) at fifteen dollars, and one at ten dollars; there would be a business manager (no salary specified) and an assistant (ten dollars a week).[22] "Financial success is not only possible," he wrote, "but necessary."[23]

Four years before he drafted the adless memorandums, Scripps had tried out the concept in an aborted experiment in Chicago. Scripps was personally on hand to direct the start of a low-budget adless paper called the *Press* in April 1900.[24] It was little more than a fling that lasted only a matter of weeks, ending when Scripps learned that William Randolph Hearst was rolling into town with a well-financed daily, the *American,* aimed at a similar working-class audience. At the time, Scripps was embroiled in costly litigation with his brother James over their brother George's estate, and E. W. was not about to risk further losses in a showdown with an aggressive Hearst paper.[25] Hearst was full of political ambition. When William Jennings Bryan and other leading Democrats approached Hearst that April about starting a daily newspaper in Chicago, hoping to counter the Republican press advantage in the Midwest, Hearst eagerly obliged.[26] In July, the *Chicago American* appeared on the newsstands, with a front-page endorsement from Bryan in the debut issue. At the same time, at the invitation of party leaders, Hearst became president of the National Association of Democratic Clubs. The opportunity to lead the association dovetailed with his personal aspirations for political office, which pointed toward the Oval Office.

Appointing an Editor

Though Scripps's plans for Chicago fell through, he thought he had just the person to lead the adless experiment—John Vandercook, editor of the organization's *Cincinnati Post.* Scripps immediately set to planning for a second try, and shifted his sights from Chicago to New York.[27] He told Vandercook to keep the plans confidential; Vandercook assured Scripps that he had "not breathed your non-advertising paper idea."[28] In a letter posted on December 21, 1904, Vandercook advised Scripps to let some other publisher try the adless paper because Scripps might see his "other papers held hostage to the advertisers."[29] Scripps disagreed at the time, though when he did undertake to publish the *Day Book* in 1911, he kept his name off the masthead and tried to keep the paper as independent as possible of the Scripps organization. Vandercook, who expressed "a faith in little things," recommended a tabloid of nine and three-quarters by fifteen inches.[30] Vandercook's favorable qualifications as an editor indirectly scuttled the second test of the adless concept. In 1906, Scripps bought Publishers Press, giving him a total of three wire services stretching across the nation. These he combined into a single wire service in 1907, United Press Associations. Others in the organization pushed for Vandercook to serve as news manager for the wire service, and though Scripps protested, because he said Vandercook was needed for the adless experiment, he gave the appointment his blessing, with the understanding that Vandercook would step aside after the operation was running smoothly and switch to the adless assignment. In April 1907, Scripps spent a whole day planning for the adless paper. The project came to an abrupt halt when Vandercook died of appendicitis in 1908.

After again surveying his stable of editors, Scripps selected Negley Dakin Cochran, who was editing the chain's *Toledo News-Bee* in Ohio, as the best candidate for the adless project. Cochran was born into a childhood of privilege in 1863, in Martin's Ferry, Ohio, the son of the judge advocate on the staff of General James S. Negley in the Civil War. He attended Lindsey Institute, a private school that served as a training ground for Harvard University. At Harvard, he ended up getting kicked out for what was obliquely described as mischievous behavior. He mended his ways enough to finish his studies at the University of Michigan. After graduation, he joined the office of his father, who was then the general counsel for Wheeling & Lake Erie Railroad, based in Toledo, and seemed bound for a career in law. The pay was excellent for a recent graduate, at $125 a month. But before long, Cochran realized that his heart was not in practicing law, and he quit the job, taking a substantial cut in pay and prestige to solicit subscribers for the *Toledo Commercial,* at twenty-four dollars a month. Writing about his experiences as a solicitor earned him a position as a cub reporter, and by twenty-seven, he had become managing editor of the paper. He later moved over to the *Toledo Bee* and served as managing editor. That paper, aligned with the Democratic Party, "created a sensation" by rejecting William Jennings Bryan, who was running for president on a free-silver platform, and as a result it "took a nose dive into the hands of a receiver."[31] Cochran and several business partners bought the *Bee* for fifteen thousand dollars in 1897, and in 1903 they sold it to the Scripps–McRae League, with Cochran retaining stock in the paper and remaining as editor. The paper merged with the *Toledo News and Times* to become the *News-Bee*.

Setting Up Shop

Under Cochran, "a natural crusader" who saw "the glaring need for a thorough scrubbing of Toledo's civic life," the paper experienced rapid circulation growth.[32] Readers were won over by the *News-Bee*'s opposition to the established political powers and its decadelong fight for municipal ownership of street cars in Toledo, which promised lower fares for riders. Cochran was viewed as "the most courageous of all Scripps Ohio editors" since the days when Scripps and Paine had personally managed newspapers there.[33] Scripps liked the fighting spirit Cochran had shown in Toledo and wanted that kind of a strong presence at the adless paper. They began talking about the experiment in 1908, and commenced with formal planning in 1910.[34] The *Day Book*, as the adless paper came to be called, was to be the full-fledged experiment—a penny tabloid dependent on circulation revenue alone. Scripps said he would limit Cochran to a budget of $2,500 per month, not including the cost of newsprint, just the amount that Scripps had settled on in his 1904 proposal. Assisting Cochran would be a managing editor, a business manager, several reporters, and a corps of young canvassers to line up subscribers. The *Day Book*, while using no more newsprint than a standard four-page paper, was going to rely on a rebuilt Potter press with a special folder to create a mini newspaper of thirty-two pages, each page eight and seven-eighths inches long by six and one-eighth inches wide.[35] Scripps was emphatic about whom the paper would serve: "It shall always be the organ, the mouthpiece and the friend of wage-earners who get small wages, and of that class who are not working for wages but still maintain themselves by daily labor of the humblest sort."[36]

Testing the profitability and effectiveness of an adless paper was only part of the experiment in Chicago. Scripps also wanted to try out a small-sized paper as the best vehicle for adless journalism. He reasoned that the tabloid form would make good economical use of paper and would appeal to readers, who could easily hold it and turn the pages, even when standing on a crowded train. But because of its unusually small size, the *Day Book* presented a special challenge in printing, which occupied Cochran in the early days of publication. Cochran referred to the paper as the first tabloid; in Chicago, for example, the other dailies at the time were usually about eighteen inches by twenty-four inches. Though it was unusually small, the *Day Book* was in some ways part of an evolution in the Scripps chain, another step in the ongoing search for smaller margins and lower paper costs. When E. W. Scripps's brother James started the *Evening Press* in Detroit in 1873, he settled on a paper that was fourteen inches by twenty inches; the second Scripps paper came in 1878, the *Penny Press* in Cleveland, and it was ten inches by sixteen inches.[37]

The offices of the *Day Book*, at the corner of West Congress and South Peoria Streets (500 South Peoria) on the west side, enjoyed good transportation links, even if the paper was in the manufacturing hinterlands. In May, soon after he found the basement space in the Kiper Building, Cochran noted that the office was only two blocks from an elevated railway station, providing a quick means to cross the river to the Loop, the heart of Chicago's central business district, into which three-fourths of a million workers commuted by train each day.[38] The elevated transit lines that encircled the business district, near the Chicago River and Lake Michigan, gave the Loop its name. The prestige and the energy came from its occupants. There were the retail giants like Marshall Field's on State Street; the blocklong City Hall between Randolph and Washington; the nearby Federal Post Office and Court House; the theaters on Randolph; the Board of Trade and banks on LaSalle Street; medical and dental offices; elegant hotels; labor headquarters; and bookstores and art galleries scattered throughout.[39] With good reason, the *Day Book*'s competitors chose to put their offices in the Loop, where a bounty of news stories were within walking distance.[40] But wanting to respect Scripps's desire for stealth and economy, Cochran set up shop a mile west of the Loop. He might have chosen otherwise if he had his way; so he found reason to cheer the ease of transportation. The office was a block away from surface railway stops on Van Buren, Harrison, and Halsted Streets, with lines running east to the Loop, west to the city limits, and for miles both north and south. In time, Cochran said, he would be able to quickly move copies of the *Day Book* to scattered newsstands for street sales across the city. He seemed eager to test the paper in the downtown district, where a "vast army of men and women"[41] ensured a big field for circulation.

Scripps Demands Secrecy

But Scripps was adamantly opposed to circulating in the Loop, and Cochran knew better than to press that point with the man who controlled the financing and was well set in his ways. Scripps had mapped out a circulation strategy consistent with those he had used to build a national chain, and that, above all else, required artfully sly tactics. In San Diego and San Francisco, in Los Angeles and Seattle, and in other cities where Scripps went, he sought to quietly build a base of working-class readers. When he started a new paper, Scripps tried to hide his ownership, reasoning that other publishers would regard him as a formidable challenge and "might engage in costly battles to stop his little newspapers."[42] Most of the Scripps papers made no mention of Scripps in the masthead, and the *Day Book* would be no exception. As part of this strategy to steer clear of rivals and avoid circulation wars and price cuts, he generally urged his editors to avoid citywide sales and instead to pursue new readers in areas where the established papers had few contacts. Most of the Scripps news-papers begun after 1898 strictly relied on home delivery by carriers to build up circulation, forgoing street sales.[43]

In Chicago, Cochran agreed to focus on house-to-house canvassing in an effort to sign up readers, beginning in the vicinity of the newsroom, and then fanning out from there; he also planned to visit various unions to win sup-porters and subscribers. Cochran said the intent would be "to build slowly on delivered circulation, and not go on the streets and newsstands until we are ready for a fight with the newspaper trust,"[44] referring to the established newspapers like the *Tribune* and the *Examiner.* To immediately look for sales on the newsstands would invite circulation wars with other publishers, and Cochran said he would not have any publicity to fight with, because others would hold such an advantage in readership. So by stealth, he hoped, the *Day Book* would build a loyal following among readers and labor unions, and after it was "strongly entrenched," then "pick the time and fighting place" to take on the publishers.[45]

In the months leading up to publication, Cochran and Scripps continued to talk of the adless paper in secretive terms. They saw the office on the out-skirts of the city as an ideal place from which to mount a surprise attack on the establishment press of Chicago. Even within the Scripps organization, the *Day Book* was to operate at arm's length from other papers in the chain and from the top executives. Scripps would provide the financing; Cochran would manage the paper. "So far as possible we want to keep entirely secret from everybody facts concerning the ownership, business methods, and the success or failure of our undertaking," Scripps told Cochran.[46] They had ini-tially agreed that the paper would be named the *Story Book,* but Cochran dis-covered that there was already a monthly publication in Chicago called *10 Story Book,* and so he settled instead on the *Day Book.* "It seems to me," he told Scripps, "our purpose is sufficiently disguised by this name."[47] Cochran thought the name would be equally fitting whether the publication evolved into a daily newspaper or a magazine, and he was not at all sure which way it would go. Even though Scripps had always talked of the undertaking as an ad-less "newspaper scheme," as the time drew close to publication both Scripps and Cochran emphasized that they were reinventing journalism, and that the result might look more like a magazine than a newspaper.

Editorial Vision on a Budget

Still a year from publishing the first issue of the *Day Book,* Scripps expounded on his editorial vision for the paper. Thus far in planning, Scripps said, he and Cochran had been so caught up in freedom from commercialism, and the kinds of uplifting articles and editorials they might write, that "we had our heads up so high that they were bumping the stars."[48] He proposed, instead, to pursue a different kind of freedom: indifference to "the contempt of all classes." Scripps said he and Cochran should not arrogate to serve as "worthy advisers and leaders" of the masses, or propose to educate them to unrealistic "higher levels of thought." The newspaper should become, he said, "the common vulgar friend and companion of the common vulgar crowd, of which if I am not a member, I would like to be." The paper should limit the preachments and lectures, he said, and print only a small amount of news that would help readers organize themselves for their own advantage. In sum, he noted, the *Day Book* should follow in the path of a dime novel or a police gazette and be heavily entertaining as it pursued "new journalism." Scripps did not explicitly say what was "new" about this brand of journalism. Indeed, Scripps papers had long followed a formula of mixing brightly written news briefs and entertaining features, without a lot of editorial preaching. It may be that Scripps did not have a specific kind of content in mind and wanted the *Day Book* to experiment with different blends of news and features until it found the combination that readers seemed most eager to pay for.

In a letter to Scripps in May, Cochran said he had analyzed the Chicago newspapers and found that all of them appeared to be published for the benefit of advertisers, employers, and the upper class, a group he readily dismissed as "the 5 percent."[49] Cochran and Scripps intended the *Day Book* to be a record of news and opinion and entertainment written expressly for the rest of the city, an amalgam of workers, "the 95 percent." Cochran said in September that the Chicago newspaper publishers appeared to be at odds in battling for circulation and advertising, but that under the surface they were united in their hostility to labor unions. "They won't publish the truth about strikes or labor troubles," he wrote.[50] Cochran said he had advised the pressmen with Hearst newspapers, who he said appeared to be on the verge of a strike, to wait until the *Day Book* was circulating, so they could count on "a newspaper that will give them a square deal."[51]

Scripps underscored his intent that the paper be published at a cost of no more than $2,500 a month, excluding the price of paper.[52] Given that constraint, Cochran said that at one level the effort amounted to "selling newsprint paper at a profit."[53] It took a pound of paper to produce fifteen copies of the *Day Book*. The cost of newsprint, at the start, was about forty dollars per ton, or two cents per pound; with delivery and related costs added, it came to just under two-and-a-half cents per pound. The *Day Book* was sold to newsboys for fifty cents per hundred, or a half cent for each paper. So when the paper reached a circulation of thirty thousand, Cochran figured, it would be self-sustaining. That circulation would require two thousand pounds of paper, and a profit of five cents per pound on the paper meant revenue of $100 per day, or $2,600 a month, based on twenty-six publishing days. The *Day Book* would not publish on Sundays. Limiting the paper to six days a week was not perceived as a major handicap; in 1911, only three of Chicago's nine dailies published on Sundays.

Operating on such a strict budget would force the paper to be efficient, which Scripps said was essential if it was to thrive. Moreover, he told Cochran, making a go of it on a fairly modest budget would prove the soundness of one of his hypotheses with regard to the adless paper: that any person able to secure a small amount of capital could publish a similarly honest newspaper that would be successful because it printed news that people would willingly pay for. That would open the way, Scripps said, for people of principle, but of modest means, to start adless papers in other cities. "We must prove that dollars, which only the capitalists have," he wrote, "are not necessary to business enterprise."[54]

Word of the venture leaked out a month before the first issue, on August 29, when the *Record-Herald* ran a short article describing the *Day Book* as a daily newspaper in tabloid form, with "much mystery attached" to it. Cochran himself did not talk with the reporter, but the president of the pressman's union had, thinking the *Day Book* would benefit from the publicity. The article noted that the *Day Book*'s pressroom, composing room, and editorial department were all in one room, and that two linotype machines had been installed and a press was being set up. Publication was said to be about two weeks away. The *Day Book* would sell for one cent a copy and would carry no local advertising at the start. Beyond that, the article said, whether the stories in the paper would be real news of the day or fiction, it was not immediately clear.

FOUR

The *Day Book's* Debut

The old Potter press had Cochran feeling testy as he struggled to publish the first issue of the *Day Book*. The press was supposed to take a single broadsheet for a standard four-page newspaper, print it, fold it three times, and produce a thirty-two-page mini newspaper.[1] But something was amiss, and a dozen people were playing press mechanic, trying to figure out what to do as the press churned out pages in the wrong order. Cochran "stormed around, trying to correct the screw-up, smearing ink on his shirt, blistering his hands handling the hot plates."[2] Finally, he came up with a jury-rigged solution that required making flat casts, sawing them apart, rearranging the pages, and recasting all four plates. Volume 1, number 1, of the *Day Book* came off the press at about 5:30 P.M. on September 28, 1911. It would take Cochran more than a week to work out the mechanical bugs, but the adless paper that he and Scripps had been planning for years was finally ready for home delivery.

The first issue of the *Day Book* did little to clarify the paper's editorial direction. Scripps had asked for vulgarity, and he got it, not in the sense of profanity, but in the tidbits of accessible news and humor and in the kind of trashy fiction that was popular in some magazines and novels at the turn of the century.[3] The paper led with a short story that had little to recommend it, a hurriedly written piece of confectionary prose that followed a formulaic plot.[4] The story told of a seventeen-year-old factory worker, Mary McIntyre, who labored ten hours a day to make four dollars a week, barely enough to support herself and her mother. Mary became engaged to a neighbor, Tom Murray,

THE DAY BOOK

500 So.Peoria St.-CHICAGO — Tel.Monroe353

Thursday, September 28, 1911.*

SOCIETY LIFE OF RICHES AND TROUBLE OUTDONE BY SIMPLE LIFE AND HAPPINESS

By John T. Watters.

Day after day Mary sat at her machine in the factory—the perspiration pouring from her brow. She was one of the faithful employes, having been engaged at the same work for four years; and now but 17 years of age.

Every morning at an early hour Mary could be seen hurrying to work; but as she retraced her steps homeward in the evening, after laboring for 10 hours, she was worn out and ready to "take the count." She would never ride in the cars, rain or shine—no, she needed all her spare change to support her mother who worked unceasingly at the washboard until she was physically unable to continue. And Mary received but four dollars a week; some weeks she would earn a trifle more by working overtime. By careful figuring she managed to pay expenses on her small salary.

Mary was never dressed like other girls. She never had the pleasure of admiring a new pair of shoes when she was a child (like all children do), and when she had grown she continued her practice of wearing shoes donated to her by friends. Her clothes were also shabby, but they were always clean. She cared nothing for shabbyness and her only ambition was to make her mother happy.

"Hello, mother dear, hope you've been as happy as I have been all day," was Mary's usual greeting to her mother as she would imprint a kiss upon her mother's lips when she returned from her hard day's work late every evening. Then she would proceed to do the housework. Being an invalid, Mrs. McIntyre was unable to do this work.

A neighboring young man, Tom Murray, had been paying a great deal of attention to Mary and she was deeply in love with him. He was just a few years her senior. Tom was always held uppermost in the eyes of Mary's mother, too, and had promised to look after the girl when her mother's death came. This was expected at any time.

Several months later she died and Mary grew tired of daily laboring as a factory drudge—She then promised to marry Tom. By this time, when she had but herself to support she was able to buy clothes and did not

The front page of the first issue of the *Day Book*. (The Center for Research Libraries)

a steady and dependable young man. But in time her mother died and Mary was promoted from the factory floor to the office, where she met Dick Kane, a polished man who promised her "clothes of the finest variety and expensive hats of the latest styles." So they eloped. But after a few months, she became disillusioned with the finery and pretense of high society, and Dick turned to drinking and gambling, striking her in his drunken rages. Forced to leave him, Mary took her baby girl to another city, secured work, and discovered that her new boss was Tom Murray. Having found, as the headline put it, a "Society Life of Riches and Trouble Outdone by Simple Life and Happiness," Mary married Tom. The morality tale, oddly enough written by the business manager, John T. Watters, was followed by material from the Scripps wire services: a feature on beauty tips ("Let us take up first the question of what not to eat. Sweets and pastries are absolutely taboo."), quotable quotes ("Some folks think that the winter twilights begin early so as not to delay the poker game."), and several pages of sports. Only then, well inside the paper, was there a run of news, a combination of briefs and short news stories, mostly about crimes committed in Chicago and across the country. Sensational accounts were preferred, like the one about a young woman under arrest in New Orleans, suspected of having killed her sister and parents to collect on insurance policies.

A four-page fictional story by Don MacGregor, about as poor an offering as the one by Watters, led the next issue, on September 29,[5] once more with a message for readers in the headline: "John Bertram Thinks of Suicide; But Decides on Marriage Instead." In this account, a handsome young man, John Bertram, is rejected by his fiancée and contemplates suicide. But he soon thinks better of it and takes a job as a deckhand aboard a lake steamer, where he meets a blue-eyed beauty, Jennie Laughton, "as erect as a young pine tree, as fearless as a god, and as careless of wind or storm or rain as a stormy petral." Such attributes are needed, because a storm comes on suddenly, and in the dark fury the boat is hit by another, and founders. Somehow John reaches Jennie in time for them to leap together into the water, and the two cling to a lone spar in the rough waters until they are rescued by a passing boat, by which time he has professed his love for her and they have sealed their engagement with a kiss. The saccharine account sets a curious tone for a paper whose founders had made so much of being adless and free to publish all the news that a democracy deserved. Once again, the inside pages contain a mix of short news and feature items, primarily drawn from Scripps wire services. Cochran also admitted to heavily borrowing news items from the morning papers during the first few days.[6]

Critique of a Work in Progress

E. W. Scripps wrote to Cochran as soon as he had looked over the first issue, and offered many suggestions, including numbering the issues and pages (Cochran later noted that he had elected to forgo numbering to give more space in the paper to news and features[7]), changing the name (Scripps did not care for the *Day Book* and mentioned the *Adless* as an alternative), and adding a table of contents.[8] Scripps suggested adding datelines, to let the reader know whether an article was local or national, and whether it was new or dated, a convention that some readers "will require as the guarantee of the quality of an article."[9] Scripps said the *Day Book* "really looks littler than I thought it would," but suggested that when advertisements, overblown headlines, financial news, and other "purely class matter" were taken out of the other Chicago papers, the *Day Book* would compare favorably in the volume of reading matter. He urged Cochran to conduct a comparative analysis, and then let readers know that "their little paper is really a very big paper." However, a comparison of the *Day Book*'s entire September 28 news package with that found on the day's front page of the *Chicago Daily Tribune* showed that only *Tribune* readers would have known about a trap laid for a Chicago prosecutor investigating gambling in the city, or that Italy had issued an ultimatum to Turkey over the occupation of Tripoli, or that twenty-one-year-old Betty Trump had been killed by a hit-and-run driver at the corner of Hermitage Avenue and Madison Street. Whether Scripps actually read the other dailies is not clear; perhaps he thought there was really no need to since he and Cochran were engaged in re-invention. Before signing off, Scripps told Cochran not to "put much weight on this advice," but rather to break with journalistic conventions and forms and see what the readers want.

For all the years that Scripps and his lieutenants planned for an adless newspaper, when publication of the *Day Book* actually began, it was remarkably still a work in progress. The opening weeks found Cochran experimenting with content and layout in fairly radical ways. After running fiction on the front page for the first two issues, as though intending to put out a magazine, Cochran shifted course and began to lead with news, but unpredictably so. The front-page article (only one article fit comfortably on the page) was about sports one day, a courtroom drama the next, then the war between Italy and Turkey. Sometimes the news was local, but more often than not it was a wire story from United Press, given prominence because of its importance or simply human interest value. On October 2, for example, the front page detailed

CITY BRIEFS.

Joseph Darflinger and George Jaborsky stole an auto. Sixty days.

James Harvey, W. 52 street, threatened to kill howling dog next door. $500 Peace bond.

Robbers held up Henry Humiston, W. Lake place—diamond stud—paste.

William Beaubien, Whipple street, dead. 76 years old—never out of Chicago.

Gaudy lights in living rooms worse than debt or indigestion. Professor J. R. Gravath told illuminating engineers' convention at Congress hotel.

Mrs. Christ Glocker W. 47 Place, ill and despondent. Poison —police surgeon—recovered.

Beggar asked Erick Hartmann, 905 Fullerton ave., for dime. Nothing doing—Hartmann badly beaten.

John Rakiesky, W. 14 Place, threw trousers on gas jet and went to bed. Asphyxiated.

Fanny Haeusgen gave husband money to buy ring and wedding apparel — married one week— Henry disappeared—divorce.

Government turns Cupid—offers Phillipine honeymoon trips to schoolmasters and "marms" who want to marry.

Friday, Oct. 13, set by judge for trial of Harry Doughty, charged with assault with deadly weapon. Doughty superstitious. Judge changed to Thursday, October 12.

Henry Prack, 44, Paulina street invented aeroplane to go up like elevator—tried to join salvation army and personally conduct trips to heaven—detention hospital.

Federal secret service agents discovered opium depot at Terre Haute, Ind. Manufactured in St. Paul.

OFFICER DISCHARGED; RESULT GAMBLING DEA?

As a result of the gambling investigation, Patrolman Charles J McClellan was found guilty of permitting gambling outside the White Sox park, Labor day, and was ordered discharged from the force. Lieut. W. W. Wash, of the 35th street station, will be confronted with similar charges tomorrow.

Attorney Ettelson, for McClellan, made a vitriolic attack on the members of the civil service commission in his closing argument.

Question has arisen over the sincerity of Raymond O'Keefe, who declared he had evidence against the police who have prosecuted the labor sluggers. W. W. Wheelock, in charge of the investigation, refused to make an appointment for an interview in a room in the Sherman hotel, claiming a trap was being laid to compromise him and weaken his position.

O'Keefe, who asserts he has sensational evidence against a certain police official, says that Wheelock is preparing to "whitewash" the department, and is afraid to handle his evidence. He adds that he will present his facts at the close of the case and make Wheelock "look foolish."

The Day Book gave local news short shrift in the first issue, presenting "City Briefs" in a staccato style. (The Center for Research Libraries) an account of a self-confessed murderer in an Oregon jail who committed big-amy and then killed his second wife (a news story, the paper said, "far surpass-ing all tales of horror in fiction"). Two days later, the front page told of Turkey invading Greece, and Italy bombing Albania. And on October 6, a photograph of Chief Myers, the .332–hitting catcher for the New York Giants, a team that was facing the Philadelphia Athletics in the World Series, took up nearly all of the page. Then a collection of news briefs ran out front on October 16, a rapid-fire pastiche of miscellaneous items that recalled features in Dana's *New York Sun* and other papers of that period:[10] "Tag! You're it"; "Earthquake in Sicily. Vengeance of Allah?" (this an apparent reference to Italy's role in the war with Turkey); "C. Parker, Kenosha, Wis., dropped dead while shaving. Shaving had nothing to do with it."

Friend of the Working Class

Even as it veered toward news as entertainment, the *Day Book* suggested that it could be quite serious about covering some issues, especially those affect-ing the rights and wages of workers, and that it would not pull punches in reporting on what it saw as the chief adversaries of labor, among them com-mercial newspapers and department stores. An editorial on October 28 took issue with an ongoing crackdown on prostitution and other vice in Chicago. The underlying problem, the paper said, was not that young women were morally bankrupt. Rather, it was that many worked for department stores for beggarly wages, and that because of this, some were "driven to degradation" because "a girl can't pay her board, room rent and laundry bills in Chicago on a measly $6 a week."[11] The solution lay not in police raids but in organizing the women into unions, despite certain resistance from store executives. Success-fully building unions, the paper said, would require standing up to powerful newspaper interests as well as to the stores themselves, because the press bar-ons in their eagerness to secure advertising would not risk siding with work-ers or printing "the truth about the deplorable conditions" in which these workers labored.

Beyond editorials, the *Day Book* did not provide much original local cov-erage of labor issues in the early going, though it certainly did prominently report such news when it was available from the United Press. The biggest na-tional labor story that fall was the opening of a trial that focused on a fierce struggle between organized workers and big business in Los Angeles, and the *Day Book* led with the trial nine times in October, all dispatches from United Press. Two brothers, John and James McNamara, well-known labor advocates and organizers, were charged with bombing the *Los Angeles Times* building on October 1, 1910.[12] The explosion killed twenty people, nearly all workers, and caused $500,000 worth of damage. The *Day Book* was absolutely clear about where its sympathies lay in covering the bombing or, for that matter, any labor news.[13] The staff was encouraged to rewrite any "cold-bloodedly exact news story" sent by United Press and color it to favor the working class, even if that meant giving it a "semi-editorial tone," Cochran noted.[14] Meanwhile, the *Day Book* was doing its best to establish ties with organized labor in Chicago. In November, the Chicago Federation of Labor requested twenty copies of the paper to pass around at an upcoming American Federation of Labor convention in Atlanta; in December, Cochran met with John Fitzpatrick, president of the Chicago organization; and that same month, the Chicago Allied Printing Trades Council endorsed the newspaper.[15] The unions, Cochran noted, especially welcomed having the *Day Book* pull back the curtain on the Chicago press: "What attracts the most attention just now is the news about Chicago newspapers. It seems to daze people—the idea of anybody having the nerve to publish disagreeable facts about newspapers."[16]

Experimenting Along the Way

Cochran told Scripps that he had purposefully turned out a paper that consisted largely of items from the Scripps feature service, the Newspaper Enterprise Association, and the United Press news service. Rather than investing resources in original reporting and commentary, he said, he was trying to help his staff settle in at the office and become familiar with the various tasks involved in putting out a newspaper. Cochran said the news items had largely been selected and condensed by his son Harold, who would serve as managing editor. This arrangement left the senior Cochran free to concentrate on mechanical problems with the press, of which there were plenty in the first few weeks, and also gave Harold training that would enable him to take over the management of the paper as needed during his father's absences, which would prove to be both frequent and extended. Moreover, Negley Cochran said, "I wanted no punch in the first issues. Wanted our weakness pointed out by readers."[17] The strategy, he said, was to lay aside convention and let the readers help to shape the paper. Responding to Scripps's gentle criticism of the name of the newspaper, Cochran said the *Day Book* was a strong choice in part because of its ambiguous label, because it "commits us to nothing and leaves everything open to make it what we please."[18]

Scripps and Cochran were still not sure whether the *Day Book* should be promoted as a newspaper, a magazine, or a hybrid all its own.[19] Their references to exactly what they thought constituted a newspaper or magazine were oblique at best; they suggested that a preponderance of news would make it a newspaper; alternatively, an emphasis on fiction and features would make it more of a magazine, especially given its unusually small size. Cochran suggested in a letter to Scripps that it definitely should not be a traditional newspaper: "Not that a newspaper is what the people really want, but that it is what they think they want. The newspaper habit is there to overcome."[20] He went on to say that the *Day Book* might print one big news story a day to give the readers their cent's worth of the news, and then "put other stuff in it that would suit them better than much of the stuff called news."[21] By way of illustration, he told Scripps about a vice commission's recently completed report on gambling, prostitution, and other illegal activities in Chicago. The report had been talked about across the country, he said, but had not been published in Chicago newspapers, which in his view were reluctant to touch it because the report indirectly blamed department stores for prostitution, by paying wages that women could not hope to live on. Cochran said he was thinking about publishing the report in installments, and also about arranging with a young woman to work undercover at Marshall Field's and then write an exposé. In early November, nearly two months into the experiment, circulation at the *Day Book* was a modest 165 subscribers, all drawn from delivery routes near the office.[22] But if he were to put published accounts of the vice report on the street, Cochran predicted, people would buy the paper by the thousands.

With such comments, Cochran let Scripps know of his eagerness to quickly expand the *Day Book*'s circulation and make an impact on the workings of government and business. But Scripps cautioned Cochran not to deviate from the usual approach, urging him to stick with the plan to slowly build up circulation within one neighborhood, and if that effort did not succeed, then revise the content or focus of the paper and try selling it in another area, until it was clear that circulation would grow. Only then, with a strong local readership base, Scripps said, should Cochran consider putting the paper on newsstands. Scripps said: "We do not want the other publishers in Chicago to even suspect that our paper may be a go until after it is running at a profit."[23] Again, Scripps emphasized the need for stealth in all matters concerning the *Day Book,* "secrecy which would even include or exclude my own sons and the chief men of our concern."[24] Scripps wanted to avoid having other Chicago newspapers retaliate against the fledgling low-cost *Day Book,* and he also did not want the adless experiment subjected to in-house scrutiny until it had started to prove itself viable. A smaller point of some dispute was whether to promote the adless aspect of the paper. Scripps wanted Cochran to consider incorporating some mention of this rejection of advertising in the nameplate, even if it was only a simple slogan like "An Adless Newspaper." But Cochran argued that "the biggest thing about it isn't that we carry no ads—rather is it [sic] that we are free from any influence at all that is evil."[25] Cochran went on to say: "We can prove we are free by deeds rather than by an advertisement that we are adless." In Cochran's mind, the newspaper's content would set it apart, and it should not have to trumpet its adless approach. Still, Cochran said, he had an open mind about it. It would take a couple of years, but Scripps finally prevailed on that point, and "An Adless Daily Newspaper" began appearing underneath the nameplate in 1914.

The *Day Book's* Most Faithful Reader

The frequent letters and expansive advice from Scripps were testament to his interest, even obsession, in seeing the *Day Book* succeed as the first of many adless newspapers across the country. His writings make clear that his commitment to adless journalism was more than a lark or idle posturing by a rich old man retired to an estate by the sea. Though the *Day Book* was the smallest of the Scripps organization's properties, and years away from hoping to turn a profit, Scripps told Cochran that it was of utmost importance: "It means more to me today than all my other newspaper properties, all my political scheming, all my readings and philosophies."[26] When the mail arrived, Scripps said, he reached first for the *Day Book,* followed by any letters from Cochran or circulation reports on the paper. Only then, he said, did he read letters from his wife or other correspondence. "The ad-less paper is to be my last job as a newspaper man," Scripps wrote, "and there is nothing concerning it that it can be too trivial to excite my greatest interest."[27] Scripps reminded Cochran of their purpose: "You and I are not trying to do anything else under the sun, than to demonstrate, that there can exist a press, free from influence of, or any sort of control by, men of wealth and position" who seek "to rule the mob of the uninformed or misinformed mass of humanity."[28] And he reminded Cochran of the scale of their experiment in the city of 2.2 million: "Even the great city of Chicago forms but an insignificant fraction of the population of the vast nation, to the interest of which, as a whole, we have devoted ourselves."[29]

As for circulation, Cochran said it continued to prove difficult to gain new readers for the adless paper by canvassing neighborhoods around the office.[30] Since the success of the *Day Book* depended upon "the 95 per cent,"[31] the public at large must know what the paper was all about, its intents and purposes.

But Cochran said publishing without ads was proving to be something of an impediment, instead of an immediate advantage, in signing up readers. He said: "As it is now, the *Day Book* is a mystery. People are suspicious. They don't understand an adless newspaper, and can't see how it can make money. Hence they wonder what our game is." To address that concern, Cochran began running short promotional notes in the paper, which became a regular, if varied, feature of the *Day Book*. In the first of these items, he introduced the *Day Book* as "a West Side daily magazine," combining magazine features that "you can't get in any daily newspaper" and "all the news you find in newspapers."[32] For a penny a day, Cochran promised a newsmagazine that would be small in size and convenient to handle and read, but "big in news." In the next issue, he ran a promotional brief warning readers that the fine print in newspapers would ruin their vision, and that the *Day Book* used larger type, all the better to protect eyesight.[33] According to Cochran's final figures, the daily average circulation for the first three months of publication showed a steady, if modest, gain: October, 77; November, 138; and December, 143.

Into the new year, Cochran continued to experiment with the *Day Book's* format. A three-page article led the paper on January 1, with the accounts of women, largely royalty, who had proposed marriage in what the paper described as "the leap year privilege of womankind."[34] Then followed a listing of the dates on which holidays fell in 1912, and an unsigned playful column on "What 1911 Saw," including "The McNamara case," "Turmoil in Tripoli," "Some books about Bernard Shaw," and "Some books not about Bernard Shaw." The next day the paper led with a wire service report on a pending strike by 45,000 laundry workers in New York City, while inside the reader found "Doings of the World Boiled Down"[35] into a series of news briefs, with editorial comments attached. One reported a judge's finding that gambling and illegal resorts were pervasive and unchecked by the police in New York City, to which the paper added, "Oh, well, Chicago doesn't stand alone." Except for staff coverage of a record cold front that gripped Chicago early in the month, killing at least twenty-one people as temperatures fell below zero for three consecutive days, the paper largely relied on wire service news from New York, Washington, and elsewhere. The newspaper's coverage of striking mill workers in Lawrence, Massachusetts, was extensive in the new year, with wire service reports providing details and *Day Book* editorials adding perspective, underscoring its commitment to labor. Workers in the cotton and woolen mills, who had earned on average sixteen cents an hour for a fifty-six-hour work week, had gone on strike to protest their pay after the State Legislature reduced the work week by two hours, and salaries fell accordingly. Women and children, some girls as young as fourteen, many of them foreign nationals, constituted the bulk of the labor force. The strike led to violent clashes between workers and the law enforcement officials who were called in to keep order.

"The Truth Without Fear or Favor"

Cochran wanted to be sure that readers were beginning to grasp what set the *Day Book* apart from other dailies in the city. In a promotional note apparently prompted by Scripps, he said the *Day Book,* described as a combination newspaper and magazine, gave readers more news of value in thirty-two pages than other papers did with many more pages, because the other papers were fattened by advertising. He said the other dailies ran big headlines about sensational crime stories to drive up circulation, not for the sake of the reader, but of the advertiser. Addressing his readers, Cochran said: "You have a cash value to the advertiser, and hence to the newspaper. The advertiser pays the newspaper to carry his advertising to you and get you into his store with your money."[36] But that same reliance on department store advertising keeps other papers from publishing any news that could hinder sales, like reports on the low wages paid to clerks, Cochran said. Since the *Day Book's* only source of revenue was six cents a week from each reader, he said, it could "afford to publish the truth without fear or favor."

Scripps's mind was on circulation early in January, knowing that Cochran was itching to have a downtown presence. He fired off a terse note reminding Cochran that under no circumstances should he consider selling the *Day Book* through newsboys or on the newsstands.[37] The only acceptable method, Scripps said, was house to house canvassing. And, in what seemed like a threat from out of the blue, he closed with this: "The chances are now three out of four that the *Day Book* enterprise will be closed up before the end of March next." Later in the month, he continued to press his point on circulation strategy, though he seemed to be in slightly better humor about it. Referring to a report in which John T. Watters, the business manager, mentioned having signed up twenty subscribers within a few hours, Scripps said, "In fact the life or death of the *Day Book* is going to depend upon the work that this three or four hours' work of Watters shows it is possible for a man to do in Chicago."[38] But a better test of Watters, he added, would be his ability to select the right kind of people to help with canvassing and delivering newspapers, perhaps a reference to Scripps's self-proclaimed success in relying on the sons of widows for circulation routes in Detroit. Or he may have had an earlier memory in mind. Scripps enjoyed telling a story from his boyhood in

Schuyler County, Ill., when he turned hoeing on the family farm into a contest that drew boys from town. While they raced to see who could finish their rows first, he managed the event from a fence rail, in Tom Sawyer fashion.[39]

Recipe for Success: Jokes and Features

In signing off, Scripps added a postscript, touching on the content of the *Day Book*: "Tonight I have looked over a number of *Day Books*. They are full of appeals to workingmen's minds—to their sense of justice or injustice. There are to be found no things, which will cause a man to forget that he has to work—and that he suffers. There is nothing to make him laugh for the pure joy of being able to laugh or to appeal to common place interests. It's all uplift, argument and scold, and no fun and frolic and no common every day plain workingman's gossip and 'chow rag.'"[40] A little levity, he suggested, would help to attract readers. Heeding Scripps's advice not to take itself too seriously, the *Day Book* offered some light touches on the front page in February, including the tale of Raleigh Wilson, a circus clown who was leaving the Vollmar Brothers troupe to become a Methodist minister; in visiting a little country church, Wilson had been mistaken for an itinerant minister and was ushered to the pulpit, where he thoroughly enjoyed delivering an impromptu sermon.[41] The next day featured a wire dispatch on a national convention of hoboes, officially a gathering of the Casual and Migratory Workers' Association. The unnamed reporter who covered the convention tried to surreptitiously gain entry as a delegate, but found his way blocked because he did not know the requisite password. He owned up to being a reporter, and the guard responded: "Why didn't you say so at first? . . . That lets you in. All undesirable citizens are welcome."[42]

The leading news story in February was the continued unrest at the mills in Lawrence, Massachusetts. The paper reported on the efforts of the mill owners and the local authorities to block striking workers from sending their children to stay with friends or relatives in other cities until the situation in Lawrence calmed and food was more plentiful. But despite the heavy coverage of the strike, the *Day Book* showed signs of scaling back its overall news content. In mid-February, Scripps laid out a detailed recipe for success: jokes, love stories, cooking features, household tips, and suggestions on how to stretch a dollar.[43] He wrote: "The thirty-second page is enough to furnish all the uplift and intellectual pablum that our duty can possibly call for. Try to give your readers something in your thirty-one pages that wont [*sic*] cause them to think, that won't even invite them to think." Cochran, always eager to appease Scripps, agreed that the *Day Book* should emphasize entertaining news and features. In a letter to Scripps, Cochran wrote: "If you have watched the *Day Book* lately, you have noticed, no doubt, the gradual disappearance of what the average newspaper prints as news. Along with this kind of news has almost disappeared the conventional editorial. The general aim now is to make every line in the paper interesting without regard to anything but interest."[44] Cochran said that he increasingly found that UP coverage, with its concentration of articles on accidents, crime, and disaster, did not meet the paper's needs. Cochran continued: "The more I analyze our paper and the others, the more I become convinced that we want stories and comedy—slap-stick comedy at that—and very little if any uplift stuff. Anyhow not while we are getting an audience. And if not while we are getting an audience, then why very much of it it [*sic*] after we get the audience?" The test of what should go in the newspaper, he said, is "common human interest." But no sooner had the *Day Book* embarked on this very course than Scripps and Cochran were forced to do an about-face. As Scripps said, "That excursion into the magazine field was a disaster pure and simple."[45] The so-called magazine approach, heavy on entertainment, short on news, proved a failure, as circulation took a dive. Cochran looked at the loss of five hundred subscribers, dropping circulation to about a thousand from 1,500, and concluded: "From all we have been able to find out they really want more of a newspaper than a magazine, and they want a tabloid newspaper."[46] And so, he began "to jam red-blooded news back into the paper."[47] The circulation debacle seemed to bring about a kind of editorial epiphany for Cochran. In one of his many typewritten letters to Scripps, he summarized what would become the guiding approach: "I am going now on the theory that we will make better headway by giving them what we think is news, handled in a more sympathetic manner toward the masses than the other papers handle it, and striking from the shoulder editorially on subjects the people are interested in and the dailies timid about."[48]

The radical turn toward a light magazine-style journalism and subsequent turnabout illustrated a management flaw that would continue to trouble the newspaper. Scripps would issue grand, and often contradictory, pronouncements about editorial policy; and Cochran would generally try to follow Scripps's advice, resulting in a *Day Book* that seemed to be zig-zagging without a clear sense of its mission. At one point after the tilt toward features, Scripps said he wanted lots of news, at least as much as in the other papers, requiring a staff large enough to cover Chicago; but he also emphasized that he wanted to run a low-cost newspaper and take advantage of United Press and Newspaper Enterprise material. Scripps hailed the contribution that an adless paper could make to democracy, by empowering voters with news and ideas that the commercial press would screen out; on the other hand, he urged Cochran to entertain his working-class readers, since they had enough personal hardships without adding to the mix weighty issues like municipal reform and labor strife, which would make them only more discouraged. But after all the experimenting that went on in the early months, Scripps and Cochran both seemed to finally conclude that the *Day Book* needed an identity, that it would probably do best as a newspaper, and that as a newspaper it needed to emphasize news.

FIVE

Critic of the Hometown Press

Only a few weeks into the *Day Book* experiment, E. W. Scripps asked Negley Cochran whether a friend of Scripps's in Chicago, Clarence Darrow, the celebrated lawyer and champion of American labor, could be of any use to the newspaper. Without hesitation, Cochran said Darrow could be of great assistance if he would recommend a lawyer ready to take on powerful interests in Chicago. Cochran explained that the *Day Book* needed the name of a fearless and independent lawyer—perhaps, he hinted, Darrow himself—who would be willing to represent the paper when it started reporting on what he regarded as the corrupt practices of some of the leading newspapers in the city.[1] The Chicago publishers, Cochran wrote, "are the most dangerous criminals in Chicago," and the *Day Book*, he said, intended to expose the dark underside of the hometown press.[2] Cochran said that two newspapers owned by Victor Lawson, the *Record-Herald* and the *Daily News;* two owned by William Randolph Hearst, the *American* and the *Examiner;* and one controlled by the McCormick and Patterson families, the *Tribune,* were engaged in fierce, and illegal, circulation battles. The newspapers had hired streetwise toughs, known as sluggers, who were assigned to so-called wrecking crews. These crews sought to put their respective newspapers at an advantage by controlling newsstands: which papers were put out for sale, how many copies were available, how prominently they were displayed. In an effort to gain the upper hand, the crews regularly beat up those who delivered the papers to stands as well as those who managed the stands, the latter in an effort to force them to take more copies of one paper than they could reasonably expect to sell or to persuade them not to accept any papers from the competition. The sluggers were able to get away with such strong-arm marketing, Cochran said, because they had "a powerful pull"[3] with the courts, thereby avoiding prosecution, and because they had an understanding among themselves that news of their exploits would be suppressed. Cochran said he proposed "to much-rake [*sic*] the newspapers, and go at them with an axe."[4] First, though, he wanted to line up organized labor behind the *Day Book* and to secure a lawyer, who, by the way, he told Scripps, should not be a socialist, because the newspaper wanted to avoid being politically labeled.

A Tough Town Gets Tougher

The circulation methods that so outraged Cochran in 1911 were not new to the business of journalism in Chicago. It was already a tough newspaper town with vigorous competition when Hearst arrived in 1900, with typical flamboyance and money to spend, ready to stir things up even more. Hearst, thirty-seven, had been named president of the National Association of Democratic Clubs in May of that year. On July 2, just in time to give Chicago readers favorable accounts of the July 4 opening of the Democratic national convention in Kansas City, he started the *American,* an afternoon paper, and would soon add the *Examiner,* for morning readers. The addition of the Hearst papers brought to nine the number of daily newspapers operating in Chicago. The leading news voice in the city was the *Tribune,* a staid paper of record that combined a front page laden with foreign, national, and local news and inside pages filled with an assortment of items, including sports, upscale fashion, and political commentary. Even so, the *Tribune,* a morning daily, did not command the largest audience in Chicago. Lawson's papers, the *Daily News,* an evening daily, and the *Record-Herald,* the morning counterpart, reached a larger number of readers, and a different cross-section of the population. The Lawson papers laced their pages with crime stories and tidbits of sensationalism, and tapped into the mass market of immigrants and laborers, a group of readers that Hearst also had his eyes on. The arrival of Hearst, who had already proved to be a formidable publisher on the East and West coasts, signaled fiercer circulation battles. The competition was soon felt on every street corner, where municipal trash cans that long carried *Daily News* placards suddenly became pitchmen for the *American.*[5]

Hearst started out in journalism at twenty-three, as the editor and owner of the *San Francisco Examiner.* Like Cochran, he had been dismissed from Harvard; Hearst's grades tumbled, leading to academic probation and eventually his being expelled. He was determined to make a name for himself in journalism (the high point of his second year at Harvard had been serving as business manager of the *Harvard Lampoon*).[6] Like Scripps, he merged personal wealth with a philosophy that favored the working class and challenged big business. The San Francisco paper had been owned by Hearst's father, George, who made his fortune in mines. Though the paper at that time was losing money and claimed a circulation of 15,000, George Hearst had used it to help promote his Democratic candidacy for the U.S. Senate. The father was elected senator in California in January 1887, and two months later the son took over the paper. In an effort to turn things around, William Hearst enlarged the paper to eight pages, brought on board people he had worked with on the *Lampoon* at Harvard, experimented with huge headlines, inserted illustrations, beefed up sports coverage, loaded up on crime stories, started crusades (e.g., to lower water rates and to check the power of the Southern Pacific Railroad, a bulwark of the Republican Party), and cooked up events to build circulation (e.g., hiring a boat to take readers for a ride in the Bay and renting a hot-air balloon to carry a couple and a minister aloft for a marriage ceremony, all generously covered by the staff of the *Examiner*).[7] The strategy worked, as circulation doubled in the first year, and climbed to about 37,000 by 1890; deficits turned into yearly profits.[8] Having found success in San Francisco, Hearst was eager to apply his methods in the highly competitive New York market, where his main rival would be Joseph Pulitzer, owner of the *World*. In 1895, Hearst paid $180,000 for the *Journal*, which had a sagging circulation of 77,000 and dim prospects in the face of growing deficits. Pulitzer hardly noticed "the gnat buzzing around his head" at first.[9] But Hearst lowered the *Journal's* price to one cent, though it meant taking an initial loss, in order to build up circulation, and he enlarged the paper to sixteen pages. He brought in top staff members from San Francisco and used higher salaries to raid Pulitzer's staff, reaching into the upper echelon. He hired Solomon S. Carvalho, the *World's* publisher, and Morrill Goddard, the *World's* Sunday editor, and then Goddard's replacement Sunday editor, Arthur Brisbane. The *Journal* focused on crime and scandal, as did the *World*, looking to such stories to build a mass audience; the *Journal* also helped its circulation drive by campaigning for war with Spain and supporting William Jennings Bryan for president, among other causes. Within a year, the *Journal's* circulation was 150,000 and rapidly climbing, and Pulitzer knew he was in the midst of what came to be called the "Yellow Journalism" war, an allusion to the "Yellow Kid" cartoons in the *World* that were known for touches of sensationalism and vulgarity. Typical of the blaring headlines in the *Journal* were "Startling

Confession of a Wholesale Murderer Who Begs to Be Hanged," "Real American Monsters and Dragons" (over a story about fossil remains), and "The Whole Country Thrills With War Fever" (in promoting action against Spain).[10]

Hearst Favors the Tried, the True, and the Muscular

So when Hearst set up shop in Chicago, sending Carvalho ahead as his business manager to prepare for publication, he hewed to the strategies that had worked for him in San Francisco and in New York. The Hearst team focused on circulation, and pledged to quickly surpass the *Daily News* and the *Record-Herald,* as well as the *Tribune.*[11] Hearst housed the *American* in an old building at 216 West Madison St., and had presses shipped from New York. In assembling a team of reporters and editors, Hearst transferred some of his staff members from New York, including Brisbane, Homer Davenport, and Jimmy Swinnerton, and snatched away some from other Chicago dailies by offering more generous salaries. A top salary for Chicago reporters was thirty dollars per week, and Hearst offered some fifty dollars or more.[12] The Hearst team put out newspapers with headlines that "varied from large to gigantic" (the latter, 480–point banners that filled the top half of the page).[13] The headlines were intended to catch the eye on newsstands. But in order to be seen, the papers had to be on the newsstands, and Hearst ran into trouble there. The other dailies, especially Lawson's *News,* tried to use their muscular circulation workers and established relationships with news dealers to keep Hearst papers off the stands.[14] Needing a forceful advocate, Hearst turned to Max Annenberg, a twenty-five-year-old assistant circulation manager who was then employed by the *Tribune,* and his brother Moses. The Annenbergs were streetwise businessmen who understood that circulation work at that time in Chicago involved more than eloquent sales pitches and subscription giveaways. Circulation managers first had to see that the papers were delivered, and then properly displayed. In the rules that governed distribution at the time, "dealers had no compunction about stealing bundles of papers belonging to a rival and throwing them into Lake Michigan or the Chicago River or setting them on fire."[15] Newspapers tried to establish exclusive relationships with dealers to keep rivals off the stands; dealers who failed to heed warnings could have their kiosks trashed and get roughed up, or worse.

As the Hearst papers mounted an offensive in the early years of the century, "the avenues were bloody and whether Max and Moe Annenberg were the instigators or the retaliators, there is no question they were full participants" in the sometimes violent competition for readers.[16] Max worked out of the

Madison Street headquarters as a circulation manager; Moe oversaw circulation in the tough neighborhood of Englewood, southwest of the University of Chicago, and eventually he was promoted to circulation manager for the whole South Side of Chicago. Moe organized a squad of circulation specialists, who were armed with baseball bats, brass knuckles, and handguns, to make room on the newsstands for the *American*. The men rode on *American* circulation wagons to give each news dealer a choice: "He could either sell the bundle of papers tossed to him or he could eat them," taking a financial loss.[17] It was leadership by example. Moe described waking up at 3:30 A.M., tucking a revolver in each of his coat pockets, and heading into Englewood by streetcar to see that the kiosks and carriers got their papers. One morning in Englewood he and a *Tribune* seller got into a fistfight that ended only after Moe had bloodied his opponent and both were arrested, an action that apparently resulted in little more than a judicial scolding.[18] The Annenberg squad consisted of prizefighters, bouncers, and mobsters in the making, some of whom became notorious. They included Mossy Enright, who was killed in a gangland fight in the 1920s; Tim Murphy, who was also killed in a mob feud; "Diamond" Dick Torpy, who was shot and slain in a private dispute; and James Ragen and Mickey McBride, who went on to help manage a racetrack newswire for Moe in the 1930s, Nationwide News Service.[19] With this fourth estate army in place, the circulation of the Hearst papers soared. Gradually, the slugging tactics settled down, and Moe headed to Milwaukee in 1906 to set up a newspaper and magazine distribution service. Back in Chicago, where the dailies fell into a kind of tense accommodation, Max continued to manage circulation for the Hearst papers.

Circulation Wars Heat Up

Then in 1910, the violence sharply escalated. The *Tribune's* management was in turmoil, with Robert W. Patterson, the president of the Tribune Company and editor-in-chief of the paper, in poor health. Patterson had taken over the paper when his father-in-law, Joseph Medill, the longtime editor-in-chief and owner, died in 1899. Patterson was reelected president of the Tribune Company and editor-in-chief of the newspaper in February 1910, but he died two months later. Lawson wanted to buy the paper, and the company directors appeared ready to consummate the sale. But two of Medill's grandsons, Robert R. McCormick and Joe Patterson, stepped forward to run the paper and block the sale to Lawson. While the sale was up in the air, Lawson had let it be known that if he could not buy the paper, the Tribune Company should prepare for a price war.[20] That June, with the sale effectively scuttled, Lawson informed the Tribune directors that he intended to cut the price of the *Record-Herald,* the morning paper, to a cent a copy, from two cents.[21] The *Tribune,* also a morning paper, responded in kind, and dropped its price to a cent, from two cents. Before that, the *Examiner* had been the only morning paper that sold for a penny.[22] With the price war underway, slugging again became the tactic of choice in bolstering circulation. The *Tribune* this time raided Hearst's staff, and hired his chief of circulation, Max Annenberg, who took some of his hard-fisted associates and his weapons with him in switching to the *Tribune* side. In October 1910, the *Tribune's* "new army" began driving through the Loop in a black limousine truck.[23] The truck would park by a newsstand and wait for the arrival of a competing daily's truck, which could be met with a round of bullets. Andrew M. Lawrence, who had become Hearst's top executive in Chicago, responded by hiring his own gang of gunmen, and Lawson papers also joined in using force to sell papers. A "new kind of circulation war"[24] raged in Chicago, as armed sluggers brutalized news dealers, trashed delivery trucks belonging to the competition, and dumped papers in the river. Despite calls from the smaller *Chicago Daily Socialist* for a grand jury, the police and prosecuting attorney largely ignored the battles, at the behest of the powerful publishers.[25] The newspapers, except for the *Chicago Daily Socialist,* did not regard the shootings as news to be covered: "The *Tribune,* the *American,* and the *Record-Herald* wrote nothing."[26]

Dailies Form a United Front Against Labor

Cochran, who began publishing the *Day Book* while the circulation war was still raging, intended to crusade against these strong-arm tactics employed by the most powerful publishers in the city. But while Cochran was settling in, the circulation dynamics in the city abruptly changed, and the alliances shifted. In the spring of 1912, labor troubles between Hearst's *Examiner* and *American* and the pressmen's union reached a breaking point, and prompted the major dailies in the city to form a united front against labor. The lead story in the *Day Book* on Thursday, May 2, reported: "Every newspaper in Chicago that is a member of the Daily Newspaper Association of Chicago [the Chicago chapter of the American Newspaper Publishers' Association]—this is the technical name of the publishers' trust—today suspended publication."[27] The action followed what the paper described as "a lockout" of the pressmen at the *Examiner* and the *American,* which was ordered by Lawrence, manager of the Hearst papers, at 9:30 on Wednesday night. By prior agreement, the *Day Book* said, the action of any one publisher against the union bound the other publishers to lend their support, or face fines from the association. The lockout amounted to an "obvious first step,"[28] the paper asserted, to dismantle the entire Web Pressmen's union, beginning with Local No. 7 in Chicago. In addition to the *Examiner* and the *American,* the newspapers in the association consisted of the *Tribune, Record-Herald, News, Inter-Ocean, Journal,* and *Evening Post.*

The reporting by the *Day Book,* which clearly showed its support of the union, was somewhat misleading. The association newspapers did not suspend publication, but they did face a struggle to continue publishing papers, with the pressmen no longer on the job. The publishing efforts were further handicapped on Friday, May 3, when the Stereotypers' Local No. 4 joined the walkout in a sympathy action, and two unaffiliated local organizations, the Delivery and Mail Drivers' Union and the Newsboys' Union, followed suit. The impact of the labor dispute was immediate, and visible on the streets. The *Day Book* reported that week that five wagons backed up to the offices of the *Daily News* and seven to the *American,* there to load up on nonunion issues of the newspapers.[29] Each wagon carried a nonunion driver, two policemen, and six sluggers. The newspapers were delivered to a few downtown corners, where, under heavy police protection, few copies sold, the *Day Book* said.

There was a wide discrepancy in accounts over what precipitated the labor troubles, and whether to say the pressmen had gone on strike or whether they had been locked out by the publishers. The choice of wording was more than an exercise in semantics, because it effectively assigned "responsibility for the conflict."[30] The Newspapers Publishers' Association preferred to characterize the action as a strike, while the unions and the *Day Book* called it a lockout. The labor dispute, in whatever terms it was couched, arose in part because of Hearst's initial desire to bolster his reputation as a friend of labor, and to increase circulation, when he began publishing in Chicago. Hearst struck out on his own in making contracts with the various unions, and agreed to more generous terms than those agreed to by the other publishers. The Hearst contracts ran for five years, until 1905, and then were renewed for another five-year term. But during that second period in the contact, the unions signed contracts with the publishers' association "on terms more favorable to management than those granted to Hearst."[31] When it came time to negotiate a new contract for the pressmen and other printing trades unions in 1910, Hearst wanted conditions in line with those of the other publishers. But the unions objected, and the pressmen and Hearst were unable to reach an agreement on wages, among other matters. The contract differences were submitted to arbitration at the Chicago Board of Trade, which reduced wages between 20 percent and 30 percent, putting them in line with the salaries of pressmen at the other Chicago dailies. But on another matter of contention, the size of press crews, the board did not go along with Hearst's wish to reduce the number of men per press. Management proceeded anyway with the crew reduction, saying only eight men should operate each Octuple press, rather than ten. At that point the pressmen refused to work, contending that Hearst could not change the size of the crew without the approval of the workers and that doing so constituted a broader attack on organized labor.

For Two Papers, an Opportunity

It was clear from the beginning of the labor strife that the *Day Book* intended to fully support the striking workers. Not only was this consistent with the newspaper's general pro-labor stance, but in this case it made smart business sense. With the other dailies handicapped in their ability to publish and distribute papers, the *Day Book* had a chance to make extensive circulation inroads. In April, its average daily circulation was 1,401; the subscriber base more than doubled in May to 3,430.[32] Only two newspapers remained at full strength during the labor battle, the *Day Book* and the *Chicago Daily Socialist,* which in the course of the strife changed its name to the *Chicago Evening World.*[33] Scripps forewarned Cochran not to change the character of his newspaper to appeal to readers bereft of their old papers and not to get carried away in seeking circulation gains. "After this short orgy is over, and you have enjoyed or suffered a period of great exhilaration or hope," Scripps wrote, "your circulation will fall with a dull thud."[34] But the *World* took a different tack, expanding to twelve pages from four, adding new presses, introducing a morning edition, and hiring more staff members.[35] With the presses racing, circulation at the *World* took off toward 300,000, representing nearly a tenfold increase from the paper's typical audience of 30,000 to 40,000.

The struggle between the unions and newspaper owners was fiercely fought, at times violently so. On a Saturday a few days into the strike or lockout, nonunion workers selling the *News* and the *American* met with a newsboy selling the *World,* who shouted that his paper was "the only union newspaper for sale on the streets of Chicago."[36] A Hearst worker struck the newsboy, and the crowd began to close in on the worker. But some thirty-five police officers then rushed the crowd, using their clubs to disperse people. At various times in 1912, newsboys for the socialist paper were beaten, shot, and even killed by sluggers from the big dailies.[37] As Jon Bekken has noted, the attacks were not really about politics, that is, capitalism opposed to socialism. Rather, the violence was "an effort to shut down one of the few newspapers not crippled" by the strike or lockout of the pressmen.[38] On May 10, the *Day Book* reported that Charles Jones, identified as a "negro strikebreaker," was trying to sell copies of the *News,* the *Journal,* and the *American* on the West Side.[39] Another black man, reportedly on the newspapers' payroll, walked up to him and bought a newspaper. A crowd of union supporters surged forward, someone tore away the newspaper just purchased, and others chased the buyer. Then people turned on the strikebreaker, throwing rolled-up paper and then a stone at him. A policeman hustled him into a tavern, where union supporters jammed the officer into a corner and beat up the strikebreaker.

Three weeks into the strike, Samuel Gompers, president of the American Federation of Labor, based in New York, sought to meet with the publishers in Chicago, but was turned away. Gompers said he was convinced that the publishers intended to enforce an open shop in every newspaper office—meaning that workers could be hired regardless of whether they were members of a union—rather than submit the issues of dispute to arbitration.[40] While in town, Gompers did meet with John Fitzpatrick, president of the Chicago Federation of Labor; Ed Nockels, secretary of the federation; Joe C. Orr, international secretary of the pressmen's union, and others. When asked to discuss any plans for winning the strike, Gompers said, "This is going to be a hard battle. It would be folly to tell how we are going to fight it."[41] At the end of May, the wives, relatives, and friends of the strikers held a rally at which they urged a boycott of any stores that advertised in papers belonging to the publishers' association. The boycott campaign, the *Day Book* reported, is "making the stores holler like stuck pigs," since many already had "not been getting returns for money paid out for advertising in the trust newspapers" after the strike began.[42] That same day, the *Day Book* reported that the largest advertisers had investigated circulation levels during the strike and determined that they were being charged full rates although circulation was less than half of what it had been before the strike began. As a result, stores pledged to cut their advertising in half.

Selling Papers by the ".38–Caliber Method"

As the strike continued, the violence turned deadly. Five *American* newspaper wagons were crossing Desplaines Street, when a union worker, George Hehr, tried to drive his wagon across the street between the *American* wagons. The *Day Book* reported that an *American* driver "drove his wagon crashing into Hehr's."[43] An exchange of words followed, and then the *American* driver drew a gun and fired at Hehr five times, hitting him in the abdomen. Hehr died shortly afterward. This was the second "murder" committed by "thugs in the employ of Chicago newspapers."[44] Earlier in the year, a street car conductor had been killed. In both cases, the gunmen had been deputized officers, granted badges by the police department to keep order on the streets, alongside special security officers employed by the association papers. The *Day Book* stated in an editorial, "This means that in a war between newspaper owners and their union employees, the law has been thrown on the side of the rich publishers and against the wage-workers."[45] In a series of front-page articles in August, the *Day Book* sought to expose the extent of the thuggery engaged in by the big dailies. With the pressmen's standoff, the papers hired "ex-convicts, thugs and sluggers"[46] and had them sworn in as deputies by the police, permitting the men to carry guns. The *Day Book* published the names of some of the so-called special policemen hired by Hearst: Charles Barrett, convicted of rape in 1905; his brother Edward Barrett, convicted of robbing the Chicago post office, 1909; Thomas Delhante, convicted of burglary, 1909; and William (Buck) Masterson, convicted of robbery, 1906. Edward Barrett, Delhante, and Masterson were among seven suspects in the killing of George Hehr.[47]

The ".38-caliber method of selling newspapers"[48] became perhaps most fierce in 1912, the year of the strike, with sluggers from the major dailies fighting with union workers, and, to a lesser degree, with the dailies still battling one another to gain readers. The effort to build circulation by brute force that year left more than two dozen news dealers dead and many more injured.[49] The circulation battles were certainly aggravated by the labor dispute with the pressmen, which sent readership plummeting. In one instance, Dutch Gentleman, who worked for the Hearst papers, was in a saloon drinking whisky when a *Tribune* slugger entered the saloon and shot him dead. On other occasions, newsstands were wrecked. Most of the violence could be traced to the special guards hired by Hearst and the other publishers to accompany their delivery trucks and monitor distribution points.[50] At least four strikers and sympathizers were killed by gunfire, and others were seriously wounded.[51] The distributors and newsboys for the Socialist paper, the *World*, were also attacked by sluggers from the association papers, and the police seemed disinclined to protect the newsboys.[52] There is no indication that the *Day Book* suffered such violence, presumably because it had largely limited its circulation to small residential areas outside the Loop and did not challenge the other dailies in sales as directly as the *World* did during the strike.

Except for the *Day Book* and the *World*, the newspapers scarcely covered the violence, and the police gave it little notice, at least in part because of the political clout exercised by the papers.[53] The *Day Book* urged Mayor Carter Harrison to stand up to the major dailies and to cancel the deputy privileges of all of the newspaper security employees. The locus of power, the paper said, is Hearst's lieutenant, Andy Lawrence, who "appears to be the real mayor of Chicago."[54] The *Day Book* said that Lawrence had Paddy Lavin, captain of the Chicago police force, placed in charge of the strike squad, "so that the police could be used as the publishers wanted them used in the fight to crush unionism."[55] The paper urged immediate intervention: "If Mayor Harrison isn't owned, body, soul and breeches by the newspaper bosses, he will order the police to disarm every newspaper slugger."[56]

City Puts *Day Book* on Notice

The strike effectively ended in November that year, when the delivery drivers and the newsboys who had walked out in sympathy returned to work, and the stereotypers signed a new contract with the Chicago publishers. The pressmen's local was left isolated and ineffective, and nonunion pressmen carried out their work at the association papers. As the established dailies began to recover the circulation that had been lost during the labor troubles, the *Day Book*'s circulation plummeted. The *Day Book* had peaked at 5,161 subscribers in September, then slipped to 5,006 in October, and 4,221 in November. Cochran was desperate to try a new tack to jumpstart the paper's growth. Though Scripps wanted to hold to the familiar strategy and build circulation strictly through canvassing house to house, Cochran determined in December, that with the other dailies back at full strength, it was imperative that he begin selling papers on newsstands in the downtown Loop. But the powers that be did not give the paper a warm reception in the business district. Less than four months later, on March 26, with circulation hitting nearly 7,000, the *Day Book* was booted from newsstands. The city abruptly removed the paper from the stands on the pretext that it did not qualify as a newspaper under ordinance No. 2471 of the municipal code, which authorized stands for the sale of daily newspapers printed and published in the city.[57] The *Day Book* said the order was given by a police captain, referred to only by the last name Gibbons, who in turn said that William Luthardt, secretary to the police superintendent, Chief John McWeeny, had made the decision. Whoever the ultimate source of the directive, the official department line was that the *Day Book,* much smaller in size than any of the other dailies, was not a newspaper at all and thus should be barred from the stands. The *Day Book* measured roughly six inches by nine inches, while most of the other papers were about eighteen inches by twenty-four inches.

In Cochran's mind, the action had nothing to do with the paper's size, and everything to do with its critical coverage of the hometown press and the department stores. The action against the *Day Book* coincided with the paper's prominent coverage of a state commission's inquiry into wages paid by businesses in Chicago, the paper said, and the reason for it was clear: "The newspaper trust, with crooked Big Business behind it, has decided that an ad-less newspaper that is free to publish the truth, and dares to publish the truth, is a dangerous thing for crooked business and slave drivers, even if it is a good thing for the people."[58] Cochran did not present evidence directly linking the newsstand action to other newspapers or businesses, but he seemed certain of it. His reasoning was that the *Day Book* had been on sale in the Loop since December 2, 1912, and there had been no interference with its delivery or sale until it began covering the commission.

When the owners of one stand, at the northeast corner of Madison and State Streets, refused to take copies of the *Day Book* on Wednesday, March 26, the business manager, J. T. Watters, placed a newsboy at the corner to sell papers. A police officer, Dennis Hayes, approached and asked whether the newsboy had a permit to sell papers at the corner. Watters said no, but that since the newsstand dealer refused to take copies, it was the only way to make the paper available to passersby. Both Watters and the newsboy were taken to a nearby police booth, where a crowd gathered, and soon both were taken to a police station and charged. Cochran contacted Mayor Carter Harrison's office, and Harrison ordered the police to allow the *Day Book* back on the newsstands, pending a ruling by the corporation counsel on whether the *Day Book* was, in fact, a newspaper. Cochran took the opportunity to champion the *Day Book* not only as a newspaper (published every day except Sunday, he noted, with a staff of editors and reporters, whose copy is supplemented with news from the United Press), but as one that stood apart from its competitors in significant ways, especially by virtue of being adless.[59] An unsigned front-page article, in extra-large type, said: "Having no advertisements, it is under no obligation to anybody but the public. Hence it is more truly a newspaper, in the best sense, than any advertising publication that is run for the benefit of advertisers and calls itself a newspaper."[60] On Friday morning, the corporation counsel's office ended the dispute, ruling, in a qualified way, that the *Day Book* should be considered a newspaper. Leon Hornstein, an assistant corporation counsel, made it clear in the decision that he regarded the *Day Book* as "very far from what is ordinarily called a newspaper."[61] Its tabloid form, for one thing, he said, made it look like a magazine. Still, he said, it carried a conventional newspaper diet of local, national, foreign, and sports news, and circulated among the general public, as opposed to having a specialized readership like that of a literary magazine or legal journal. In a less than ringing endorsement, he concluded: "It, therefore, must be construed as a daily newspaper."

The downtown newsstand battle underscored the uniqueness of the *Day Book,* which was just what Cochran wanted. It was that quality of being different, especially in the absence of advertising, that Cochran sought to emphasize throughout the life of the paper. The *Day Book* frequently ran promotional items along the lines of this one in January 1912: "The *Day Book* is interested most of all in its readers. As it accepts no advertising, it does not have to suppress news and grant special privileges to advertisers. And it can and does tell the truth, no matter where it strikes."[62] The *Day Book* rarely passed up an opportunity to highlight the ties—usually described as financial dependence and editorial subservience—between its competitors and their advertisers, especially the department stores.

SIX

Sandburg and Company

To be a newspaper reporter around the turn of the century in Chicago was to hold a job rich in life experiences but wanting in many other respects. Each of the city's ten largest dailies employed some eight to twenty reporters, as well as six or more editors and assistant editors.[1] Reporters, many of whom were young and saw in journalism a chance for adventure, were assigned to cover City Hall, the courts, the police, and other beats. As a group, they were mostly white, single men, who entered the field in their teens and left in their thirties and forties, often moving on in search of more money and better job security.[2] Whatever the shortcomings of the job, reporters in the early 1900s did enjoy a growing sense of status and glamour, especially those who found work on metropolitan papers, even modest startups like the *Day Book*. A reporter at the smallest of papers in Chicago could go from asking the mayor questions at a news conference to covering a trial with a national following, and write about it all, with a couple of bylines as proof of the day's work. A. A. Dornfeld, who got his start at the City News Bureau, a collective news service that kept Chicago's dailies supplied with local stories, described the intoxicating feeling that a cub reporter had in being on the inside as events unfolded. "He could pick up the telephone at any hour of the day or night," Dornfeld said, "and talk to politicians, bankers, industrialists, and be received with attention. However, to most of the young reporters these solid citizens were not half as interesting as the pimps and prostitutes, the madams and the murderers."[3] As one of the nation's financial and political centers, Chicago promised reporters opportunities to meet the wealthy and the power-ful, as well as those who measured success outside the bounds of law. The novelist Theodore Dreiser described the city as "a giant magnet, drawing to itself, from all quarters, the hopeful and the hopeless—those who had their fortune yet to make and those whose fortunes and affairs had reached a di-sastrous climax elsewhere."[4] Reporters, with or without a college degree, and few had one, enjoyed front-row seats by the stage where these fortunes were made and lost.[5]

Beyond the excitement of the job, many reporters also saw their work as a kind of mission carried out in the public interest, for which they would willingly make sacrifices. Elections needed to be covered, politicians held to account, and the public's tax dollars spent wisely. The reportorial ethos understood reporters to be essential watchdogs on government and vital conduits of important information for the public. When reporters emerged as a distinct work group at the end of the nineteenth century, as gatherers and writers of news, Marianne Salcetti noted, they developed certain "service ideals" linked to "the notion of sacrifice on behalf of the story, or the public interest."[6] The hours might be long, and unpaid beyond a certain point, but, as E. W. Scripps put it, reporters were there "to fight the battles of righteousness against unrighteousness."[7] Investigative and reformist journalism was in full force in muckraking magazines of the era like *Harper's* and *Scribners,* and also in newspapers like those owned by Scripps. In standing by the common people, Scripps newspapers aided the Progressive movement's efforts "to check the excesses of industrialization by wresting political and economic power from the elites and returning it to the masses."[8] Newspaper reporters joined in exposing abuses of power on the part of both government and industry, and advocating goals like municipal ownership of utilities and pure food legislation. The journalist was indoctrinated, said Hugh Dalziel Duncan, "with the belief that the voice of the subscriber was, like the voice of the people, the voice of God. The people must be reached, and they must be reached by good leaders."[9]

Low Pay and Long Hours

But journalists, especially those who worked at smaller news organizations, had no misconceptions about their own dim prospects for securing material security as they followed this calling. As a general rule, the pay was modest, the hours long, and the job tenuous.[10] One study of journalists of the late nineteenth and early twentieth centuries portrayed these early reporters as hard-working (twelve to fourteen hours a day, six days a week) but undercompensated.[11] At the turn of the century, reporters generally received no overtime, no medical insurance, no paid vacations, and no severance pay.[12] Moreover, reporters were commonly fired with little or no notice when the economy stumbled or they missed assignments or took to drinking.[13] In describing the "grim reality" of newsroom conditions at the time, William S. Solomon noted "the ease with which newsroom managers fired or reassigned people on the spot; journalists often could not count on a job from one day to the next."[14] At the City News Bureau in the early years of the century, many reporters worked twelve- to sixteen-hour days, for as little as ten dollars a week, and only in the 1920s did reporters begin to get one day off each week instead of one day off every two weeks.[15] The news bureau, as a press service, was at the lower end of the remuneration scale. At one of Chicago's dailies, the *Inter-Ocean,* reporters earned $15 to $27.50 a week in 1907 (the managing editor was paid considerably more, at $65 a week).[16] According to one survey, reporters at daily newspapers in Chicago were paid $15 to $35 a week, with an average salary of $25.[17] One of the first reporters hired by Negley Cochran at the *Day Book* was Carl Sandburg, who was brought on board at $25 a week. At that time, in 1912, Sandburg's salary (about $1,250 a year) would have roughly corresponded to that earned by clerical workers in manufacturing ($1,209) and by federal employees ($1,128).[18] While salaries varied from one newspaper to another, Fred Fedler found that "some reporters were poor and some comfortable, but few were rich."[19] Reporters could generally afford decent food, shelter, and clothing. But reporters who were young and single had an easier time getting by than those who had families to support. Though without beepers, journalists were very much on call, with breaking news setting irregular hours. As Hugh Dalziel Duncan noted, "While this life gave them an unsurpassed knowledge of the city, it gave them very little knowledge of family life."[20] A survey of journalists in Chicago at the turn of the century found that 43.3 percent were married, widowed, or divorced, compared with 85.8 percent for the nation's adults as a whole; moreover only 15.6 percent of the journalists had been born in Illinois, suggesting a highly mobile work force.[21] They were young (36.8 years old on average) and nearly all male (93.6 percent). And only 7.8 percent owned their own homes, compared with 25 percent for the city as a whole and 64.4 percent across the nation.[22] For many reporters in 1911, when the *Day Book* began publishing, the goals of a decent wage, reasonable work hours, and job security remained, as Marianne Salcetti observed, "elusive work factors."[23]

Sandburg as Party Organizer and Aspiring Writer

The experiences of Carl Sandburg as a journalist reflected the mobility, and the job insecurity, of the day. He had come to Chicago from Milwaukee in 1912 to take a position with the *World,* a socialist daily. When the pressmen's strike had curtailed the operations of most of Chicago's dailies, the *World* and the *Day Book,* which did not belong to the newspaper publishers' association in the city and so were not party to the labor troubles, found themselves in a position to make circulation inroads. The *World,* in particular, embarked on a rapid expansion, hiring reporters and other staff members in an effort to broaden its coverage and win over readers from the striking dailies. Sandburg, who had worked at a socialist daily in Milwaukee, the *Leader,* was among a group of journalists associated with the party who seized the chance to advance their careers in Chicago. But newspaper jobs at the *World* proved as short-lived as they were easy to find. When the pressmen's strike was settled in the fall of 1912, competition returned in full force to the Chicago newsstands, and the *World* found its rapid expansion untenable. Its circulation had increased to nearly 300,000 from about 30,000 before the lockout, but even then the newspaper was still losing money.[24] Its advertising revenue—from socialist publishers, patent medicine manufacturers, and small businesses—was modest; the department stores ran their large and lucrative ads in the capitalist dailies.[25] In November 1912, Sandburg's paycheck bounced, and in December, when the *World* was about $125,000 in debt and had filed for bankruptcy protection, he was out of work.

Sandburg, then thirty-four, certainly knew what it was to be between jobs. A tall, athletic man who was both a gifted speaker and writer, he had spent years trying to find "one clear course for his life," often torn between his literary ambitions and his wish to have enough money to support himself and a family.[26] He first left his hometown of Galesburg, Illinois, in 1897, at 19, to join a wave of tramps and hoboes and vagabonds riding the railroads West for adventure. He washed dishes in Kansas City, threshed wheat on farms in Kansas, and chopped wood in Nebraska. When the United States declared war against Spain in the following year, Sandburg joined the Illinois militia and caught glimpses of exploding shells in Puerto Rico, but saw no action in the brief war. After attending Lombard College back in Galesburg, he set out on the road again, wandering through Michigan, Wisconsin, New York, New Jersey, and Pennsylvania, scratching out a living by selling stereoscopic photographs and 3–D viewers, publishing poems, and giving speeches. And always, wherever he went, he filled pocket notebooks with ideas for poems or articles, bits of conversations overheard, quotations from books.

Promoting the Socialist Vision

Given his early and instinctive interest in reforms that would ease the hard life of many American workers, like better wages and shorter hours, Sandburg was drawn to the socialist movement in Wisconsin, led by the Social-Democrats. He vaguely knew the theories of Marx and Engels, but, as Penelope Niven said, his was more of "a personal, instinctive, eclectic socialism."[27] He had seen his father labor long hours for small wages on the railroad, and he had seen children as young as nine years old put to work in factories. Wisconsin's socialists emphasized the welfare of society and the value of each person, offering a vision that Sandburg shared: reformed government, the right of women to vote, higher wages, tax reform, and pensions. In 1907, the Social-Democrats hired Sandburg as a district organizer, and he traveled widely to recruit members and promote the party's platform, work that left him thin and disheveled and usually with only a few dollars, if that, in his pocket. He stopped by party headquarters in December of that year to chat with Victor Berger, the statewide party leader. Sandburg had to wait because someone else was in Berger's office, a party member and schoolteacher named Lilian Steichen, whose considerable proficiencies included an ability to translate socialist literature in German and French into English for the party. They were introduced, and within days began writing letters, first as comrades exchanging ideas, and then, increasingly, as two people in love. They were married later that year—he was thirty, and she twenty-five—in a brief ceremony in the home of a Congregational minister and party member in Milwaukee.

Carl Sandburg continued to dedicate himself to the socialist movement in Milwaukee, captivating audiences with fiery oratory and lyrical turns of phrase. Married life in the early years, though, was not what Lilian, whom Carl called Paula, had expected. She traveled some of the time with Carl, but more often than not she stayed behind at her parents' farm, harvesting apples, making apple butter, and typing Carl's handwritten articles and poems for submission while he crisscrossed the district. The strain that both of them felt over the long periods of separation eased somewhat when they moved their things from the Steichen farm to an apartment in Appleton, in the heart of Sandburg's district. In the spring of 1909, though, they decided they could no longer subsist on Carl's irregular income as a campaign worker, amounting to an average salary of twenty dollars a month. He resigned his job as an organizer, and they moved to a larger apartment in Milwaukee. For six weeks, he wrote advertising copy for Kroeger's Department Store, and then took a job with the *Milwaukee Journal* as a feature writer. He later switched to the *Milwaukee Sentinel* and then returned to the *Journal.*

As Milwaukee's municipal elections approached in 1910, the socialist party sensed the potential to win a major victory. Recognizing an opportunity to give concrete expression to their socialist ideals, the Sandburgs campaigned tirelessly for Emil Seidel, a councilman who was running for mayor on a pledge to improve the lives of the working people of Milwaukee. Seidel was elected on April 5 with 27,608 votes, outdistancing a Democratic candidate (20,530) and a Republican (11,346), to become the first socialist mayor of Milwaukee.[28] Seidel had seen how effectively Sandburg reached out to people, individually or in groups, and chose him to be his private secretary. The party thought that having a daily newspaper in the city would be crucial for its continued success, and so Berger founded the *Leader* on December 7, 1911. Sandburg joined the paper as a labor reporter and columnist, promoting the socialist vision. In practical matters of governing, however, Seidel and the Social-Democrats faced several hurdles, including state laws limiting municipal autonomy in Milwaukee and the challenges of meeting voters' high expectations for a better quality of life; they also found themselves contending with a more formidable political opponent, when the city's Democrats and Republicans combined forces. In 1912, after two years in office, Seidel and the Social-Democrats were overwhelmed at the polls, and Sandburg, disheartened by the defeat and by quarrels within the socialist movement, headed for Chicago, where, he had heard, the *World* was hiring.[29]

A Door Opens at the *Day Book*

The *World* gave the Sandburgs an opportunity to relocate to Chicago, but little else. Carl and Paula, who had a year-old daughter, Margaret, faced a grim winter after the paper went out of business. The three of them were settled in a small apartment in Ravenswood, a neighborhood in the northwest part of the city. As the holidays approached, they were without an income and without a nearby network of relatives or close friends to whom they might turn for assistance. Sandburg sought work at the *Tribune, La Follette's* in Wisconsin, the *St. Paul News* in Minnesota, and other newspapers,[30] but without success, and was left feeling as dispirited as ever.[31] The literary circles in Chicago offered little prospect of help; Sandburg was still several years away from publishing his first major book of verse, *Chicago Poems,*[32] and he had few contacts among established writers and editors in the city. The couple would later refer to this time as their "Dark Period."[33]

As the new year opened, Sandburg, thirty-four, visited the offices of the *Day Book,* crowded into a basement newsroom on the corner of Congress and Peoria Streets.[34] The editor, Negley Cochran, was looking to add a reporter, and he hired Sandburg at twenty-five dollars a week, about five times what Sandburg had been earning as a party organizer in Wisconsin, but still a modest salary. Cochran had made his mark as a social and political progressive editing the *News-Bee,* the Scripps newspaper in Toledo, Ohio, and he and Sandburg immediately hit it off as fellow reformers. They joined forces in sympathetic coverage of labor and withering treatment of big business, the political establishment, and the mainstream press. In March 1913, for example, around the time Sandburg was hired, the *Day Book* filled the paper with reports and commentary on an Illinois Senate hearing on low wages earned by girls and young women working in Chicago department stores. The paper also carried out its own investigation of the conditions that workers confronted.[35] In what may have been his first article for the *Day Book,* Sandburg noted that a city ordinance required businesses to file police reports for every accident that required the use of an ambulance.[36] But despite the

Carl Sandburg, left, in the offices of the *Day Book,* around 1913–14. (University of Illinois at Urbana-Champaign)

law, he noted, department stores routinely failed to report accidents on their premises. Days earlier, for example, an electrician had had his leg crushed in an elevator in the Carson Pirie Scott store, and at the Hillman's store a woman died after falling down an elevator shaft. In the case of the electrician, Sandburg said, there was no police report and no mention of the accident in any paper excepting the *Day Book;*[37] as for the woman's death, he said, most of the papers that reported the accident kept Hillman's name out of the news, describing the location only as "a building on the southwest corner of Washington and State streets."[38] Sandburg issued an indictment by implication: shoppers were at risk of injury or even death, but the stores, because of their financial clout, maintained a sanitized image conducive to doing business.

Young Reporters in Charge

Cochran managed a small staff, primarily consisting of a managing editor, a business manager, and several reporters.[39] At the outset, he brought in his son, Harold, to be the managing editor.[40] Cochran let Harold edit the paper largely on his own for months at a time, including, somewhat surprisingly, the first few weeks of publication. In a letter to Scripps, Cochran said that Harold had selected and condensed many of the features and news articles from the wire services as the paper got underway.[41] Cochran said that gave him time to solve the mechanical problems with the press and gave Harold editorial training so that he could take over as needed during Cochran's absences. At times Cochran said he knew he would need to travel back to Ohio to tend to business at the *News-Bee,* of which he remained the editor and a part owner, and during those times, Harold Cochran would run the paper. This became something of a sore point with Scripps, who seemed concerned that Cochran was failing to provide sufficient leadership and was turning over too much authority to inexperienced hands.[42] A year into the experiment, Cochran sought to assure Scripps that he remained fully in charge of the paper and was not overly delegating authority to his son Harold or to anyone else: "[Harold] never was editor, had only considered himself an aide to me and a sort of managing editor. Both he and I figured on [Donald] MacGregor doing the editor's work if I wasn't here. He knows and I know that he isn't ready to tackle any such job as editor of the *Day Book.*"[43]

But a review of letters exchanged by Negley and Harold Cochran suggests that Harold was indeed, for long stretches at a time, the de facto editor. In the spring of 1912, for example, Harold Cochran, writing from Chicago, sent letters to his father back in Ohio on March 3 and 21, April 18, May 16 and 20, and

June 5.[44] During that stretch, John T. Watters, the *Day Book's* business manager, also had regular correspondence with Negley Cochran in Ohio, dating letters on March 20, April 30, and May 23. In one letter to Harold, Cochran said he would "leave you boys largely to your own resources in building up the *Day Book*," and assured him that "you have had enough experience in making up the paper, as you have made up every issue since the beginning."[45] Negley Cochran also left little doubt in his correspondence with Watters that the two young men were to manage the paper: "You and Harold will have things largely in your own hands now, for I am going to be here most of the time and watch you from a distance."[46] The following month Cochran sent Watters another letter in which he gave the date for his expected return to Chicago, and noted that he had been away from the *Day Book's* operations for two weeks. "You can do nothing to please me more," he wrote, "than to make it a good thing for the *Day Book* for me to keep out of Chicago except for occasional flying visits."[47]

The relatively small size of the staff, as well as Negley Cochran's hands-off management style, presented ample opportunity for employees to try out different roles in the newsroom. Watters, who was hired as the business manager, discovered that openness in the first issue when he wrote the syrupy short story that led the paper. The story established, beyond any doubt, that Watters's best contributions to journalism would lie elsewhere. There is no indication that Watters wrote after that inauspicious debut, though it is difficult to determine that with any certainty because the paper consistently printed articles by staff members without any byline at all.[48] Figuring out who on the staff wrote a given article often ends in speculation. Watters concentrated most of his efforts on circulation, supervising canvassers whose job it was to sign up subscribers, though at times making the rounds himself. He regularly sent circulation reports to Miramar to keep Scripps abreast of where readership stood.

Harold Cochran also tried his hand at writing as well as editing, often contributing a kind of folksy poetry that gave prominence to the rhyme, even when it forced awkward word choices. For example, in his ode to the "American Kid," he wrote:

A school kid looks more like himself,
When dirty are his hands and face;
And comfort is a ruling thing,
If his necktie's out of place.[49]

And when the Chicago police roughed up waitresses who were on strike at

Henrici's restaurant in 1914, Cochran complemented the paper's regular news coverage with a poem that began:

> My Country, 'Tis of Thee,
> Sweet Land of Slugging Cops,
> Of Thee We Sing.
> Land where the cops can't see,
> To treat girls humanly,
> But wrench them terribly,
> Has freedom come?[50]

Though he wrote such pieces from time to time, Cochran too seemed to recognize that his strengths lay elsewhere—in his case, editing and managing, and he largely kept to that.

Whether on the business side or the news side, nearly all of the employees at the *Day Book* were men, as was true of the industry as a whole. When women began entering newsrooms after the Civil War, in small numbers, most were assigned to cover topics seen as appealing to women, like food and fashions. If they drew a general news assignment, they might have been asked to write an emotional sidebar to accompany a main news story.[51] In the midst of the male force assembled in the *Day Book*'s newsroom, one reporter stood out, and only partly because she was a woman. Jane Whitaker established herself as a sterling editor and reporter, and a top assistant to Harold Cochran. In 1913, Harold Cochran noted that he had reorganized the desks in the office and placed the reporters in a line along the wall.[52] He said that Whitaker's desk was first in line. "I am getting copy from Jane all day long so wanted her desk closer to mine," he said. At the time, she was editing telegraph news and rewriting items from other Chicago papers. She expressed an interest, he said, in doing more reporting out of the office, and Harold said he wanted another reporter to pick up some of her work in the office so she could go out on assignments. Such opportunities followed, and Whitaker filed regular reports on labor strife and workplace conditions, including a series of articles on the strike by waitresses at Henrici's. In those articles, Whitaker helped readers get to know the waitresses, and the reasons they were on strike; the primary goal was a one dollar raise in weekly pay, to eight dollars. Whitaker interviewed one waitress on the picket line who said she had been ticketed numerous times by the police, who accused her of disorderly conduct in front of the restaurant. But she said she would not be intimidated because she needed the raise: "After I paid my room rent and my laundry I had between $2 and $2.50 a week on which to

Staff members of the *Day Book,* around 1913–14. Sandburg is second from the left. (University of Illinois at Urbana-Champaign)

live. Some days I spent 10 cents for food. Other days when I got tips I was able to get meals. But my meals depended on the tips I got."[53]

A Brand of Advocacy Journalism

Another reporter hired by Cochran early on, Don MacGregor, struggled with drinking and health in Chicago, never emerging as the solid editor that Cochran was betting on.[54] In 1913, Cochran shipped him to Denver, hoping that the change of climate would restore his health.[55] Once out West, MacGregor worked for another Scripps paper, the *Denver Express.* He ended up camping with striking miners in May 1914 at one site of labor tensions, in Walsenburg, Colorado, and led several hundred of them in a battle with National Guardsmen. He recounted the scene in an article published in the *Day Book:* "There were two hundred and fifty militiamen. There were over one hundred mine guards. They had nine machine guns. We had the advantage of [a hilltop] position, but they outnumbered us, they had the machine guns, and were better organized."[56] Both miners and militiamen died before a truce was called at Walsenburg and Federal troops moved in, MacGregor reported. For the miners, the rallying cry was Ludlow, site of the famous massacre on April 20, in which several dozen people, including women and children, were shot or burned to death. After he was indicted for murder by a Colorado grand jury, MacGregor took off for Mexico, in the apparent hope of joining the forces led by Francisco "Pancho" Villa, the revolutionary who took up arms in his advocacy of social reforms.[57] Villa had fought against the dictator Porfirio Diaz in 1910 and helped bring about Diaz's fall. Successors followed in short order, with Venustiano Carranza eventually taking power. By 1914, Villa was seeking to topple the Carranza government. But Villa had also threatened to kill gringos, and in 1916, when his men took over a Carranza stronghold in Manaca, they shot one of their own in spirit, Don MacGregor, as he left the hotel where he had been staying.[58]

Writing in 1929, Sandburg remembered "this fair haired Scotch boy with a soft heart, beautiful dreams and rare courage of both instinct and mind."[59] It had been a long time, he said, since they both had napped on tables at City Hall during the 1912 pressmen's strike. Sandburg paid homage to MacGregor in the poem "Memoir of a Proud Boy," and, with ample poetic license, told how it all turned out:

Named by a grand jury as a murderer
He went to Chihuahua, forgot his old Scotch name,
Smoked cheroots with Pancho Villa
And wrote letters of Villa as a rock of the people.

How can I tell how Don MacGregor went?

Three riders emptied lead into him.
He lay on the main street of an inland town.
A boy sat near all day throwing stones
To keep pigs away.

The Villa men buried him in a pit
With twenty Carranzistas.[60]

Sandburg failed to note that MacGregor had actually been shot by a Villa officer; and that it was townspeople in Manaca, not the Villa men, who buried the young reporter.[61] Displaying a looseness with the facts that would sometimes color his reporting, Sandburg the poet shaped the story to fit his vision of how it should have turned out: "the revolutionary is killed by reactionary forces and buried by radical forces."[62]

Just as MacGregor had left the *Day Book* after a short stay, Sandburg too felt compelled to leave soon after he was first hired in 1913, though for different reasons. On his improved but still modest salary at the *Day Book,* Sandburg and his wife, Lilian, continued to struggle to pay the bills, and he looked for ways to supplement his earnings.[63] During his nights at home that winter, when he often wrote poetry, Sandburg also turned out a couple of articles for *System: The Magazine of Business,* a national journal published for administrators, salesmen, and factory managers.[64] The articles were well received, and the trade journal offered him a job as associate editor at thirty-five dollars a week, which represented a raise of nearly 50 percent. He accepted the position in March, though it is apparent he felt somewhat uneasy working for a voice of industry. He often used a pseudonym for the articles he wrote on the high cost of government, but reverted to his own name when an article focused on a subject of concern to workers, like accident prevention. He was aware of the credibility risks of "a socialist writing for a capitalist trade journal."[65] His job at *System* did not last long. In the fall of 1913, he was dismissed by the editors, who recognized Sandburg's writing ability, especially his creative powers, but thought he was out of place at the trade journal. After being fired, Sandburg briefly edited another trade journal, the *American Artisan and Hardware Record.* By the spring of 1914, he was back at the *Day Book* to stay.

A Clear Message in a Folksy Style

Sandburg's writing in the *Day Book* reflected the kind of breezy, slangy style that Scripps and Cochran thought would appeal to workers. For example, under the headline "Willum Is Working A Fine Little Game," Sandburg wrote about patent-medicine ads that ran in a Hearst paper: "Willie Hearst's afternoon paper, the Evening American, solemnly told us last Monday that never-r-r again would advertisements of patent medicines, known or suspected to be fakes, be published in the valued (?) American."[66] The article then lists some of the advertisers and their promises that ran in Hearst's morning paper, the *Examiner,* like Pape's Cold Compound, which "breaks a cold in a few hours" and can be taken with the knowledge that "there is nothing else in the world which will cure your cold or end grippe misery as promptly." One envisions Sandburg sitting down at a typewriter and hurriedly banging out his copy, reserving more thoughtful and judicious editing for his poetry at night. In fairness to Sandburg, Cochran would likely have tossed out any articles that did suggest literary pretensions. If Scripps had his way, the editor, and no doubt the entire staff, would have been "forbidden to read anything better than could be found in a farm journal or dime novel."[67] Cochran drilled his reporters on certain fundamentals of journalism, like economy and simplicity of words. He found an attentive student in Sandburg, who later said: "I never hesitate about saying that probably the best single course of instruction I ever had as a writer was working along with you on the *Day Book*."[68]

Sandburg's contributions as a poet and a biographer, for which he received Pulitzer Prizes,[69] are well documented, but his journalistic work, especially at the *Day Book*, remains largely unexplored.[70] Two librarians, N. Frederick Nash and Gwenna Weshinsky, took an initial step in 1982 in compiling a list of Sandburg's articles in the *Day Book* from 1912 to 1917.[71] Nash and Weshinsky were hard-pressed to identify all of Sandburg's writing for the *Day Book* because of the paper's questionable policy of nearly always omitting bylines, a move intended to free up more space for news on the small tabloid pages.[72] While Sandburg received more bylines than anyone else on staff, excepting possibly the editor, Negley Cochran, more often than not his articles appeared unsigned. Nash and Weshinsky succeeded in identifying 135 articles by Sandburg in part by drawing on clippings in his personal files, some of which had bylines and some of which he had marked or initialed to signal authorship.[73] More than a quarter of the articles attributed to Sandburg were published in 1917, when he added a signed column called "War Notes" to his news beat assignments. The *Day Book* published at least four of his poems that were not published elsewhere.[74]

Sandburg Helps to Redefine News

Nash and Weshinsky observe in a brief introduction to the list that it is doubtful whether the articles, written in a kind of folksy style well suited to the *Day Book,* "in and of themselves are to be considered valuable as literature."[75] But the articles, they would allow, do open a significant window on Chicago journalism in the early 1900s, and on the meaning of news as Sandburg and his colleagues understood it. Sandburg was a lead contributor in the *Day Book's* effort to redefine news by intentionally focusing on the struggles of the working class and the dispossessed; as the *Day Book* saw it, the mainstream press took a top-down approach, covering (generally favorably) the activities of powerful players in government and business. By contrast, the *Day Book* established itself as a champion of those on the lower rungs: the factory workers, department store clerks, and others it counted among the struggling majority. The paper's favorite targets included department stores, especially Marshall Field's, the commercial lord of State Street, and other newspapers, which were seen as courting advertisers at every turn (reflected, for example, in the failure to report on accidents and other troubles in department stores). Sandburg set the tone. In a passionate and sometimes confrontational voice, Sandburg, in nearly every article, challenged the industry standard of detached and objective reporting presented in the inverted pyramid style, with the most important information in the lead paragraphs. His approach, at the *Day Book* and later at the *Daily News,* required finding the larger meaning in a news story, and making that plain.[76] As a journalist, and as a poet, he believed that he had to speak the truth as he saw it, and the *Day Book* gave him a platform to do just that. And the truth was, he believed, that Chicago's most powerful and wealthy citizens were oppressing the majority—"the 95 percent"—and the system cried out for reform.

Given his socialist credentials, Sandburg comfortably filled the role of senior reporter for a paper that saw itself as a faithful advocate of the working class. Some of his articles harshly criticized the State Street department stores over safety, working conditions, and wages; he faulted the mainstream Chicago press for its coverage, or lack of coverage, of the news; some articles focused on living and working conditions around the stockyards; city government and city officials, especially the mayor's office and police department, also came under fire. Two favorite targets were the Marshall Field family and the publisher William Randolph Hearst, who were portrayed as oppressive representatives of the wealthy, capitalist class. Sandburg was never one to practice detached, neutral reporting. In his view, for example, giving equal time to store owners and store workers would have resulted in a distorted picture of reality and represented a failure to tell the truth about inequities and injustices that daily confronted the workers. But his unbending advocacy could also risk distorting the truth. As a labor reporter for the *Leader,* Sandburg once went to cover an expected strike by streetcar employees who were aggrieved by their working conditions.[77] As he waited at a station, the cars kept running along, without any sign of a labor action. As Sandburg recounted the story, he approached one motorman, determined to get him to walk off the job. When words failed, Sandburg said he grabbed the motorman's right arm to pull him off the car; the company manager stepped forward and grabbed the motorman's left arm, intent on keeping the car running. The two engaged in a tug-of-war until Sandburg, aware of a growing audience, gave up the effort.

An Eager Champion of Causes

Such intervention was no doubt rare, but as a rule, Sandburg did not hesitate to engage in social commentary or to champion people or causes he believed in, as many of his articles in the *Day Book* make clear. In 1916, he wrote obituary essays for two men whom he admired. The first was a tribute to Henry Favill, a physician and "man of light and vision"[78] who fought for safer and healthier conditions for American workers. Describing Favill's face, Sandburg wrote, it had "the sad, stern power written on faces of some of the finest Indians—the deep, quizzical thoughtfulness of a Lincoln face." Favill regarded the human body as a temple, Sandburg wrote, and railed against the Chicago mills and workshops that contaminated so many bodies, leading to premature death. The "chief message of his life" was that employers had "a direct control over the health of the thousands working for them through control of the air supply, the working hours and the wages that dictate housing conditions." Sandburg linked his own work to Favill's crusade, noting that as a reporter he wrote about "the white plague" of tuberculosis victims who had toiled in Mandel Brothers' second-basement salesrooms and Oscar Heineman's silk mill, "where girls get headaches breathing in foul air and then Heineman gives them Bromo Seltzer free gratis to cure their headaches."

Two months later, Sandburg wrote another obituary essay to celebrate the life of a doctor who sought better working conditions and health care for workers. The doctor, Theodore B. Sachs, regarded tuberculosis as "a creeping terror" that could be stopped if society would give science "a chance to use what it knows."[79] Cook County, Illinois, had 3,500 tuberculosis deaths in 1915, according to Sandburg. Few of those who died were bankers, he wrote. Rather, "wherever there are low wages and long working hours"—in cigar shops, garment factories, department store basements, granite cutting shops—"the white plague reaches its highest batting average in mortality." Sachs, who managed a public hospital, committed suicide. He killed himself in part because he wearied of political accusations of mismanagement at the hospital, Sandburg said. But more than that, Sachs was done in by watching "wholesale murder working through the slow process of consumption, a preventable disease, checking off its victims with the regularity of a clock."

Around that same time, Sandburg wrote an opinion piece for the *Day Book* in which he roundly criticized Arthur Brisbane, "the Hearst editorial star," over two columns that Brisbane had written offering advice to workers on saving money.[80] The thrust of the columns, as Sandburg related it, was that workers should be frugal, or else risk ending up in the poorhouse. Sandburg pointed out that the columnist who would counsel laborers was "known as a spender who slings money right and left, has dozens of shirts in his wardrobe, lives in a big house with men-servants to tend his laundry and feel of the water before he takes his bath." The reason Brisbane was urging struggling workers to save, Sandburg said, was because "the bankers want that advice fed to the poor." Sandburg left it up to the readers to infer why it would be that bankers would want the poor to hear that message—perhaps so the working class would believe that the way to get ahead was through personal thrift and economy rather than a collective demand for an increase in the minimum wage or other reforms in the economic system. But Sandburg saw little reason to put stock in savings as an antidote to the struggles of workers: "As wages run in most industries today, the poor don't have a chance to know the value of a dollar because they live on nickels and dimes. They eat fried mush when they need eggs."

Sandburg invariably kept a focus on the working class in covering political campaigns. One piece proceeded as a straightforward question-and-answer column on Frank O. Lowden, a Chicago lawyer, who in August 1916 had the inside track in the race for the Republican nomination for governor in Illinois.[81] Lowden had married into the wealthy Pullman family and served as a director of the family's railroad concern. Sandburg asked him about his plans for road construction, home rule for Chicago, and the elimination of some state offices. Then he asked Lowden what plans he might have to help "the workingmen of Illinois."

> Sandburg: "Do you have any special ideas on the minimum wage? Would you care to say whether you would stand for a law giving at least $8 a week to the girls in the State Street stores?
> Lowden: "No."
> Sandburg: "Would you care to say anything about a nine-hour day for women workers?"
> Lowden: "No."

Without directly offering his own opinion of Lowden, Sandburg, through carefully selected questions and answers, let the *Day Book* readers know that the lawyer of means and connections was not their candidate.

> Sandburg: "As a director of the Pullman Co. you tried to work out there the same principles of efficiency and humanity which you stand for as a candidate for governor?"
> Lowden: "Yes."

Having established Lowden's commitment to "efficiency" in business, Sandburg ended the interview. In November of that year, after Lowden had been elected, Sandburg suggested a need for campaign finance reforms so that those with "the unlimited moneybags" of a Lowden cannot simply buy whatever office they are seeking.[82] Sandburg itemized some of the $750,000 or so that Lowden spent in the campaign, including at least $100,000 on newspaper advertising, $75,000 for pictures on billboards and poles, and $50,000 for brass bands.

Though Sandburg primarily reported on news in Chicago, he commented on events abroad at times, especially when there were direct links to or shared philosophical interests with workers in the city. He praised a speech by President Woodrow Wilson in April 1916 in which Wilson forcefully rejected calls for the United States to send troops into Mexico. Sandburg wrote: "If Woodrow Wilson is some day classed as a man who shouldered his load and handled his power for masses of people in the same way that Abe Lincoln, amid doubts and accusations, was the lonesomest man in the nation—it will be on the basis of his action in Mexico, refusing to hand over the Federal government to the plunderbunch of capitalists hunting new fields of exploitation."[83] When mass meetings were held in Chicago that spring to raise money for Jews in Russia, Poland, and Palestine, Sandburg took to task some of the leaders of the relief effort, especially Julius Rosenwald, whom he referred to as "the Sears-Roebuck head and the largest income taxpayer in Chicago."[84] Sandburg did not object to the fund-raising effort, he said, but he did accuse some of the leading campaigners of seeing desperation abroad and ignoring the plight of Jewish garment workers in Chicago who had been on strike for "the right to organize and be paid a living wage." Rather than paying decent wages, he said, business owners were investing money in "private detectives, spies, gunmen and sluggers" to intimidate the strikers.

Blending of Poetry and Journalism

Sandburg's work in journalism often provided raw material for his poetry, some of which focused on social and economic conditions, and some of which was apolitical and imagist. As the biographer Penelope Niven observed, he "sat with equal ease with the poets on Cass Street and the reporters at the *Day Book*."[85] Niven describes Sandburg leaving the *Day Book* office one day headed for the Loop to interview a juvenile court judge.[86] He passed through Grant Park and there saw the fog move across the Chicago harbor. When the judge later kept him waiting in the anteroom, Sandburg took out a pencil and paper and wrote his own American version of Japanese haiku:

The fog comes
on little cat feet.

It sits looking
over harbor and city
on silent haunches
and then moves on.[87]

The little work of twenty-one words became Sandburg's most quoted poem.[88] His Chicago poems have been described as "a kind of daily diary," drawn from his time spent wandering the streets, covering meetings, and hanging out at the bohemian Dill Pickle Club (which displayed a cartoon of a man shouting "We gotta change the system").[89] In "Mill-Doors," he writes of a workplace where "you are old before you are young" and in "A Fence," describes a house on the lakefront where the iron bars would "shut off the rabble and all vagabonds and hungry men and all wandering children looking for a place to play."[90]

When Henry Holt published Sandburg's first major work of poetry, *Chicago Poems,* in 1916, the *Day Book* printed a review that was distributed by Scripps's Newspaper Enterprise Association, the national syndicated service for features and opinions. The review, which may have been written by Cochran but did not carry a personal byline, described the poems as constituting a portrait of "the real America" seen through "honest, comprehending eyes" and written for "the common man as well as the highbrow."[91] The volume of verse, the review said, celebrated real-life experiences: "They are not about the romance of the France of Louis XIV or of the England of Milton; rather they concern the pig-stickers of the stockyards, the clerks of Marshall Field's and the folks who go to picnics on boats like the Eastland."

SEVEN

Watchdog on State Street

The Marshall Field store on State Street in Chicago stood as a thirteen-story granite monument to retail trade, one of a cluster of department stores that made State Street the city's prime thoroughfare for dry goods, indeed "the shopping center of the entire Middle West."[1] Neighbors of the Marshall Field store included Carson Pirie Scott, Mandel Brothers, and the Boston Store, as well as The Fair, home of the bargain bazaar. But the largest of the retailers on State Street was Marshall Field's, the "Cathedral of all the stores,"[2] occupying a massive main store that had been built in five stages, from 1893 to 1914. At the time of its completion, the store encompassed some thirty-five acres of selling space and more than thirty-one miles of Wilton carpet, with long aisles running past showcases of jewelry, laces, handkerchiefs, neckwear, and dress trimmings; displays of imported China and American pottery; acres of furniture; picture galleries, and models wearing Parisian gowns. The physical plant and related services included seventy-six elevators, 23,000 automatic sprinklers, a telephone exchange equipped to handle 10,000 calls a day, and 142 wagons and 375 horses at the beck and call of customers who wished to take advantage of home delivery.[3] The importance of Marshall Field's to the economy was not lost on the executives of the commercial establishment as they searched for an apt description: "The position of a great store as a factor in civilization, the meeting-point of supply and demand, the clearing-house for the handicraft of the nations, the stage upon which is played an important [role] in the great drama of distribution!"[4]

While other Chicago newspapers generally raved about the variety and quality and price of the goods, as they did so effusively at the Marshall Field grand opening in 1907,[5] the *Day Book* largely ignored the items for sale to focus on the employees who did the unpacking, sorting, arranging, and selling. The paper consistently urged Marshall Field's to worry less about profits and more about raising the standard of living among its employees, calling on the store to embody the ideals of its own slogan: "To do the right thing, at the right time, in the right way."[6] The newspaper had an unusual relationship with Marshall Field's, and all other department stores, because it published no advertising. It was an effort out of sync with the newspaper industry, which viewed advertisers as deserving of special treatment. Common business sense dictated as much; the percentage of revenue from advertising had risen from about 50 percent in 1880 to 64 percent in 1910, eclipsing circulation income.[7] At the same time, the space devoted to advertising doubled in most dailies, reaching 50 percent by World War I.[8] The nation was shifting from a producer to a consumer society, with a movement of labor from farms to factories, and advertising served as "the single most useful tool to promote consumption."[9] Department stores used elaborate visual displays on site and in newspaper pages to reach buyers. For example, in Philadelphia, Wanamaker, the largest retail dealer in men's clothing in the country, used ads to "create an intimate relationship with each customer," selling "one pair of gloves at a time."[10] Department stores held "a preeminent role in local advertising" from 1890 through the 1980s.[11] As the major provider of revenue for newspapers, they sought, often successfully, to influence news coverage and editorial opinion.[12] Scripps believed that advertisers, given any say, would make more and more demands for control, including advertisements disguised as news articles and the suppression of important information. The result, he believed, would be news content shaped to please a powerful minority, big business, rather than a deserving majority, the working class, which was the primary audience for Scripps papers. Scripps said he wanted his newspapers to be "the servant of the common people and not of the money class and especially not of the advertising public."[13]

Linking Low Wages to Crime

With no advertisers to be concerned about and with its target audience as the working class, the *Day Book* served as a fierce watchdog on State Street, looking for any signs of mistreatment on the part of department stores, even if the details were sketchy.[14] The newspaper consistently railed against remuneration that was so low, in its view, as to make it immoral. When a member of the Anthropological Society (who was never identified) rose at a meeting to accuse Marshall Field's, Carson Pirie Scott, and other retailers of driving young women into prostitution because their salaries were too low to cover reasonable living expenses, the *Day Book* put the accusation on the front page, despite the absence of any salary data or other supporting evidence, under the headline "Marshall Field and Carson, Pirie, Scott Wages Named as Cause of Vice."[15] And when three young women who worked at The Fair for less than six dollars a week were brought up on charges of stealing, the newspaper pointed out that what they stole was food—bologna, sausage, cheese, and canned beans—and that they were driven to such a desperate measure because they needed to eat.[16]

Though it spared no department store in its criticism of wages paid to workers, the *Day Book* reserved its strongest words for Marshall Field's. To many of the accusations made by the *Day Book* in regard to workers' pay and benefits, Marshall Field himself might have willingly pleaded guilty. He was a steadfast advocate of low pay who believed that thrift on the part of workers and management was crucial to business success and that largesse in wages would be the ruin of character. "Remember," he would tell clerks in passing, "the five, ten, or fifteen cents a day that is squandered, while a mere trifle apparently, if saved would amount to thousands of dollars in a few years."[17] When he started off at the store in 1856, Field might have pointed out, he lived in a cheap rooming house and saved half of the four-hundred-dollar salary earned that year. And as far as shopping, he might have added, he bought a pair of overalls in that year, but little else.

For the roughly 2,000 workers in Marshall Field's employ around the turn of the century, wages varied. Elevator operators received four dollars a week; clerks, many of them young women and girls, earned five dollars or less; beginning salesmen earned eight to ten dollars a week, with bonuses; women in upstairs workrooms got nine to twelve dollars; the top wage was about twenty-five dollars a week.[18] In 1910, the average wage across industries in the United States was about twelve dollars a week; among the lowest paid were farm laborers and domestics, who earned about six dollars and fifty cents a week, still more than store clerks; many office workers in manufacturing and with federal agencies were earning about twenty-one dollars weekly, and finance and insurance workers twenty-five dollars weekly.[19] It was generally acknowledged that Marshall Field's paid a little less than other stores for comparable positions, but in the eyes of many workers the store conferred added prestige, which made it an enviable place to work. As one Field employee said: "You were considered low class if you clerked in some other store. Besides, it was pretty nearly true—as our bosses kept telling us—that if you worked for Field's for half an hour you could go to New York or Philadelphia and get a job almost at once."[20] Whatever their salary, for most workers at Marshall Field's, their buying power fell short of what was needed to shop for clothes and finery at the company store. A tailor-made suit, at fifteen dollars, might easily have required nearly two weeks' pay; a dress hat could run $7.50, good for one week's labor; if pressed, one could move down the price ladder: dress shoes, $2.96; a sweater, $1.90; everyday shoes, $1.79; or a chased gold comb, twenty-five cents.[21]

Lobbying Marshall Field's for a Bonus

The *Day Book* waged its most sustained campaign to boost the pay scale at Marshall Field's in 1917, beginning ten days after Christmas. In a series of articles, Marshall Field and Company stood accused of having shortchanged its workers in a year when its revenues soared. The *Day Book* opened its case on the front page on January 4, 1917. The banner headline read: "Marshall Field Xmas 'Present' to Help Joke of State St." During a drive to record profits in 1916,[22] the *Day Book* reported, Marshall Field executives "posted notices praising their employees and urging them on to greater effort."[23] Inspired by this rallying and by intimations that their work would not go unrewarded in such a lucrative year, the newspaper said, employees expected the store's management to express its gratitude through a bonus, following the example of a smaller, downscale store in town, The Fair.[24] But instead, the newspaper reported, Marshall Field's gave to its workers only another letter, on December 29, this one commending them for their diligence and reminding them to focus their energies on the new year. Marshall Field's holiday greeting concluded:

> 'The Store of Christmas Spirit' fully justified its title by the atmosphere of cordiality and good will which was everywhere in evidence, and we sincerely hope that this spirit will continue as one of the permanent characteristics of this store. The year 1917 now before us is teeming with great and pleasant possibilities. To the full utilization and enjoyment of these we now direct your best thought and energy.[25]

With that, the newspaper account ended, without any direct comment on the contents of the letter. Evidently, the *Day Book* regarded the letter itself as sufficiently self-incriminating; the store had posted its miserly ways for all to read.

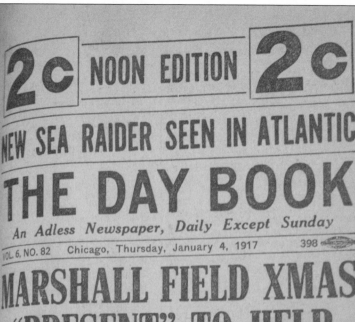

NOON EDITION

NEW SEA RAIDER SEEN IN ATLANTIC

THE DAY BOOK
An Adless Newspaper, Daily Except Sunday

VOL. 6, NO. 82   Chicago, Thursday, January 4, 1917   398

MARSHALL FIELD XMAS "PRESENT" TO HELP JOKE OF STATE ST.

Biggest Department Store Kids Its Employes Along to Great Efforts by Smiling Hints—Finally Give Them a Neatly Prepared "Present"—Urges Harder Work in 1917.

1916 was a big year for Marshall Field & Co. It is understood that more money passed into the youthful mitts of the Field heirs than ever before. From time to time during the latter part of the year M. F. & Co. posted notices praising their employes and urging them on to great-er effort.

So much pleasant urging on the part of the bosses started a rumor that the biggest State street store planned to follow the example of one of the smaller State street stores, The Fair, and give the employes a Christmas present in the shape of a bonus.

Dep't managers smiled and en-couraged the workers on to even more desperate efforts in the pre-

The Day Book's favorite target, Marshall Field's, brought to task, this time over the absense of a Christmas bonus. (The Center for Research Libraries)

The next day, the *Day Book* again led with Marshall Field news, this time focusing on the reaction of employees at the store to the article that ran in the newspaper the previous day. A *Day Book* reporter—following its usual style format, the newspaper did not identify the reporter—went to the store to take a measure of the response to the news coverage. The reporter found that "the spirit of the workers" was "broken," with many left "peeved and disappointed."[26] The main topic of conversation, as the newspaper reported it, was the *Day Book* itself, and its account of the bonus that it said should have been. On the ninth floor, the reporter observed a young woman leave the executive offices, take the elevator down to the street level, buy several copies of the *Day Book*, and return with them to the ninth floor. From the sales floors to the executive suites, it seemed, everyone was following the news at the "Cathedral of All Stores."[27]

Giving the Marshall Field story prominence for a third day running, Negley D. Cochran then published an open letter in which he took to task the president of Marshall Field's, John G. Shedd, in a way that left no doubt as to how disgraceful he held the store's actions to be. Without citing company figures or estimates, which surely would have given his argument more authority, Cochran said the store had received inflated war prices for what it had sold and had sold more than ever before.[28] The scores of employees who bought, sold, arranged, and delivered the goods did the bulk of the work, but most of the profits, Cochran continued, went to two people. He wrote: "Marshall Field III and Henry Field, the polo-playing, society-buzzing, lazy-loafing heirs of old Marshall Field, didn't do a thing."[29] At the same time, "every employe [*sic*] in the big store had to pay war prices for everything they ate and wore and used in 1916. You knew how the cost of living had soared, and why it was harder for every employe to make both ends meet. . . . Did you do anything to make 1916 the most profitable year in THEIR lives?"

Then Cochran sought to place responsibility for the welfare of the workers directly on the shoulders of Shedd, who he thought had lost touch with the workers as he had climbed the management ladder at the store. Shedd had started off at Marshall Field's in 1871, a farm boy from New Hampshire who got a job as a stock hand in the wholesale division, earning ten dollars a week.[30] Working with linens, laces, hosiery, and gloves, he packed goods and set up stock and tracked down salesmen for waiting customers. He rose through the ranks, to salesman, then general manager of wholesale, and he took over the presidency when Marshall Field died in 1906. Shedd was in his mid-60s when Cochran sought to use the fear of God to goad him into giving bonuses to the workers. Cochran called Shedd "an old man" without much time to live. He challenged Shedd to consider "what you have done to make the lives of those employees happier and better." He wrote, "I know you are rich, and that you are a bank director, a railroad director and a man of high standing in business circles. But how do you stand with humanity? How do you stand with yourself?" The only right course, in Cochran's mind, was for Shedd to use his position and power to redistribute earnings so that more of the money reached the workers. "If you do that, John Shedd," he wrote in closing, "you'll have a right to die happy."

Though the *Day Book* failed to persuade Shedd and Marshall Field's to reverse course and distribute bonuses, it did find a large audience for its coverage and efforts on behalf of the workers. Circulation soared that first week in January, even as other newspapers ignored the Marshall Field story.[31] The business manager of the *Day Book,* J. T. Watters, reported that in that week the paper experienced its largest single-day spikes in circulation since its founding.[32] On the Thursday the news coverage began, the newspaper sold about 2,500 more copies than usual in the Loop business district; and on Friday, when the *Day Book* focused on the reaction of employees, it sold an extra 8,000 copies. The sales that Friday represented about a 50 percent increase above the average daily circulation, which was 15,966 for the month of January.[33] The largest increase in circulation was near the Marshall Field store. Watters wrote, "When the store closed at 5:30 P.M. Friday it took seven of my boys to help the stand man sell his *Day Books.* There were hundreds of people fighting to get near the news stand to buy papers. This one man alone made about $15.00 profit on the *Day Books* in 15 minutes. A mounted policeman who saw the crowd drove up and wanted to know what happened. I told him what was going on and he went away when I gave him a *Day Book.*"

The *Day Book* consistently contended that the salaries at Marshall Field's and other stores were so low that workers were driven to desperate measures, including crime. In the winter of 1912, the newspaper gave prominent play to accusations made by the Young People's Civic League that prostitution resulted in part from low wages paid to workers. The paper printed excerpts from a letter sent by the league to officials of department stores, and then took some editorial liberties in its unsigned news article: "They also charged and gave facts to prove the charge that many girls had found their way from department stores to the vice district because they couldn't live decent lives on the salary they got. The stores never answered that charge. There was no answer. They won't answer the charge of the Young People's Civic League. There is no answer, except that the charge is true and easily proven."[34]

An editorial a week later pointed to some of the ads being run by department stores looking for girls fourteen and older.[35] The Fair is seeking "girls" ages sixteen to eighteen, as cashiers, inspectors, and wrappers; Marshall Field's wants young women from eighteen to twenty, "good education essential"; the Boston Store wants girls at least fourteen years old to work as cash girls, errand runners, and wrappers; Rothschild wants one hundred girls sixteen to eighteen (experience not necessary; but must have a grammar school education and live at home). "But there are mighty few of the ads," the newspaper said, "that tell what wages the big business men will pay for bright, strong, rapid, educated girls. The average, however, will not go over six dollars a week. All the same the market for girls is active, and the newspaper ads invite the family to dump their girls, their bright, strong, educated girls, into the big business mill to be ground up into more dollars for millionaire men."

Steadfast Opposition to the Merchant Class

What the paper saw as its freedom to tell the truth sometimes seemed like reflexive antagonism on its part toward the merchant class, regardless of the circumstances. For better or for worse, the paper invariably criticized the stores, taking what it saw as the workers' side (in matters of wages and strikes) or the small taxpayers' side (when Chicago considered tax breaks or permit approvals for the stores) or the customers' side (in reporting accidents at stores or safety regulations governing the stores). One of the most stunning examples of the paper opposing the princes of State Street despite mitigating evidence came in the case of Margaret McManus. The paper, at least indirectly, seemed to advocate a kind of Robin Hood social code that justified illegal action if the victim of a crime was wealthy and the beneficiary was poor.

Margaret McManus was a young woman who admitted stealing fifty dollars from the Marshall Field store in 1912. She was a twenty-two-year-old clerk at the time, making first five dollars a week, then six, and then seven. She shared a room with another young woman and between the rent costs and other expenses, her debts mounted. Faced with financial pressures, she stole the money from Marshall Field's, never to return to her job. But a year later, detectives hired by the store tracked her down, and she was indicted. When the McManus case came to trial in 1914, her lawyer, John D. Farrell, acknowledged that she had taken the money and then appealed to the jurors to weigh the case based on scales of justice devised outside of the established law. Farrell said: "The conditions in this case are such that if the jury believes the girl was not paid enough wages it becomes a question of morality. And it is up to you to decide who is guilty—the Marshall Field store for paying starvation wages or this working girl for taking some of the ill-gotten gain. Everyone has a right to enough wages to live decently. Marshall Field robbed this girl of that right by not paying her a living wage."[36] The jury brought in a verdict of not guilty, as did the *Day Book*. In announcing the verdict in an article that ran with his byline, Negley Cochran switched to the first-person to affirm the jury's decision. Cochran said he would not advocate that people steal, but in some cases, he said, it was justified. He wrote, "I do say that I have a mighty kindly feeling for the human beings who sat on that jury and had the clear vision to see through the meshes of the law and find justice. Had I been on that jury I would have voted as those jurymen did. . . . The real verdict of that jury was that the Field store was guilty of paying starvation wages; and that guilt was greater than the technical guilt of Margaret McManus in stealing."[37]

The *Day Book* was an equal opportunity prosecutor on behalf of those employed in the department stores. Though Marshall Field's was the serial defendant, when there were labor troubles or concerns at other stores on State Street, the newspaper responded just as vigorously. In December 1913, for example, The Fair, a store known for its low prices and sidewalk sales, required several hundred clerks to work on Sundays, for fifty cents each in extra pay, to get the stock ready for shoppers during the week. On the third Sunday of this arrangement, The Fair served a store dinner as payment instead of the fifty cents, and several hundred of the workers noisily objected and demanded wages. Some scuffling ensued, and one of the clerks, a policeman's son, tumbled down the stairs along with a store detective. Apparently, no one was hurt.

The *Day Book* had a good story to tell, and it intended to tell it well, even if that meant fudging details that might get in the way of an engaging narrative line. The flair for drama was apparent in the headlines on the two days of coverage, which clearly sided with the store clerks: "Fair Employes [sic] Strike Against Slaving on Sunday"[38] and "Officials of The Fair Try to Force Employes [sic] Into Submission."[39] The articles called the action at the store a strike, but the reporting clearly shows more spontaneous protest than organized strike, as the workers raised their voices at the prospect of not being paid in cash for a day's work. And at first the newspaper said the clerks had worked for several Sundays with no pay; but the second article corrected that report and said they had been paid for two Sundays and then the meal was offered as compensation only on the third Sunday. When a reporter for the *Day Book* called on E. J. Lehmann, president of The Fair, to ask for a justification, Lehmann said that the work needed to be done and that employees each received "a nice lovely dinner," easily worth seventy-five cents.[40]

Crusading for Workplace Safety

Apart from its campaign for higher wages, the *Day Book* also became a crusader for workplace safety, extensively covering accidents inside the department stores. The articles often required enterprising reporting because the police generally had no information—or at least, no information to share—on the accidents, the newspaper said. Moreover, in some cases, the *Day Book* was the only newspaper that seemed to regard the accidents as priority news and worth tracking down, even if the police had nothing to say. In Cochran's view, the omission of such coverage in other newspapers confirmed his belief that they were suppressing news so as not to alarm shoppers or alienate advertisers. For example, three days before Christmas in 1912, a freight elevator fell in the Siegel, Cooper department store, injuring ten and possibly killing two, the newspaper said.[41] Details were sketchy because the police said such an accident had not been reported to the police department, and store executives declined to say much beyond confirming that there had been an elevator accident and asserting that four people were involved. The newspaper, however, said that about forty people were on the freight elevator, which was pressed into action to take shoppers to the toy section during the holiday season and was believed to have fallen eight stories. The last paragraph lays claim to an exclusive: "The *Day Book* is the only paper which has printed a line about this accident. The trust papers don't dare to."[42] The next day the newspaper reported that the police had "investigated"—the word appeared in quotation marks—the elevator account and determined that there had not been any such accident.

As 1913 got under way, the newspaper continued to focus on accidents and suspected abuses among department stores. A front-page story on January 8 reported that an engineer, Jim McMinnehan, had been crushed beneath a freight elevator at Siegel, Cooper. The accident was not reported to the police, nor was there any mention of it in the other newspapers, the *Day Book* said.[43] Then on January 14, the newspaper reported that an elevator repairman was hospitalized after an accident at the Carson Pirie Scott store, and that days earlier, on Christmas Eve, a decorator at the store had fallen fifteen feet from scaffolding. Both men were said to have remained hospitalized. Though the *Day Book* said it had confirmed the accounts with several workers, A. J. Cronin, security chief at Carson Pirie Scott, denied that either accident had occurred. Once again, the newspaper said, there was no record of a police report or coverage in the other dailies.[44] After speaking with doctors familiar with the treatment of the workers, the newspaper's unnamed reporter headed back to Cronin and asked whether it was company policy to "suppress information about industrial accidents" in the store. Cronin responded: "We don't have any accidents. We haven't had any in a long while. I don't know how long it's been since we had an accident here." The reporter told Cronin that elevator operations and safety conditions were subject to state and city laws, and that the City Council could appoint a committee to inquire into such accidents. "The city has a right," the reporter said, "to ask if you are treating your employes [sic] and customers properly." Cronin responded: "The public has no more right to know what is going on here than it has to know what is going on in your home." Cronin huffily directed the reporter to a Mr. Wood, the general manager. Wood was unavailable, and his secretary directed the reporter back to Cronin's office. Cronin reiterated his contention that no one had been hurt and said, "wait a minute—I'll be back." While waiting for Cronin, the reporter spied a store booklet on the counter, "The Etiquette of Entertaining." Glancing through it, the reporter read: "The art of entertaining, of making one's guests feel thoroughly at ease . . . this gentle art is worth cultivating." Cronin never returned, the reporter noted.

An elevator accident that month proved fatal for a shopper at Hillman's department store. At about 3 P.M. on January 13, the shopper, Mary Dorf, fell through the open door of the elevator shaft on the fifth floor and plummeted to the ground. Apparently, the *Day Book* reported, a gate by the elevator shaft had been left open instead of being closed, and Dorf approached, thinking she was about to enter the elevator, but instead fell through the shaft. A witness said: "She screamed as she went. I noticed that she had on white stockings and black shoes. That was the last I saw."[45] Two weeks later the *Day Book* reported on the front page that a forty-year-old woman from Maywood, Ill., had been injured, perhaps fatally, in an elevator accident in Mandel Brothers department store. The woman, a Mrs. J. Weinbauer, began to enter an elevator at the basement level, but the operator closed the door on her arm, leaving Weinbauer pinned on the outside. As the elevator rose, she was lifted along with it until her head struck the ceiling, and she tumbled to the floor. When questioned by the *Day Book's* reporter, a store manager at first denied that such an accident had occurred, the newspaper said, and acknowledged that it had only when it became clear that the reporter had independently gathered details.

On the same day that the *Day Book* reported on Mrs. Weinbauer's accident, it presented its case, in an editorial, for covering such news. By giving attention to accidents and hazards in department stores and offices, the newspaper said, it puts pressure on city officials and store executives to see that safety regulations are in place and observed. For example, an elevator injured six people the day before Mrs. Weinbauer's fall, at a loan and trust company building owned by Marshall Field and Company. Field executives notified the press (the editorial said this was only because the *Day Book* had been on a campaign for full disclosure); news of the injuries, all relatively minor, was widely reported; and the city building commissioner put the elevator out of service until it had been inspected. But the city failed to order a similar halt in service in December when a dozen people were hurt in an accident at Seigel, Cooper, the adless paper said, because "all the newspapers except the *Day Book* so kindly suppressed news of the accident."

An examination of causes of death in Chicago during the years in which the *Day Book* published shows that while elevators were not the leading cause, they did pose a significant hazard. In 1916, for example, thirty-six people died in elevator accidents; this compared with 598 deaths by suicide; industrial accidents, 558; asphyxiation, 502; falls, 455; homicides, 312; streetcar accidents, 136; and horse and wagon accidents, 119.[46] The number of elevator accidents in Chicago from 1905 to 1916 totaled 426. Of the thirty-six elevator deaths in 1916, a majority, nineteen, were attributed to falling down the shaft; others died when they were crushed between the elevator and a wall or floor, or crushed in a pit. And by no means were all of the elevator accidents confined to stores. In that year, eight of the thirty-six deaths occurred in stores, with the rest at factories, offices, hotels, and restaurants.

Vigorous Coverage of Store Owners

It was the *Day Book*'s contention that the press extended special privileges to the department stores in ways that went beyond a filtered coverage of accidents and labor disputes, to the very people who owned the stores. A case in point, the newspaper said, concerned the death of Marshall Field II. At the time, the official account had Marshall Field II accidentally shooting himself while cleaning his gun at his home on November 22, 1905.[47] He remained alive for another five days and in that time rumors spread that he had been shot by a young woman at the Everleigh Club, a notorious social venue with private rooms in the red-light district of Chicago, or that he had shot himself because of business or health troubles. The verdict of the coroner's jury, however, was that Field shot himself accidentally.

The Associated Press and United Press International moved a story across the wires on Saturday, November 22, 1913, eight years to the day of the shooting, reporting a woman's claim that she had shot Field in the Everleigh Club with his own revolver after they had quarreled.[48] The woman, Vera Prosser, said that the elder Field gave her $25,000 in return for leaving Chicago and keeping quiet about the matter. But her standing as a witness in 1913 was somewhat compromised because she made the statement from the city jail in Los Angeles, where she was being held on charges of extorting money from businessmen. Moreover, two days later, she recanted and denied a role in the shooting.[49] In a front-page article under the headline "The Field Family Gets Special Privileges in the Newspapers," the *Day Book* said the confession of Vera Prosser had been suppressed by the other dailies in Chicago out of deference to Marshall Field and Company, the advertiser.[50] If the victim had been a labor leader in Chicago, the *Day Book* said, the Chicago dailies would surely have printed the accounts that went out over the AP and UPI wires. The newspaper went on to say: "But to Chicago papers there appears to be something out of the ordinary, if not sacred, about the name of Field. When the late Marshall Field, the merchant prince, was alive . . . he was made one of Chicago's gods, through the influence of the newspapers that got monthly checks from the big store for newspaper advertising."

The *Day Book* said the important point about the Prosser confession was not whether she really shot Field or he shot himself; it was that the absence of coverage in this case illustrated the tendency on the part of the press to protect advertisers by ignoring or downplaying news of accidents in stores and the wages and benefits provided there. The *Day Book* laid claim to the high ground of publishing "the truth" and "real news," but its claims in this case were diminished somewhat because of weaknesses in the news account. In its eagerness to promote itself as a different and unique voice, the newspaper arguably overplayed the Field article, putting it on the front page three days out of five that week. The other papers could have countered that the circumstances of the confession dictated a more patient course of waiting for corroborating evidence before linking Field's death to a tête-à-tête at the Everleigh Club, and that, in any case, Prosser abruptly changed her account and denied any role in the killing. At the same time, the *Day Book* did expose an apparent reluctance on the part of the commercial press to print negative news about the Field family, even when there was enough information to merit a qualified account. If the Chicago press suppressed this news, what else were they suppressing?

A Willingness to Get Personal

The *Day Book*'s approach to journalism could be intensely personal, as John Shedd discovered when Marshall Field's decided not to pay bonuses at the end of 1916. Like the institutional retailers themselves, the executives and heirs of department store fortunes were often called to account. The leading candidate for this kind of personal journalism was Marshall Field III, who was in line to inherit at least $400 million, which was to be poured gradually into his accounts until age fifty, when the full inheritance would spill over.[51] The Field estate had vast holdings in land in Chicago and substantial investments in gas, electric, and telephone utilities, along with its department store interests. As Cochran observed, "Every incandescent globe, every arc light, every advertising sign in Chicago is twinkling off the pennies for this boy, night after night."[52] In 1915, at age twenty-one, Field was back in Chicago, having completed his schooling in England. In honor of his return, a ritzy bachelor party was held in January at the Blackstone Hotel, done up with a "Palm Beach" theme. The centerpiece featured mounds of sand and miniature palm trees, surrounding a mirror that represented Worth Lake; miniature yachts served as place cards.

In typical Cochran fashion, the editor set out in an open letter to instruct young Field in the ways of the world beyond fancy dinners and country clubs. It was likely, Cochran said, that Field learned something in British classrooms, but doubtful that he learned much at all about humanity. Cochran wrote: "It's about a hundred to one shot that young Field will be one of the most conspicuously useless members of the human colony known as the City of Chicago. Yet this boy has a chance to be a real MAN."[53] The suggested course, Cochran said, would have Field get to know all of the companies from which he draws money, and especially get to know the men, women, and children who labor in them. He should know what work people do and how much money they earn and how long are the hours of their day. From the conductors on the street railways to the clerks in the department store, How are things for them? "If he starts out on his business career in this manner," Cochran concluded, "he may become a MAN. Blackstone dinners may make of him only a social MONKEY."

EIGHT

Champion of Labor

Every Scripps newspaper, beginning with the *Detroit Evening News* in the 1870s, staked its success on the support of the working class. One of the parent organization's most ambitious efforts to court the labor vote came in 1889, by which time the organization, then called the Scripps League, had expanded its newspaper holdings to four cities. In May of that year, the Scripps papers announced a plan to sponsor a delegation of forty American workers to study European working conditions and industrial innovation at the Paris International Exposition.[1] Nominations for the delegates poured in, including one from Samuel Gompers, head of the American Federation of Labor. Labor groups sent their thanks, on behalf of the American workers, for this interest shown by the Scripps papers. The Scripps League spent $25,000 underwriting the trip, officially called the Workingmen's Expedition, a large expense for a business operation that pinched pennies even when it came to pencils (one editor was told to buy his own) and toilet paper (old newspapers would have to do). Clearly, E. W. Scripps viewed the expedition as a shrewd self-promotional investment that would win the loyalty of American labor, and boost circulation as well as advertising. The expedition coverage in the Scripps papers "praised organized labor at a time when many newspapers (and Americans) found collective bargaining and strikes to be anathema."[2] Even so, Scripps knew that the nation's workers, standing shoulder to shoulder, formed a lucrative and underserved market. Most newspaper publishers tried to build circulation by appealing to readers who were well-off enough to frequent the department stores that anchored the advertising pages. But, as Gerald Baldasty points out, Scripps figured that what workers lacked in individual wealth they made up for in collective purchasing power, and that made them appealing to advertisers as well. And given their large numbers, workers could provide a strong circulation base that was itself an important source of revenue. For the *Day Book,* of course, the size of the working class was the vital statistic, since all of the paper's revenue came from circulation.

Seeking to Serve the "95 Percent" in Chicago

To win over these readers, Scripps papers "relied on explicit advocacy" in editorials, editorial cartoons, personal columns, and news articles.[3] Specifically, Scripps papers championed reforms for the common people through government legislation and corporate change and sought close ties with labor unions. The *Day Book* was fully committed to the Scripps strategy, an approach that Cochran knew well from his days as an editor in Toledo, where he had campaigned for lower streetcar fares and reforms in municipal government. As Cochran expressed it, the success of the *Day Book* "depends upon the 95 percent—It must be really THEIR paper,"[4] using the favored Scripps term for the working class. Through both its original reporting and its tailored use of national and foreign news from Scripps's United Press, the *Day Book* immediately established itself as a faithful advocate of the working class. In Chicago, the paper urged the startup of unions in places where workers were unorganized, and an increase in membership in places where unions already existed. By joining collectively in that way, the paper argued, workers across industries would be in a better position to secure higher wages and better benefits, to which they were entitled. The paper's push for organizing workers was especially intense among department stores, whose clerks were often paid six dollars a week or less. The *Day Book's* sympathetic portrayal of workers contrasted with the typical coverage found in other general-circulation dailies. While the mainstream press often ignored labor unrest or called for restoring order by force, the *Day Book* consistently urged that workers be allowed to carry out strikes, including sympathy strikes, and to picket and publicize their case in pursuit of fair wages and safe working conditions. Cochran had little patience for Hearst's claims to represent the interests of working class. As Cochran saw it, Hearst advocated the cause of workers only when they were in places where the Hearst company had no financial interests.

Cochran relied on the *Day Book's* own modest union force, the men who handled stereotyping and other mechanical work, as well as union locals across the city, to serve as informal advisers—an early version of focus groups—to help shape the paper's content in a way that would resonate with the working class. Having talked daily with trade unionists in the opening weeks of publication, Cochran said, "I find I haven't been as close to the 95 per cent as I thought I was."[5] He began training the head stereotyper to help out in the newsroom, and the same stereotyper wrote an editorial in the November 2, 1911, issue that was titled "Yes, Organized Labor Has Done Much, But There Is Still Much More to Do." In one of his frequent letters to Miramar, Cochran described the stereotyper to Scripps: "He is full of fire and ambition, and knows human nature and the labor game thoroughly—is president of the Stereotypers' union, and a fighter from Fighterville—for principle."[6] Even as he established labor ties in Chicago, Cochran was careful to keep his distance from the Socialist Party.[7] In his view, the Socialists, though they might advocate on labor's behalf, were too constrained by party doctrine and too intellectual. The leading party newspaper in the city, the *Chicago Daily Socialist,* which became the *World* during the labor troubles in 1912, printed largely party propaganda and little news unrelated to the party, in Cochran's view. The *Day Book's* goal, he said, was to bypass all parties and as a political independent deal directly with the trade unions, represented by the Chicago Federation of Labor. Just as Cochran did not want the *Day Book* to be controlled by one political party, so too did he not want the paper to be seen as a puppet of labor, however much it might need the support of workers. Cochran said they were "not pushing the paper as a labor organ, or any other kind of an organ, but one that will publish the truth."[8] What seemed to impress the union men the most, at least in the early going, in his view, was that the *Day Book* was willing to critically cover the other dailies. "It seems to daze people," Cochran wrote, "the idea of anybody having the nerve to publish disagreeable facts about newspapers."[9] Such coverage resonated among the pressmen and other newspaper unions, which had supported Hearst's efforts to start newspapers in the city a decade earlier. But relations between Hearst and the workers had soured, and tensions culminated in the newspaper strike and lockout of 1912.

Ally of the Trade Unions

Throughout the *Day Book's* existence, both Cochran and the trade unions had interests that would be served in joining as allies: the paper would be assured of a circulation base, and the unions would be assured of favorable coverage. Early on, Cochran called on John Fitzpatrick, president of the Chicago Federation of Labor, and Ed Nockels, the secretary. This relationship was strong enough that Nockels would send a telegram from an American Federation of Labor convention in Atlanta asking to have Cochran immediately send twenty copies of the paper to show the national delegates.[10] Cochran and other staff members regularly met with union locals to promote the *Day Book*. After one meeting with the Chicago Allied Printing Trades Council, representing some 30,000 printers, the delegates wrote up a resolution of endorsement that was to be sent to other unions across the city.[11] There was strong interest on the part of workers in attaching themselves to a paper that would promote their interests. In December 1911, during a strike by Illinois Central workers, a supporter of the strikers, the Rev. C. H. Doolittle, visited the newspaper to drop off a press release, which Cochran then printed. Doolittle said he had had trouble getting the strikers' comments in the other papers in the city. He called back later to say that some of the strikers wanted to subscribe to the *Day Book*. Cochran had to tell them to wait, because, in keeping with Scripps's strategy, the paper was circulating only in the immediate neighborhoods around the office, and most of the strikers were based miles away. For Cochran, it was another reminder of how Scripps's favored circulation strategy was handicapping the *Day Book:* he was hearing from workers across the city who wanted to read the paper but could not find it anywhere. Cochran said such workers might consider mail subscriptions, but the drawback there was that it would effectively double the price of the paper, since a one-cent stamp would be needed to mail each paper. But Scripps was adamant about focusing on house-to-house canvassing for subscribers near the office and dismissed mail subscriptions, newsstands in the Loop, and distant home deliveries (such deliveries would require renting depots for newspaper dropoffs, as well as hiring regional circulation managers and separate crews of carriers) as surefire ways to lose money. While reaching out to unions certainly helped the paper forge ties with working-class readers, Scripps also believed it was fueling Cochran's interest in delivering the paper in the Loop and in other parts of the city. So a little more than a year into the experiment, Scripps brusquely told Cochran to "give orders that there shall be no more propaganda, nor talking to unions, or any work of any description done, except a house to house canvass for subscribers."[12]

Scripps's advocacy of the working class in his newspapers was somewhat at odds with his treatment of his own employees. He was notorious for his penurious ways: the cheap offices, the used presses, the shrunken salaries. Scripps made it abundantly clear that he would not lavish money on the *Day Book* and its editorial staff. While he was quick to point to a need to raise the quality of life for workers as a whole, when it came to his own businesses, he emphasized the ascendancy of sound business principles, among them that wasteful spending had an injurious effect on a company and that creating financial hardships led to greater efficiency and character building (he and Marshall Field could have had a very agreeable conversation on this point). In describing to Cochran the kind of people who should be hired, he noted that one kind would be "such men as care more for the opportunity of serving the masses than they do for gaining salary."[13]

Covering the McNamara Trial in L.A.

Whatever its internal shortcomings, the *Day Book* had an early opportunity to establish its credentials as an ally of those who toiled for a living when a trial opened in Los Angeles in 1911 focused on a fierce struggle between organized labor and big business. The *Day Book,* as well as other Scripps papers, took a keen partisan interest. John and James McNamara were accused of committing the "Crime of the Century"[14] in attacking a powerful employer, the *Los Angeles Times,* which had fought against efforts to organize unions in the city. The McNamaras were charged in the bombing of the *Times* building, on October 1, 1910. The explosion had killed twenty people, nearly all workers, and caused $500,000 worth of damage. Moreover, unexploded bombs were discovered at the homes of Harrison Gray Otis, the publisher of the *Times,* and Felix Zeehandelaar, the secretary of the Merchants and Manufacturers Association, which represented business owners in the city. The *Day Book* put the trial on the front page nine times in October, carrying dispatches from the Scripps news wire service, United Press. The coverage, including the choice of illustrations and the wording of headlines, was generally sympathetic to the two brothers. Scripps had no interest in staying neutral in his coverage of the trial, and conveyed that to Cochran. He told Cochran that Clarence Darrow, the eminent Chicago lawyer who was representing the McNamaras, had called in October and requested that Charles Edward Russell be assigned to cover the trial for United Press, apparently on the assumption that Russell's reporting would be, at the least, fair to the defense.[15] Darrow had visited with Scripps twice at Miramar. Amenable to the suggestion, Scripps said the appointment was approved. Completing the exchange of favors, Scripps said, Darrow had pledged to write a letter to organized labor in Chicago endorsing the *Day Book* and to write a separate article for the paper on the Los Angeles trial. Looking further down the road, Scripps and Darrow had even talked of teaming up to start a weekly newspaper, of which Darrow might be editor. But that October, Darrow's journalistic aspirations were on hold as he focused on a case that had come to represent a challenge to all American workers. Organized labor had rallied behind the McNamaras, convinced that big business was framing the brothers in an effort to enervate the labor movement. Gompers, a founder of the American Federation of Labor, had pursued the lawyer he thought could best defend the McNamaras and save the reputation of organized labor. Darrow was regarded as a powerful courtroom persuader, as well as a faithful advocate of labor and the poor. He had agreed to accept the case, provided that the AFL let him turn it into a national crusade and that he had at least $150,000 to spend in the defense effort and $50,000 to keep as a retainer.[16] Gompers agreed to Darrow's terms.

The publisher of the *Times,* Otis, and his son-in-law and eventual successor, Harry Chandler, were part of the city's wealthy elite and the Republican coterie that controlled city and county politics. Over the years they had successfully fought unions at the *Times* and promoted the ideology of the open shop, which called for each worker to bargain individually with an employer. Otis helped to form the Merchants and Manufacturers Association, which came to represent 80 percent of the firms in the region and presented a united and effective front against unionizing.[17] In the eyes of the unions, then, Otis loomed as the "chief enemy."[18] In early 1910, the American Federation of Labor began an effort to organize workers across the city, and there followed strikes, fights, attacks on strikebreakers by union men, and attacks on pickets by the police.[19] The bombing came at the height of the tensions, and within months prosecutors had developed a case against John J. McNamara, who was secretary-treasurer of the International Association of Bridge and Structural Iron Workers, based in Indianapolis; his brother James, and an associate named Ortie McManigal. Investigators gained McManigal's cooperation, and he identified James as the dynamiter and John as the planner of the bombing.

On the eve of the trial, the *Day Book* printed a statement from John McNamara on the front page, alongside his picture, which showed him wearing a jacket and tie and looking self-assured. His statement read in part: "I appreciate the opportunity, through the United Press, of reiterating to the thousands of wage-earners of the country my absolute confidence of acquittal. Kidnaped without warrant, my innocence has upheld me through many trying hours, and I am glad the time is approaching when the extent of the gigantic conspiracy which deprived me of my liberty will be shown before people."[20] When the trial got under way on October 11, the *Day Book* reported that huge crowds besieged the courtroom.[21] All entrances were guarded, and credentials were required to gain entry. The McNamara brothers were brought in, handcuffed to deputies, with city policemen standing by as guards. John McNa-

THE DAY BOOK

500 SO. PEORIA ST.   398   TEL. MONROE 353

Chicago, Tuesday, October 17, 1911.

McNAMARAS LEAVING JAIL TO FACE TRIAL

Brothers, accused of murder in Los Angeles Times case, snapped by Day Book correspondent, while being taken, handcuffed, to Judge Bordwell's court to face trial.

The *Day Book* ran the McNamara trial on the front page several times. (The Center for Research Libraries) mara was favorably described as "heavily built, with his long gray-tinged hair thrown back on his forehead and his clear-cut, cameo-shaped face expressive of the highest intelligence."

The judge in the case, Walter Bordwell, ruled that prospective jurors could be examined with regard to their views on unions. The trial would likely be a long one, the newspaper's United Press dispatch predicted, with jury selection expected to last three months. But instead, less than two months later, the brothers shocked the nation, and angered many supporters, when they changed their pleas to guilty.[22] Many in labor, having raised huge sums of money for the defense, felt betrayed by Darrow when the brothers pleaded guilty. Looking to make the best of a case that cast a shadow on organized labor, the *Day Book* printed a statement from William Jennings Bryan on its front page. Bryan wrote: "Organized labor is not to blame for [the McNamaras]; on the contrary, it is stronger for their elimination and only those who encouraged them or defend their conduct ought to share their condemnation. Organized labor has learned a lesson: it will be more careful in the selection of its leaders and society may well pause and inquire if there is anything wrong in the conditions which led these men into so dastardly a conspiracy against life and property."[23]

Standing By Mill Workers in Massachusetts

The *Day Book*'s commitment to the working class was highlighted again a few months later in its coverage of striking mill workers in Lawrence, Massachusetts Workers in the cotton and woolen mills, many of them women and children, had earned on average sixteen cents an hour for a fifty-six-hour work week; they had gone on strike after their salaries fell when the state legislature reduced the work week by two hours. William M. Wood, the multimillionaire president of the American Woolen Company and head of the wool trust, said that to pay fifty-six hours' worth of wages for fifty-four hours of work "would be equivalent to an increase in wages, and that the mills cannot afford to pay."[24] Some disputed that position, given that Wood's company had reported a net profit of $4 million in 1911.[25] A front-page article on Thursday, January 18, was headlined "Mill Owners Seek Trouble,"[26] and described a tense situation growing more serious by the day. On Wednesday, the paper reported, the militia had "attacked" a "peaceful, quiet procession" of men and women workers and chased them from the streets.[27] On Thursday, mill owners called for additional National Guard units and urged a declaration of martial law. Reports were bruited about—by agents of mill owners, the *Day Book* said—that strikers planned to dynamite the mills and the home of the governor. In contrast to the owners' portrayal of "bloodthirsty" strikers, the paper said, was a meeting of 5,000 strikers, mostly women and boys, who held in their hands only symbolic weapons, U.S. flags, in a battle to win public support. But the authorities said on Saturday that they had found dynamite among the workers and arrested six men and one woman. A front-page photograph the next Tuesday showed a fire hose that had been trained on men who were striking to keep them from crossing a bridge to reach the mills, where strikebreakers had replaced them. The report notes that women strikers, led by Anna Kiani, rallied at the bridge that same day.[28] As the women strikers gathered at the bridge, they faced six companies of militia, equipped not only with fire hoses, but with bayonets and cannons. "Even Anna Kiani was awed by the cannon," the unsigned report says, "and the women workers did not sweep across the bridge, and throw themselves upon the soldiers' bayonets, or tear down the mills, or anything serious like that."

In the midst of the Lawrence coverage, an unsigned editorial, presumably written by Cochran, championed the cause of organized labor and laid out the stakes. The struggle was worldwide between "Big Business," which sought to keep wages low, destroy unions, and "enslave humanity," and organized labor, which in some quarters was not organized enough.[29] "The vast army of underpaid clerks, bookkeepers, stenographers and others who have similar employment, have not seen that the reason they are underpaid is that they are unorganized," the editorial stated. Instead, the store clerks and others had accepted wages and benefits on the terms of management, believing themselves to be a step or two above mechanics and laborers, and so in less need of unions. But the editorial argued that all workers would rise or fall together, and that unless workers of all types were organized, the result would be that "one percent of the people will be bosses and the remaining 99 hired hands."[30] As if to buttress the editorial, two days later the paper printed an undercover investigation of the conditions faced by working women in Chicago. The author, Zelia Emerson, was described as a wealthy woman from Jackson, Michigan, who became active in the Women's Trades Union League in Chicago. She took a job first at Rothchild department store, where she found that state laws were kept, but "the wages of the girls were pitifully small."[31] Saleswomen received six dollars a week, cashiers and wrappers five dollars, and cash girls, the majority of whom were about age 14, two dollars and fifty cents. (Each had to spend a day's pay to buy an apron for work, and upon leaving the store had to give back the apron without getting any money in return, she noted.) Next, Emerson worked at Knab's restaurant, as a dishwasher, for two days. She found that the restaurant had violated the spirit, if not the letter, of the state law limiting work days to ten hours, because even though it promised girls an hour for lunch in an eleven-hour day, the girls usually needed to work most of that hour or there would not be time to clean the dishes and floors between the noon and evening rush periods.

The leading news story of the month was the continued unrest at the mills in Lawrence, Massachusetts. The *Day Book* reported on the efforts of the mill owners and the local authorities to block striking workers from sending their children to stay with friends or relatives in other cities until the situation in Lawrence calmed and food was more plentiful. Believing that keeping the hungry children in town would serve as a powerful inducement to workers to call off the strike, the paper reported, the mill owners, "the real commandants," pressured the police and militia to stop the departure of children.[32] On one morning the police and soldiers pulled fifty children from their parents' arms as the children were about to board a train to Philadelphia, and hauled them to patrol wagons. The reporter described one particularly bitter exchange: "One woman, seeing her little girl in the arms of a policeman, attacked the man viciously, digging her nails into his face. A soldier saw her. He drew a baton and clubbed her over the head until she sank down on the ground, moaning and half-conscious."[33] A few days later, seven mothers and their children were arraigned on criminal charges, that of neglect. The paper vividly described another scene: 10,000 strikers, most of them women, gathered for a rally on Common Street and joined voices in "The Star Spangled Banner." They began to march toward the business district, with police officers following in cars. Up ahead, other officers gathered, and as the strikers drew near, the police charged, and the clubbing began. The paper reported: "Men, and women, and little children felt the weight of the wagon spokes. They could be seen to fall down on the street, and to rise again, bleeding from their wounds."[34] Still, the strikers continued to march, singing as they went, and the officers continued to meet them with clubs, and hauled scores to jail.

Cochran had heard enough. In an editorial, again presumably his, the *Day Book* urged federal and state authorities to promptly intervene in Lawrence before any more strikers were clubbed, or the nation would risk a justified uprising. "If the government shall fail to act as promptly, as efficiently, as thoroughly in the Lawrence case as it has in the Los Angeles case," the editorial stated, "then who can blame the man who, declaring anew that the law is for the rich, shall defy the law and throw a bomb."[35] If the authorities failed to act decently, the editorial continued, violence would ensue, "for America will not sit quiet when mothers are clubbed." And in an editorial a few days later, the *Day Book* addressed the charges against parents who tried to send their children out of town on a train, but were hauled off to jail. The editorial likened the efforts of "the mill lords of Massachusetts,"[36] who sought to block the exodus, to Southern slave owners, who shared their "greed" and benighted regard of the value of human beings. The sixty-three-day strike ended with the mill owners agreeing to a modest pay raise (one cent an hour for those earning twelve to twenty cents per hour).[37]

The case of the mill workers in Lawrence returned to the *Day Book*'s front page at the end of August, with the announcement that William M. Wood, the head of the wool trust, was arrested on charges of conspiring with other mill owners to plant dynamite in the homes of strikers that winter.[38] The plan was not to set off the dynamite, but to discredit the strikers' cause by having it appear that they intended to resort to violent means. Two others, including the president of a textile mill whose name was not disclosed, were also indicted on the same charge. A week earlier, the paper noted, Ernest W. Pitman, the millionaire head of the W. W. Pitman Co., one of the biggest mill construction companies in the world, shot and killed himself after he had confessed to conspiracy in the case. Wood was tried and acquitted.

The Wages of Department Stores

The *Day Book* had an opportunity to focus on the hardships of the local labor force in 1913, when an Illinois Senate commission conducted an inquiry into the wages paid to girls and young women in Chicago. The paper had pursued the subject in articles and editorials for well over a year, but heightened its coverage in 1913. Of particular interest to the commission on white slavery, as the workers' situation was called, was whether low wages might be responsible for driving some from department store jobs and into prostitution or other crime. Lieutenant Governor Barratt O'Hara, chairman of the Senate commission, made it clear that he was prepared to question a long line of Chicago's biggest employers: "I do not care how many millions a man may have; I do not care what his social standing may be; I intend that he shall explain himself to this committee if he be one of those who drives girls to shame and ruins the womanhood of Illinois by the low wages he pays those who have helped to make his millions."[39] Before the commission called the first executives to testify, the *Day Book* spoke with two store executives, and put their views on the front page, presented as incriminating evidence. Augusta Lehmann, chief owner of The Fair department store, was quoted as saying, "Girls who work in department stores get too much money now. They haven't got brains enough to deserve what they are getting."[40] When asked why girls turn to prostitution, she cited improper home conditions and "cheap dance halls and nickle shows." Julius Rosenwald, president of Sears, Roebuck, told the paper: "Low wages never made any girl bad. Improper home conditions is the chief cause of the fall of girls." The following day, in a news article on the views of a Chicago municipal judge with regard to wages and corruption, the paper took some editorial license. The judge, Jacob H. Hopkins, said that girls throughout the city were underpaid and overworked, and that many turned to prostitution or other crime to fill an empty stomach or buy some decent clothes. "I don't know how a working girl, who is alone in the world, gets along on $6 a week," Judge Hopkins said.[41] The paper said that the average wage in department stores was six dollars a week, and for many factory workers, less than that. The article then repeated some of the comments made by Lehmann and Rosenwald the day before, both of whom, the paper said, evidently did not care about the plight of working girls. The reporter—Cochran or someone else, it is not clear—issued a harsh judgment: "Nations do not depend on the Mrs. Lehmanns and the Rosenwalds; such as they are merely commercial incidents. Nations must necessarily depend on the great mass of the people, the 95 percent, and that includes just such girls as those who work in the department stores and factories of Chicago."

The Senate commission summoned Chicago's leading department store owners and executives to testify, and ordered them to bring along the financial books and payrolls of their respective stores. Among those called before the commission were Julius Rosenwald of Sears; Augusta Lehmann, president of The Fair; Edward J. Lehmann, vice president of The Fair; Joseph H. Basch, general manager of Siegel, Cooper; James Simpson, vice president of Marshall Field; Edwin F. Mandel, president of Mandel Brothers; Henry G. Hart, general manager of the Boston Store; John Pirie, of Carson Pirie Scott; George Lytton, treasurer of The Hub; and George R. Thorne, first vice president of Montgomery Ward.[42]

Before the questioning of executives began, M. Blair Coan, an investigator retained by the commission, estimated that more than 50,000 girls and women in Chicago earned five dollars or less per week, and that many were underfed, with half getting by on two meals a day, of the "ten or fifteen cent variety."[43] At five dollars a week, a young woman would earn at most $260 a year. As a point of comparison, $1,200 to $3,000 was regarded as a comfortable middle-class income at the turn of the century, and the city's payroll included laborers earning $600 a year; stenographers, $900; patrolmen, $1,000; department heads, $3,000 to $6,000; and the mayor, $10,000.[44] The first executive to face the commission, Rosenwald of Sears, suggested that although wages paid to girls and women might be low, it might not be quite as bad as Coan had portrayed it. The average wage for the 4,732 female employees at Sears was $9.12 weekly; he said the lowest wage in the company was five dollars per week, paid to 119 girls, ages fifteen and sixteen. The *Day Book* gleefully reported that the commission had produced a former employee who said she was paid only $4.50 a week and proved him a liar.[45] Don MacGregor covered the hearing for the *Day Book* and seemed to delight in skewering the executives and their powerful enterprises, especially Marshall Field. When Jimmy Simpson, vice president of Marshall Field, appeared before the commission, MacGregor (in a front-page story appearing with a rare byline) said of the Marshall Field store: It was "shown as an oppressor of womanhood; a payer of starvation wages" and was "held up before the eyes of all men as a thing of horror."[46] But nowhere in the story did MacGregor report details of Simpson's testimony, including wages paid to workers. That same day Lieutenant Governor O'Hara had his sergeant-at-arms go into the tenderloin, or red-light district, and choose some of the women at random to tell the commission how they came to prostitution. One who returned with the sergeant told the panel members that she had a job in a store paying five dollars a week—doing what, the article does not say—and found that it was too little to support her and her children. By taking up prostitution, she said, she was able to make twenty-five to thirty dollars a week and put her children in a private school. Still, O'Hara asked her, "Would you live a decent life again if you were assured of a respectable job at $12 a week?" She answered: "Governor, I'd grab the chance."[47] As the hearings proceeded, commission members repeatedly tried to pin down store executives on where they stood with regard to a minimum wage bill for women. A Senate bill had proposed such a wage, of twelve dollars a week. Simpson declined to disclose Marshall Field's exact earnings, but said the store was profitable and would be well able to pay twelve dollars a week as a minimum wage, if such were the mandate. Cochran supported O'Hara and the inquiry in frequent editorials and urged the passage of a state minimum wage law. He said that other Chicago papers had shown "a very gentle handling of the story,"[48] not wanting to offend their advertisers and yet unable to ignore a significant news development. He said the two organs of modest progressivism in his view, the *Tribune* and the *Post,* had been relatively fair, if timid, in their coverage. But the *Day Book,* he said, would stand apart, for "no advertiser has any string tied to this paper, and I'm with Gov. O'Hara and that committee as long as they stick to the fight."

NINE

Struggling in the Shadow of War

By the spring of 1914, in Scripps's view, the *Day Book* had become "a model production."[1] In an informally conducted content analysis, Scripps said that the paper had nearly achieved the right balance between high-brow and low-brow, and that any improvements should be only in the details. Once again, he praised Negley Cochran for all of his personal writings. (On March 6, for example, Cochran had written a front-page article about Chicago businesses siding with Henrici's restaurant during a waitresses' strike, and followed that on March 12 with an editorial note criticizing the businesses.) Earlier, Scripps praised the emphasis on local coverage, and in particular Cochran's "Personal Notes." Cochran had begun running his own signed opinion pieces, including columns that demanded better street railway service and higher wages at Marshall Field's and elsewhere. Of these editorial notes, Scripps wrote, "Perhaps you will be surprised when I tell you that these articles are exactly in line with the idea that I had from the origination of the adless paper, and that I felt I was absolutely unable to communicate to you. What I mean when I say your articles are in line with my idea, is that that they express the fact that a personality, a man, is running the paper."[2]

Scripps was less than flattering with regard to Harold Cochran's latest poetry—"Some of Harold's other verse has been much better"—but said that the "light jolly grin provoking spirit" of the poetry helped to balance the senior Cochran's commentary and the news. He praised a regular feature (from the organization's Newspaper Enterprise Association) called "Confessions of a

Wife" for its "homely human interest material." And while he said that he seldom read any of the short stories and never read any sports, he recognized their popularity with the masses. He reminded Cochran that "the roughest kind of horse play in humor"—as, for example, that found in the comics "Oscar and Adolph" and "Everett True"—is "more attractive than the most subtle wit." Scripps's analysis was notably lacking in comments on news content; his main interest seemed to be the mix of features. In this focus on entertainment fare, he may have been looking to lighten his own load; he obliquely referred to family troubles, saying he had "little heart during these days for any sort of business." (Scripps's middle and favorite son, John Paul, who had been editorial director for the family business, came down with a mysterious illness in 1913 and gradually wasted away, dying in April 1914, at age twenty-six.) Once again, he urged Cochran to hold down expenses and to do all in his power to ensure that the paper reached 30,000 circulation and that it would be able to break even at that level. This is important not only for the paper itself, he said, but "far more essential on account of the *Day Book* being a working and proved model."

Growing Optimism, for a Time

In a sign of his growing optimism over the prospects for the *Day Book*'s success, Scripps traveled to Chicago in the summer of 1914 and spent nearly two weeks with Cochran and his staff. Circulation growth had been steady in the first half of the year, climbing from 13,828 in January to 16,483 in June. A careful review of the circulation figures during his visit that June convinced Scripps that it would be possible to reach a circulation of 500,000, and he authorized Cochran to buy land on which to build a one-story newspaper plant sufficient to house all departments and turn out a paper of that size.[3] During his stay, Scripps even drove around the West Side looking for a suitable lot on which to build, but failing to find one that seemed just right, he directed Cochran to keep up the search. Scripps opened a checking account in Cochran's name in San Diego and instructed his organization's business managers to honor any of Cochran's drafts for money to buy land and put up a building. In a subsequent hunt with a real estate agent, Cochran found a parcel of land that he liked, and authorized its purchase. But the escalation of tensions in Europe that summer and fall (Archduke Francis Ferdinand of Austria-Hungary was assassinated in Sarajevo on June 28, 1914, triggering a chain of events that would lead to World War I) gave Cochran pause. He anticipated that the wartime economy would drive up the cost of paper, making it increasingly doubtful that the *Day Book* could become profitable, even with a 30,000 circulation. In an executive decision that likely signaled his own lukewarm commitment to the adless venture, Cochran canceled the land deal.

An Absentee Editor

Given Cochran's personal attachment to Toledo, he was no doubt reluctant to formalize the ties to Chicago by purchasing land in place of renting. Even after the *Day Book*'s launching, Cochran remained an editor and owner of the *News-Bee* in Toledo, Ohio. He was committed to ensuring that the *News-Bee,* from which he drew his income, remain on solid financial footing, and that was a main reason for his frequent and lengthy stays in Ohio; his wife's decision to remain at the family home in Ohio only added to the continuing pull eastward. Early on he acknowledged to Scripps that he had not given as much attention to the *Day Book* as he should have: "I haven't edited this paper as it should be edited, and the idea hasn't had a fair trial. It isn't fair to the idea for me to try to edit this paper and have my family responsibilities and my bread and butter supply in Ohio." He added: "If I were out of debt and had an income of $10,000 a year coming to me not as salary from anybody, but as dividends or interest on something I owned, I would volunteer to come here to Chicago and give my undivided attention to making this paper go, and without caring a darn whether I ever made a cent out of it; but I don't happen to be situated that way." At various times he intimated that he would be willing to be relieved of the Chicago duties, ready to step aside should Scripps have someone else in mind to serve as editor. But he hastened to assure Scripps that he remained in charge in Chicago and was not overly delegating authority to his son Harold or anyone else: "[Harold] never was editor, had only considered himself an aide to me and a sort of managing editor. He knows and I know that he isn't ready to tackle any such job as editor of the *Day Book*."[4] Scripps was convinced early on that the paper's slow start stemmed from Cochran having delegated too much authority to his son Harold and having spent too much time in Ohio. He wrote: "I chose you as the editor of the *Day Book*. But you chose a young, unproved man, your son."[5] He continued: "You have never yet been really the editor—the whole thing—the man in the office who made and selected and directed every line and every word in it."

Despite such criticism, as time passed, the *Day Book* remained under the leadership of Harold Cochran. Negley Cochran noted in the fall of 1915 that he had been back in Ohio for two months and that during that time Harold had served as the managing editor and city editor, assigning all the articles,

editing, handling rewrite over the phone, writing editorials, and occasionally, as he put it, breaking forth in verse. Such had been the pattern, Cochran said: "I haven't bothered about attempting to handle the staff for nearly
a year, and all of the members know that Harold is the boss on the job."[6] Still,
circulation continued to grow: it reached 22,130 in October, before dipping
over the winter. But there was a hint of defensiveness on Cochran's part about
having turned over management of the paper as he hastened to assure Scripps
that Harold was up to the task. In the November 8 letter to Scripps, Cochran even included a note from Sandburg, at thirty-seven "the oldest man on
the staff," that read as an encomium on demand.[7] Sandburg said of Harold
Cochran, "Hal can handle the *Day Book* probably better than any all-round
executive you might hire as managing editor. For work and rapid-fire action
and meeting events I would stack him up against Roy Howard or any of the
slim young stars of the Scripps organization." Whatever misgivings Scripps
might have had, Harold Cochran continued to largely manage the *Day Book*,
as his letters to the senior Cochran indicated. Harold Cochran would write
about attending council meetings to stay abreast of the news (November 8,
1915), thinking of strategies to bolster circulation (April 6, 1916), and having
to dismiss a reporter, Jack Malloy, who could not stay sober (June 1, 1917). In
November 1916, the *Day Book's* editorial staff consisted of Harold Cochran
and five reporters, including Malloy and Carl Sandburg, on a weekly payroll
of $165.[8] The office staff consisted of the business manager, Watters, a book-
keeper, a mailer, and two others, all of whom shared $114 per week. The *Day
Book* also employed about thirty boys between fourteen and sixteen to deliver
papers by streetcar to 746 newsstands across the city; the boys who worked
all day were paid five to seven dollars weekly (a wage that the *Day Book* found
highly objectionable when paid by the department stores), and those who
began work after school received $2.50 to three dollars weekly.

Sandburg Promotes "World's Greatest Newspaper"

For his part, Sandburg remained bullish on the *Day Book's* prospects for success. A November 11, 1915, letter to Alfred Harcourt of Henry Holt and Company (who the next year would bring out Sandburg's first collection of poetry,
Chicago Poems), reflected his optimism: "I am helping build the *Day Book* here
into what we believe will be genuinely 'the world's greatest newspaper.'"[9]
That same day he wrote to a friend, the writer and editor Louis Untermyer,
telling of his commitment to the paper and of how he was pouring all of his
energy into it:

Building the *Day Book*, recent live events in politics and labor, have kept me out of poetry and art interests. Then too, I had begun to feel what your letter calls "the difficulty that a real radical has to get a hearing." There is such an aloofness from life and the people on the part of most of the poets and most of the publishers that I have begun pouring all my oaths of love and hate and beauty into my newspaper writing. I'm going to help build this adless daily newspaper to a point where we can handle with proper strokes those white rabbits who classify themselves as "publishers."[10]

A month later, in a letter to Alice Corbin Henderson, associate editor of *Poetry*, he was most effusive: "The *Day Book* is smashing ahead, making its place. Many of the Best People who know all the other Best People are getting so they don't feel they know all that's going on unless they read the *Day Book*."[11]

Signs of Declining Support

For anyone paying close critical attention, though, signs of trouble at the *Day Book* were apparent, especially with regard to its chief proponent and financial backer. For about the first three years of the experiment, Scripps regularly indicated that of all his newspapers, he paid most attention to the *Day Book*. In the spring of 1914, preparing for a trip to the East, he told Cochran that "I hope no one will talk to me or try to get me interested in any other part of the Scripps newspaper business than the Day Book."[12] Indeed, he said that he "considered that the Day Book was a more important proposition than the election of any man to the presidency."[13] Less than a year later, however, Scripps said he was no longer regularly reading the paper, and he faulted his editor for not contributing enough to the editorial page ("I am sure that it has been proven a number of times that an article a day by you means more for the growth of the paper than all the rest of the stuff in it").[14] Moreover, the paper was giving too much space to what Scripps termed propaganda. He likened a reform-minded *Day Book* to classical music, saying both would appeal to only "a certain small percent of the public."[15] "Are laboring men interested in reading about hours of labor, wages scales, the progress of labor unions, and legislation for laboring people?" On the contrary, Scripps said, they would rather be entertained and have others fight their battles. To underscore that point, he conveyed the criticisms of his wife, who he said got worked up during a drive from Baltimore to Washington: "Don't you know what's the matter with the *Day Book* Ed?" Why is it trying to reform somebody and something and everything? It is trying to reform all the time. . . .

Just have him run a newspaper with all the things that other newspapers have in; and no advertising and no reform. Why everybody will read the paper. We don't want to be reformed."[16] By the following summer, Scripps was ready to call it quits, but he held off, in large part because Cochran insisted on more time. Scripps wrote to Cochran, "I feel that I am too old and that you are not young enough any longer to continue the effort in developing the idea of an adless newspaper."[17] Cochran responded, asking for a few more months, and Scripps agreed to continue subsidizing the paper. As late as September 1915, despite his bouts of misgivings, Scripps regarded the paper as a sound business proposition, citing its steady circulation growth, and predicted that it would become self-supporting in two years. He told John Watters, the business manager, "I believe that an analysis of the whole Scripps business, considering time and the money invested, would show that the *Day Book* is at least up to the average, if not a little ahead of the average."[18] But a year later, Scripps was clearly losing interest in the paper, and any hope of profitability was fading with the rising cost of newsprint. In October 1916, Scripps wired Cochran a note that came across as a harsh dose of reality: "Stop grieving. Bury your stinking pride. No one can always win."[19]

Fallout From a Price Hike

Just as Negley Cochran had relegated management to his son Harold, so too had E. W. Scripps turned over control of the Scripps business to his son James. Whereas E. W. had long viewed the *Day Book* in grand terms as reinventing journalism along more democratic lines, James had less of a personal and philosophical stake in the venture. James Scripps was a businessman who saw little chance that the paper, especially selling for a penny, would ever break even. Rising newsprint costs, beginning in 1916, dimmed the paper's chances. Contract prices for newsprint paper across the country had been generally between two and three dollars per hundred pounds, delivered; by the end of the year, though, prices had doubled, running as high as six or seven dollars per hundred pounds.[20] Publishers across the country protested the hikes, and the Federal Trade Commission began an investigation.[21] In Chicago, Cochran was feeling pressure from James to increase the retail price of the *Day Book*. James Scripps had concluded that the margin of profit on white paper was so small that it would take "a long time" to put the *Day Book* in the black if it continued to sell for one cent.[22] The wholesale cost of *Day Books* had risen from fifty cents per hundred copies to $1.20 per hundred; with the paper still selling for a penny, or one dollar per hundred copies, it was losing twenty cents on every hundred copies sold.[23] Under increasing pressure from the national organization's bean counters, Cochran reluctantly raised the price of the paper to two cents, on November 20, 1916. As he expected, circulation took a nosedive, dropping from 22,804 in November to 15,689 in December. Despite that falloff, the higher newsstand price meant that revenue actually increased, to $3,905.26 in December, from $3,899.55 in November. For the entire year, the paper showed an average monthly deficit of $1,270.46; that was less than half the $2,690.44 average deficit recorded in 1912, the first full year of operation, but still a ways from the goal of being self-sustaining. In January 1917, the paper showed its first and only profitable month. With a circulation of 15,966, the paper had a revenue of $4,230.11 and showed a profit of $319.65.[24] The *Day Book* was the first newspaper in Chicago to begin charging two cents per copy, but given newsprint hikes, others would follow suit.[25]

Harold Cochran had fully exhausted his hopes for the *Day Book*. He said the staff was as talented and dedicated as any that could be assembled, and that the paper had played all sorts of stories on the front page, and still circulation lagged. He reflected on the struggle, "I have tried time and again to find what there was that readers of the *Day Book* do not like. But they always say, 'Oh, I like the little sheet all right.' But they don't buy it regularly."[26] Despite professing broad support for the paper, many union workers were slow to part with the money to buy it, he said. Harold Cochran concluded that the two-cent price had hurt, and that readers liked the large "scare heads on the war" that ran in the broadsheet newspapers. Finally, in what Scripps would have regarded as sacrilege, Cochran suggested that many readers really did want to read advertisements, and that they turned to the other papers for them. Cochran concluded, "To go on with the *Day Book,* knowing what I do, from past experiences, seems to me simply a waste of money, time and the energy on the part of all those employed on the paper."

"Good Night Edition"

A few weeks later, on July 6, the front page of the paper carried this message to its readers: "Good Night Edition of The Day Book: N. D. Cochran Tells Why This Is the Last Issue of the First Adless Daily." Cochran said that because of the war and the Scripps organization's decision to have him help coordinate coverage from Washington, he needed to close the paper. "With some reluctance," he wrote, "I must say good night and good bye. I can't be in Washington, Toledo and Chicago at the same time, and have discovered that there is

Negley Cochran, editor
of the *Day Book* until it
closed on July 6, 1917,
around 1920. (E. W.
Scripps Archive, Mahn
Center for Archives and
Special Collections, Ohio
University Libraries)

a limit to what one man can do." As for adless journalism, he added: "There is nothing wrong with the idea. It was thoroughly practical then. It was possible to publish an adless daily newspaper that was under no obligation to advertisers and free to publish the truth." But the war and higher paper costs intervened before the *Day Book* could reach 30,000 circulation, he said, when it could have been self-sustaining. Not enough people, he added, were ready to spend two cents for a free press. The number of subscribers continued falling in 1917: 14,482 in March, 13,697 in April, 12,051 in May, and 11,957 in June.[27] Cochran steadfastly professed his belief in the soundness of the adless concept, but all of the time he spent in Toledo and his willingness to basically turn over the *Day Book* to his son Harold from the start suggest that his personal interest was only half-hearted, or at least not enough to outweigh the pull of financial and family interests in Toledo. As he did with so many of the paper's operations, when it came time to close up, Negley Cochran assigned the task to one of his lieutenants. He had John Watters write to James Scripps right after the final issue for instructions on how to dispose of the physical remains of E. W. Scripps's greatest experiment, including nine typewriters, a safe, three desks, sixteen kitchen tables that served as desks, a Potter press with a Hoe magazine folder, and 48,000 pounds of paper.[28]

Day Book Staff Moves On

The alumni of the Cochran school of journalism at the *Day Book* went on to achieve success elsewhere, though none would match that attained by Sandburg. Harold Cochran, the managing editor, became editor and publisher of the *Denver Express* and later the art director of the Scripps organization's Newspaper Enterprise Association.[29] Scripps's nephew Thomas E. Sharp, a reporter, founded the *El Paso Post* for Scripps (it later became the *El Paso Herald-Post*) and served as editor; afterward he was editor of the *Memphis Press* (which later merged with the *News-Scimitar* to become the *Press-Scimitar*) and then the *Buffalo Times*. The longtime business manager, John Watters, became business manager of the *Youngstown Telegram*. It is not clear whether Jane Whitaker remained in journalism after her work at the *Day Book*.[30]

As for Sandburg, he was out of work when the *Day Book* ceased publication in July 1917. For about a month, he covered strike mediation talks in Omaha for the National Labor Defense Council. Back in Chicago, he was hired by Hearst's *Chicago Evening American* to write editorials for $100 a week, with a promise of freedom to write as he pleased. But Sandburg, who had railed against Hearst as the antithesis of his hero Abraham Lincoln, soon felt pressure to tilt his editorials this way and that. He resigned after a few weeks, and took a job writing editorials for Lawson's *Daily News*, at half the pay, but with his integrity intact. He found himself quite at home there, in the company of journalists like the reporter and novelist Ben Hecht, and eventually he became the paper's movie critic. Sandburg's literary ascent continued as he produced an immense body of work: books of poetry, children's stories, the six-volume Lincoln biography. He won a Pulitzer Prize in history in 1940 for the *War Years* portion of the biography and a second prize in 1951 for his *Complete Poems*.

Sandburg continued to correspond with Cochran over the years, and paid him many a compliment. Of Cochran's instruction, Sandburg said it taught him that news should be pared down to its essentials and that, even then, all news is colored by opinions. Sandburg's deep affection for Cochran was apparent in a letter written in 1932 after Sandburg had finished reading Cochran's book on Scripps. In commentary that said more about their relationship than Cochran's literary reach, he wrote: "I doubt whether 5 or 10 years from now I will revise my present judgment that the book belongs alongside Lincoln, Jefferson, Franklin, Thoreau, Emerson, Whitman. You were thoughtful so many ways from driving a car and cooking steak to opening beer bottles and talking like an honest Quaker that the day went like a long session in a saloon where I had my natural religion deepened."[31]

Conclusion

Three months after the United States entered World War I, Negley Cochran published the last issue of the *Day Book,* with a banner headline that read: "Good Night Edition."[1] In an open letter to subscribers in that issue, he explained that the Scripps organization needed him to concentrate his efforts on wartime coverage as an editor at large, based in Washington, rather than as editor of the *News-Bee* in Toledo or the *Day Book* in Chicago. He portrayed the demise as yet another casualty of the war. "So I'm through," he said. "I'm going to Washington. I've enlisted for the war; and from now on will serve where it seems to me I can render the most service."[2] While the proximate cause for closing the paper was his having to relocate to Washington on Scripps's orders, Cochran noted that economic pressures had made such an ending inevitable. The spiraling cost of newsprint had forced the paper to double its price, to two cents per issue, in December 1916, and circulation slid quickly in the wake of that price hike. On top of that, Cochran said, the cost of white paper was expected to rise again in August. In his biography of Scripps, published sixteen years after the last adless issue in Chicago, Cochran said "publication of the *Day Book* would have continued if the World War had not completely changed conditions, notably the price of newsprint."[3] Cochran, however, for reasons never made clear, did not give readers the full story on the newsprint paper troubles. He suggested paper costs rose simply because the war made such resources scarce. In fact, the Federal Trade Commission found that manufacturers had "banded together to secure unreasonable profits" in 1916.[4] As it turned out, the commission reported, there had been "no real shortage of paper," though the balance between supply and demand was close. And in March 1917, about four months before the *Day Book* ceased publication, the commission agreed to set paper prices, naming $2.50 per hundred pounds as a reasonable charge, effectively cutting the price in half. The commission noted that "some small publishers have already been put out of business and more are likely to suffer the same fate." The *Day Book* was among them: evidently having given up hope, Scripps and Cochran found no reason to reverse course in the face of the Federal Trade Commission's intervention.

Despite the *Day Book*'s modest run, totaling about six years and including only one profitable month, Cochran felt strongly that the newspaper had succeeded in its mission. In announcing the closing of the paper, he said, "There was nothing wrong with the idea. It was thoroughly practical then. It was possible to publish an adless daily newspaper that was under no obligation to advertisers and free to publish the truth."[5] Sixteen years later, he remained as convinced as ever about its viability. The "laboratory experiment in journalism," he wrote, "had proved that an adless newspaper could be made a business success."[6] But however strong his convictions on this point, Cochran never marshaled the evidence or provided the compelling analysis necessary to give his conclusions the weight of authority. Readers were left to infer that if the *Day Book* was in any sense financially viable, the proof was in the steady decline in monthly financial losses, a pattern, which, if it had continued, would seemingly have led to profits. The average monthly deficit for 1912, the first full year of publication, was $2,690.44; the monthly deficit had declined by half, to $1,270.46, by 1916.[7] But Cochran's optimistic reading of the data should be understood as an expression of faith in things unseen: the *Day Book* never had a profitable run, only the hope of one.

E. W. Scripps, like Cochran, linked the paper's closing to the prohibitive hike in newsprint prices as well as the need to have a war news editor in Washington. But Scripps could have chosen another editor to replace Cochran in Chicago, and he gave little consideration to that option in the last year of publication, even though he suspected that the reason the *Day Book* foundered was "just because I and Cochran were not able to put it over."[8] They were too old, he thought, and Cochran was too well educated and too well connected socially to effectively reach out to the working class. When all is said and done, Scripps said, "autopsies in such a case as this are certain to bring about disputes and disagreements between the attending doctors."[9] Then too, a dark personal cloud hung over all of Scripps's assessments in the final months. Scripps sounded weary, if not clinically depressed, in his letters to Cochran: his body was aging, his daughter Nackey had eloped, his son John's death still grieved him, and he continued to feud with his wife. In a biographical introduction to Scripps's collected disquisitions, Oliver Knight dismissed Scripps's comments on the closing of the *Day Book* as "a confused assessment."[10] Knight said his reading of Scripps's correspondence suggested that the publisher had "simply lost interest" in the experiment, and used the war as a pretext to summon Cochran to Washington. Regardless of any rationalizations offered by Scripps and Cochran, in Knight's view, the *Day Book* "must be reckoned a failure as an experiment in adless journalism."[11]

Second-Guessing the Choice for Editor

Scripps's questioning of whether Cochran was the right person for the job bears further scrutiny in any postmortem. From the earliest days of the *Day Book* in 1911, Cochran conveyed his ambivalence, especially to his son Harold, about the undertaking. Negley Cochran's wife and primary business ties were in Toledo, Ohio, and he continued to direct the operations of the *News-Bee* in Toledo throughout the 1910s. The way Scripps set up the finances, Cochran did not collect a salary in Chicago; his income, and that was substantial, came from his part ownership of the *News-Bee*. The incentives for divided loyalties were certainly in place. Cochran spent long stretches of time in Toledo and encouraged Harold and the other *Day Book* staff members to take the initiative in shaping the paper. This meant that the senior newspaper executive who was assigned to guide the adless newspaper experiment in effect turned over the operations to novices in the field. Harold had little newspaper experience outside of the *Day Book*. Would the *Day Book* have built up its circulation faster if the senior Cochran had overseen more of the day-to-day operations and news coverage? Would the content have been more focused and substantive, especially in the early months, if Negley Cochran had been a mainstay in Chicago?

In a biography of Scripps, Vance H. Trimble, a former Scripps–Howard editor and reporter, concludes that the fatal flaw in the experiment was having Cochran serve as editor, and not necessarily because he spent so much time in Toledo. Trimble portrays Cochran as ill-prepared for the job and then erratic and wishy-washy in running the paper. For example, he cites the time a woman canceled her subscription with a complaint about the number of murder stories in the paper, and Cochran told the staff to go easy on crime and accident coverage.[12] Trimble contends that Cochran failed to produce the kind of interesting paper that Scripps recommended, and that he sabotaged Scripps's circulation plan of canvassing homes around the office, block by block, to gain a loyal readership base. Perhaps most damning of all, however, is his claim that Cochran was "a pretty good elbow-bender"[13] who in all likelihood filled the wastebasket by his desk with a good many empty bottles. Scripps himself expressed concerns about Cochran's drinking to Dana Sleeth of the *Portland News:* "There is one thing that you and Cochran have in common. You both indulge in booze. . . . If Cochran's [health] doesn't break down, it will be because he has been more careful than I was and more careful than you are."[14]

In fairness to Cochran, it should be noted that for many years, until health problems became an overriding concern, Scripps drank whiskey heavily, and was fond of exaggerating his capacity. He liked to say that he drank a gallon of whiskey a day for many years, though apparently no one ever believed this story.[15] It may be that Scripps overstated Cochran's drinking, as he did his own. Also, Carl Sandburg, who worked for Cochran for years and kept up a correspondence with him after the *Day Book* folded, gave no indication that he thought Cochran was anything less than an estimable editor; alcohol, though present, was not seen as diminishing Cochran's work as a journalist. Sandburg made references to sharing a drink or two with Cochran and wishing him many more rounds ("may there be Canadian ale whenever you call for it,"[16] Sandburg wrote in a note to Cochran). But over and above all else, Sandburg praised Cochran without fail over the years.

Of more concern than Cochran's drinking, then, would be his style of leadership. Cochran was away from Chicago too much of the time, including a stretch of weeks at the end, when he was dispatched to Washington before the paper closed and Harold again served as editor. Negley Cochran showed moderate enthusiasm, at best, for the assignment in Chicago. Indications in his correspondence are that he felt compelled to see the assignment through, knowing how important the experiment was to Scripps personally. Though Cochran hinted to Scripps that he had important work remaining in Toledo and would not protest too greatly if replaced in Chicago, he was not about to disappoint the man who controlled his livelihood, by refusing to go when called. Nevertheless, Cochran's half-hearted leadership represented an early and continuing handicap for the experiment.

Struggling Against Historical Currents

Even if newsprint prices had not soared and even if Cochran had provided more effective leadership, the *Day Book* would still have found itself struggling against historical currents. In hindsight, Scripps and Cochran narrowly mistimed the start of the experiment. Between 1880 and 1900, the number of daily newspapers published in Chicago doubled, to thirty-seven, and the number continued to rise.[17] But most of the growth after the turn of the century came in the foreign language press, riding the wave of immigration. The number of English-language daily newspapers published in Chicago peaked at eleven in 1900; by 1918, the city had six such papers.[18] The *Day Book* went against the trend when it became the tenth English-language daily in 1911.[19] The *World,* formerly the *Socialist,* closed in 1912, and the *Inter-Ocean* merged with the *Record-Herald* in 1914. In the next two decades, the *Daily Tribune,* the *Daily News,* and the Hearst papers would squeeze out the rest of the competitors. The decline in daily newspapers in Chicago was consistent with trends across the state and the nation.[20] The combined number of morning and evening newspapers peaked in 1909, at 2,600.[21] Between 1916 and 1920 alone, the country lost 137 dailies and 2,268 weeklies.[22] John Nerone notes that most of the failures came about because of overall economic trends and wartime shortages, but "left-leaning papers," of which the *Day Book* was certainly one, "stood a far greater chance of failing than the average publication."[23] At the highest levels of government, the nation carried out an antiradical campaign, effectively barring leftist publications from the mails and encouraging the infiltration of labor organizations and other kinds of vigilante action. The *Day Book* never suffered such a direct attack on its business, but early on it had spoken out forcefully against the war and as a rule allied itself with labor and the left, and that may have contributed to the slip in circulation as the nation turned to the right.

Redefining News

Even so, circulation figures and balance sheets provide a limited measure for judging the success of the *Day Book*. What Knight and Trimble (as well as Scripps and Cochran) largely overlooked in taking stock of the adless paper was the degree to which it redefined news. The *Day Book* covered the violent circulation battles at a time when the mainstream dailies had largely suppressed the news. While the Chicago press raved about the quality of goods for sale at Marshall Field's and other department stores, the *Day Book* focused on the standard of living for those who labored in the stores. The paper urged Marshall Field's and other stores to worry less about profits and more about the health and welfare of their employees, and railed against the employers repeatedly for their failings on that score. The *Day Book* also campaigned for safer working and shopping conditions, publishing accounts of accidents that other papers ignored. These examples, among others, suggest that the content of the *Day Book,* rather than its limited lifespan, may in fact be the best measure of its contribution to the practice of journalism. Regardless of its dwindling circulation, the *Day Book* remained a steadfast ally of the working class and the dispossessed, and a primary source of news on their struggles, news that often could not be found elsewhere. The newspaper established itself as a champion of factory workers, department store clerks, and others it counted among the working class, and it showed how a newspaper might keep a vigilant watch over stores and other powerful advertisers when it was no longer dependent on them for revenue.

Scripps took note of Charles Dana's innovative separation of advertisements from news and editorial matter in the *Sun,* and he went one step further.[24] He eliminated advertising altogether, as Dana had wanted to do. Both publishers saw that step as a necessary corollary for newspapers that had gained independence from political parties. In the early nineteenth century, newspapers began to sever their political ties and strive for nonpartisanship, reflected in a neutrality in political coverage. By the 1890s, Janet Steele noted, as Scripps was building his chain, "American newspaper editors prided themselves on their freedom from political parties."[25] But what has generally been left unsaid, by editors and the scholars who write about them, she continued, was that "the press had simply traded in one form of dependence for another." While the patronage of politicians was no longer needed, advertising was, and the expectations of advertisers influenced content.[26] Advertisers and the press were in a partnership to make money. The *New Yorker* critic A. J. Liebling urged a separation of what he regarded as an unholy alliance. Such a separation would be made possible by independent financing like that provided by Scripps (to the *Day Book*) and Marshall Field III (to the later ad-less daily, *PM*), but under even more generous terms. Liebling envisioned a newspaper that would be endowed, much like a university, and "devoted to the pursuit of daily truth," not forced "to stake its survival on attracting advertisers of ball-point pens and tickets to Hollywood peep shows."[27]

Online Opportunities

The prospects for such an endowed newspaper would seem brighter today than ever because of the Internet, an ideal delivery system. The digital revolution has made possible interactive and relatively inexpensive communication. It is hard to imagine a better engine of democratic communication, one that can carry information and ideas to any home or any commuter. When Scripps shut down the *Day Book,* he pointed to the cost of newsprint as a major cause. With news delivery on the Web, that expense is eliminated. The primary costs are those associated with news gathering, writing, editing, and design. Online media pioneers such as Slate and Salon, as well as digital operations of the major media companies, have struggled to turn a profit because ad dollars have been limited and because readers are hesitant to pay for subscriptions when so much else on the Web is free.[28] The easy part has been finding an audience. The Washington Post Company purchased Slate from Microsoft in 2004, with analysts suggesting it was a sign of the online magazine's respect as a brand name and growing ability to draw advertising dollars.[29] Salon, meanwhile, was offering an ad-free Salon Premium for thirty-five dollars a year, in which contributors were invited to "make a difference: exposing hypocrisy, shedding light on issues that the timid mainstream media shies from and making this a more informed election year."[30] The question of whether enough readers would pay for such information remained to be answered.

The Internet is showing signs of success in attracting more young people to news. In "The State of the News Media 2004," a report by the Project for Excellence in Journalism, affiliated with the Columbia University Graduate School of Journalism, researchers said that the Web was the only news media, apart from the ethnic and alternative press, that was enjoying audience growth, with more than 55 percent of Internet users (eighteen to thirty-four years of age) getting news online in a typical week.[31] But as David Mindich discovered in his research on young Americans and their consumption of news, the biggest draw of the Internet, by far, was e-mail and chatting.[32] As with television in the 1990s, he said, "entertainment and personal interests seems to be making news a smaller and smaller part of the Internet's universe."[33] Moreover, the "State of the News Media" report pointed out that Internet journalism still offers minimal original content; most online news consists of material from "old media."

Robert W. McChesney argues that if the Internet is to constitute a meaningful and effective public sphere in which people are kept well informed on all matters affecting their lives, there must be a place for independent and presumably subsidized journalism, which "provides the oxygen for democratic discussion."[34] That financing could come from various sources (e.g., private foundations, wealthy individuals, or pooled gifts from donors of modest means). The goal would be to foster a more independent form of journalism, subject to pressure neither from political parties nor from advertisers. Since Scripps personally financed the *Day Book's* operations, with a subsidy of up to $2,500 a month, he was in a position to terminate the paper at a moment's notice, for any reason, and he often seemed on the verge of doing so. Toward the end of the *Day Book's* publication run, Scripps said an adless paper should not be held hostage to advertisers or financiers: "For the same reason that I am opposed to a press supported by advertisers, I am opposed to a press that is supported by men who have private axes to grind—whether the axes have moral or immoral blades."[35] He clarified his overarching intent: "There is one great principle at stake in the *Day Book,* and only one, and that is the founding of a newspaper to be successfully supported by the reading public, as distinguished from the advertising public."[36]

An alternative approach would be an endowed newspaper for which money is invested in a news venture up front and for the long haul, and with assured independence from the funding source. Like the *Day Book,* an endowed newspaper would be free to redefine news. If Scripps were in charge, one could imagine an editorial page that would champion earners of modest wages and newspapers that would critically cover company layoffs, salaries of executives, health insurance, the distribution of wealth, corporate tax breaks, and working conditions. It would be a newspaper that treated readers as citizens in a democracy with rights to be safeguarded. It would be, as Scripps described his vision of the *Day Book,* "a newspaper fairly and honestly conducted in the interest of the great masses of the public."[37]

Epilogue

The two major efforts in the twentieth century to publish profitable newspapers without advertising both have connections to Chicago.[1] In a curious turn of events, considering the *Day Book*'s front-page berating of the Marshall Field department store and the "lazy-loafing" Field heirs, it was Marshall Field III who beginning in 1940 largely financed an adless venture even more ambitious in its size and scope than Scripps's effort with the *Day Book*. Field, the grandson of the founder of the department store and an inheritor of great wealth, invested $200,000 in the adless venture, called *PM*.[2] Field knew of the *Day Book*, though it is not clear whether he read it as a youth or simply learned about it after the fact. In his 1945 book on press freedom, Field expressed admiration for the way in which Scripps stood up to advertisers, especially in publishing the *Day Book*, and Field clearly saw himself supporting a similar brand of editorial independence.[3] The two publishers reached different conclusions, however, about the viability of such journalism in the wake of their adless ventures. Whereas Scripps remained convinced that adless journalism was practicable, Field emphasized the limitations to the *PM* and *Day Book* models. Advertisers, Field said, must usually share in the cost of production and distribution so that subscription prices can be kept as low as possible for readers. Without advertising support, he continued, the press may turn to special interests and the government for subsidies, and one form of control will simply have replaced another. The best course for most papers would be to accept advertising but keep those who pay for it at arm's length, "by allowing the staff to focus its attention so fixedly upon producing a paper to which subscribers are devoted that advertisers will either be forced to purchase space or face the consequences of forgoing an excellent avenue through which to extend their sales efforts."[4] This was the strategy of the *Chicago Sun,* which Field began in December 1941 to challenge the conservative *Tribune*'s monopoly. Field said the *Sun* had to compete with an established paper that sold for only two cents and provided many pages of news and ads, as well as enticing extras like comics, and it would have been unrealistic to expect to make inroads without advertising revenue. Moreover, he noted, readership surveys showed that many people like to read ads, a finding that was apparently lost on Scripps.

Like an earlier daily called the *Sun,* this one based in New York, *PM* intended to cover the news from a decidedly liberal worldview and as a trailblazer among established dailies. Not only did *PM* eschew ads, it set out to redefine other newspaper conventions, including news content (e.g., assigning staff members to report on labor and on the news media) and design (e.g., the creative use of high-quality photographs and art on high-grade paper). The undertaking was much more ambitious than Scripps's shoestring venture in Chicago, in which Negley Cochran had to play mechanic with the used printing press before the first issue could be published and made do with only a few reporters. Whereas Scripps alone financed the *Day Book,* Field initially teamed up with sixteen other wealthy and well-connected business leaders to back *PM,* investing $1.5 million in total. The original stockholders included Marian Stern (Sears Roebuck heir), $200,000; Garrett Winston (corporate attorney), $100,000; and Lincoln Schuster (book publisher), $50,000.[5] Not all of the investors felt as comfortable as Field with the liberal agenda of the editor, Ralph Ingersoll, but most bet that Ingersoll's "reputation as a publishing genius"[6] would ensure a good financial return.

Broad Support Among Journalists

Ingersoll, a Yale alumnus who achieved professional acclaim in helping to develop the *New Yorker, Fortune,* and *Life* magazines, was the driving force behind *PM,* which early on took the journalistic world by storm in a way that also sharply contrasted with the low-profile *Day Book. PM* enjoyed "the enthusiastic support of virtually all the working reporters in the country," and the prepublication publicity attracted more than 10,000 job applications.[7] The prospect of putting out an ad-free paper was the biggest draw for most of the staffers, who saw an opportunity to report and write with a rare degree of latitude, and many also liked the prospect of exercising that freedom with a liberal slant.[8] With hirings that tapped academia, book publishers, newspapers, and magazines, Ingersoll assembled a high-powered mix of intellectuals ready to try their hand at journalism and accomplished journalism professionals, a combination that at times would prove combustible. The Nieman fellows who joined the experiment included Hodding Carter, who had published his own paper in Mississippi; Volta Torrey of The Associated Press; and William P. Vogel of the *Herald Tribune.* (In response to Ingersoll's invitation to suggest a good reporter to cover City Hall, Mayor Fiorello La Guardia of New York recommended Vogel.) Leo Huberman and James Wechsler left the *Nation* to cover labor for *PM;* I. F. Stone supplemented his *Nation* paycheck with regular contributions to *PM.* Margaret Bourke-White and Mary Morris, the photographers, joined *PM.* Others who would become well known in journalism or the arts also came on board, including Theodor Seuss Geisel (Dr. Seuss), Ernest Hemingway, Benjamin Spock, and James Thurber. Journalists were not the only ones pleased by the prospect of a newspaper dependent on sales and subscriptions alone. President Franklin D. Roosevelt sent Ingersoll a congratulatory letter a month before the first issue: "'Your proposal to sustain your enterprise simply by merchandising information, with the public as your only customer, appeals to me as a new and promising formula for freedom of the press.'"[9] Roosevelt was complimenting a paper that shared his New Deal vision and would prove to be one of his staunchest supporters among the press.

In a confidential memorandum distributed to the staff in May 1940, a month before the first issue, Ingersoll described *PM* as "a new kind of newspaper" that would provide complete news coverage dedicated to the proposition that people would want and need to know what was going on, and that the job could best be done without the indirect support of advertisers, whose primary interest was in selling a product or service.[10] Ingersoll said he harbored no philosophical prejudice against advertising, but felt that the existing commercial operation in newspapers often ill-served readers—"tending to limit the editors' freedom of action, making the paper cumbersome and inconvenient physically, and constantly distracting the publisher from devising new ways to make his paper more valuable to the reader."[11] Knowing that some readers would miss the information in advertising, *PM* designed a daily digest that presented the information the same day it appeared in ads in competing New York papers. There were other innovations, as *PM* introduced beats covering labor, radio and the print press, modern living, and food, all of which would become standard fare in most newspapers. *PM* was the first to provide complete movie listings and a guide to radio programs. Like the *Day Book, PM* was to have thirty-two pages, though the page size was larger, at approximately fourteen inches by eleven inches (the *Day Book* published pages of about nine inches by six).

Circulation Troubles

Given the prepublication fanfare, eager readers mobbed delivery trucks when *PM* printed its first issue on June 18.[12] People were paying scalpers up to fifty cents for an issue marked for sale at five cents. The paper sold more than 400,000 copies on the first day. Not until later would it be learned that the most loyal readers, the 150,000 charter subscribers, who had committed to regularly buying the paper, had been left without papers as others snatched up copies of the first issue. As it turned out, *PM* would have had a hard time delivering to those charter subscribers anyway because the list of such subscribers was missing. It would be months before the paperwork could be sorted out, and in that time *PM* lost some of its most valued readers. *PM* saw its circulation drop to 31,000 within eight weeks, far below the 200,000 needed to break even. Before the year was out, in October 1940, Field, then forty-six, bought out the paper's other investors at twenty cents on the dollar.

Though Field was *PM*'s primary financial supporter, staff members said he did not seek to influence it editorially. That is not to suggest he was always in agreement with the paper's coverage and positions, and he was excoriated for having Communists on staff. Stone said Field caught a lot of flak in his social circle for supporting "a bunch of nondescript radicals and pinkos" who put out the paper.[13] On one occasion Field did intervene, indirectly, in the paper's operations.[14] Ingersoll had been called up for the draft in 1942, suggesting a draft board conspiracy to some because other editors were being granted exemptions and Ingersoll was forty-one at the time. Without Ingersoll's knowledge, Field appealed to General Lewis Hershey, director of Selective Service, for an exemption, which was subsequently granted. However, Ingersoll, who vigorously campaigned for American intervention in the war and an all-out effort to halt fascism, later enlisted and took a leave from the paper.

Accusations of Communist Ties

As with the strain between the intellectuals and professional journalists on staff, the relationship with Communists proved troublesome for *PM* from the outset. Ingersoll's position was that no one should be excluded from the paper because of affiliations with the Communist party; he himself had belonged to a Communist study group, and though he eventually found himself unable to abide by the party line and dropped out, he shared with the party stalwarts a commitment to the poor and the labor movement. Still, for *PM* workers as well as for himself, he insisted on a commitment to disinterested journalism, in the sense of independence from any party ideology. Some of the paper's early contributors—including Dashiel Hammett, Dorothy Parker, Heywood Broun, and Lillian Hellman—had links to Communist organizations. For a short time, the paper employed a writer recommended by the head of the American Communist party. Rumors circulated that the paper was being secretly financed by Moscow. Publications like the *Saturday Evening Post* ran tallies of the number of known Communists working at *PM*—"as many as sixteen at one count."[15] Ingersoll felt obliged to run an item in the Press section of the paper that responded to an unsigned handbill circulating in competitors' offices and purporting to list twenty-four staffers who were party members or sympathizers; *PM* published photos of all twenty-four with a copy of the circular, and invited the FBI to investigate. The FBI did have a file on *PM*, but evidently took the staff to be what it was: "a random collection of predominantly liberal newspaper men and women of varying political persuasions and sympathetic to the labor movement and other causes also supported by the Communists in the 1940s."[16]

As printing and other costs continued to rise, Field grew impatient with losing $25,000 a day. In 1946, Field decided that advertising was necessary to turn a profit and that Ingersoll was no longer the best person to lead the paper, and Ingersoll resigned. The man who had confounded so many in the industry was welcomed back in the circle. To other publishers, John Tebbel said, "it became in time a comforting reassurance" that adless newspapers do not succeed.[17] An advertising rate card was published on November 7, 1946, but not until the following year would the ad flow become significant. Paul Milkman, who wrote the definitive history of *PM,* comments at length on how the appearance of boxy ads and the paper's shift to a more traditional tabloid format abruptly ended Ingersoll's vision of a beautiful newspaper.[18] But it was no longer Ingersoll's paper, nor would it be Field's for long. Though *PM* had achieved a steady circulation of just over 150,000, it had cost Field about $7 million in the first six years of publication.[19] Field was concerned not only about the relentless losses, but also that the controversial *PM* might be hurting his ad sales in Chicago. Moreover, the *Sun,* which merged with the *Chicago Times* to form the *Sun-Times,* was really his paper in his town, and he decided to sell *PM.* The change in ownership came on May 1, 1948, with the new owners, Bartley Crum and Joseph Barnes, renaming the paper the *New York Star.* Still unable to attract advertising, the paper folded on January 28, 1949. The presses were sold to a

Pennsylvania newspaper, and the building soon after was occupied by a new tabloid called the *Daily Compass,* which went bankrupt in 1952.

Postmortem for an Adless Paper

Over the years, many analysts, from former staffers to journalism professors to Ingersoll himself, have weighed in with their views on why *PM* failed to survive. A majority of staff members who responded to questionnaires in a 1949 study cited editorial mismanagement, bad business decisions, and biased news coverage.[20] Some faulted Ingersoll and his brand of personal journalism; Ingersoll, on the other hand, pointed to financial impediments, believing that more money would have meant more talent on staff and, in the end, more readers. The more recent analysis is Milkman's, who said the most compelling reasons for the paper's demise may be found in Roosevelt's death and a political shift in which the Cold War came to be the prism of choice in Washington. The "war for political and economic democracy was in retreat,"[21] signaling an end as well for the liberal and antifascist crusader *PM.* Milkman also noted that the paper faced unfavorable odds in trying to break into a market already crowded: the city had eight daily newspapers at the time, and in the ensuing years several other papers also folded. He concluded that *PM*'s demise was typical of the fate of many newspapers across the nation and should not overshadow its journalistic successes, including innovations in photography, graphics, and news coverage. In its daily coverage, *PM* "legitimized the struggles of American labor and the nation's black citizens, affording eloquent news, feature, and pictorial coverage to outsiders the traditional press ignored."[22] In its investigative work, *PM* crusaded with rare verve, exposing watered meat, exorbitant interest rates charged by installment loan companies, price fixing in the milk industry, and profiteering by American defense firms during World War II.

Appendix A: Chronology

1911 Carter Henry Harrison Jr. elected mayor of Chicago. (April 4)
      The *Day Book* begins publication. (September 28)
1912 Legal prostitution in Chicago is abolished.
      The magazine *Poetry* started by Harriet Monroe in Chicago.
      Titanic sinks in mid-Atlantic on maiden voyage from England.
      (April 15)
      Theodore Roosevelt survives assassination attempt in Milwaukee.
      (October 14)
      Textile strike in Lawrence, Massachusetts.
      Woodrow Wilson elected 28th president of U.S.
1913 16th Amendment empowers U.S. Government to collect income
      taxes. (February 25)
      17th Amendment allows for popular election of U.S. senators. (May 31)
1914 Hostilities between the U.S. and Mexico. (April 21)
      Archduke Francis Ferdinand of Austria-Hungary assassinated. (June 28)
      U.S. declares neutrality in World War I. (August 4)
1915 Lake passenger steamer Eastland sinks off Chicago River. (July 24)
      William Hale (Big Bill) Thompson elected mayor of Chicago. (April 6)
      Germans sink British ship Lusitania with 128 Americans on board.
      (May 7)
      U.S. Marines land in Haiti. (July 28)
1916 Woodrow Wilson wins re-election with slogan "He Kept Us Out of
      War."
1917 U.S. merchant ships arm for self-defense against German submarines.
      (March 13)
      Congress declares war on Germany. (April 6)
      The *Day Book* ends publication. (July 6)

Appendix B: Newspapers in Chicago in 1911

NAME	ESTABLISHED	PUBLISHER	SCHEDULE	CIRCULATION
The American	1900	W. R. Hearst	P.M.	315,335
The Day Book	1911	E. W. Scripps	P.M.	143*
The Evening Post	1890	J. C. Reilly	P.M.	28,000
The Examiner	1900	W. R. Hearst	A.M.	187,021
The Inter-Ocean	1872	H. H. Kohlsaat	A.M.	80,000
The Journal	1844	Chicago Journal Co.	P.M.	126,685
The News	1876	V. F. Lawson	P.M.	327,634
The Record-Herald	1854	V. F. Lawson	A.M.	200,000
The Socialist	1906	Workers' Pub. Soc.	P.M.	N.A.
The Tribune	1847	Tribune Co.	A.M.	226,000

Source: N. W. Ayer and Sons, *American Newspaper Annual and Directory,* 1911.
*As of December 1911, three months into publication.

Appendix C: Rise and Decline of the Number of Newspapers

Table 1: Number of Daily Newspapers and Periodicals in U.S.

1880	909
1885	1,207
1890	1,662
1895	2,056
1900	2,190
1905	2,326
1910	2,433
1915	2,447
1920	2,324
1925	2,283
1930	2,219

Source: Alfred M. Lee, *The Daily Newspaper in America,* 722–23.

Table 2: Number of Daily Newspapers in Illinois

1840	3
1850	8
1860	23
1870	39
1880	74
1889	121
1899	197
1909	194
1919	168
1929	120

Source: Alfred M. Lee, *The Daily Newspaper in America,* 716.

Table 3: Number of Daily Newspapers in Chicago

1840	2
1850	4
1860	5
1870	5
1880	6
1890	10
1900	11
1910	9
1918	6
1930	6

Source: Elizabeth Dewey Johns, "Chicago's Newspapers and The News: A Study of Public Communication in a Metropolis." Ph.D. diss., University of Chicago, 1942.

Notes

Introduction

1. E. W. Scripps, Non-Advertising Newspaper Scheme, 2 November 1904, Scripps Papers, subseries 1.2, box, 7, folder, 5, p. 5.

2. Ibid., 8.

3. Ibid., 12.

4. Ibid., 9.

5. Ibid.

6. E. W. Scripps to Negley D. Cochran, 28 July 1913, Scripps Papers, subseries 1.2, box 19, folder 6.

7. E. W. Scripps to Negley D. Cochran, 12 December 1913, Scripps Papers, subseries 1.2, box 19, folder 11.

8. Ben H. Bagdikian, *The Media Monopoly*. 6th ed. (Boston: Beacon Press, 2000), 147.

9. Frank Luther Mott, *American Journalism: A History of Newspapers in the United States Through 250 Years: 1690 to 1940* (New York: The Macmillan Company, 1947), 551–54.

10. Willard Grosvenor Bleyer, *Main Currents in the History of American Journalism* (Cambridge, Mass.: The Riverside Press, 1927).

11. In *The Press and America: An Interpretive History of the Mass Media* (8th ed., Boston: Allyn and Bacon, 1966), Michael and Edwin Emery offer a cursory treatment in wording strikingly similar to Mott's. Robert E. Park, in "The Natural History of the Newspaper," in *The City*, a book co-authored with E. W. Burgess and R. D. McKenzie (Chicago: University of Chicago Press, 1925), overlooks Scripps entirely in a listing of major historical figures in journalism. In contrast, Alfred M. Lee's *The Daily Newspaper in America* (New York: Macmillan, 1937) provides a more extensive historical record of Scripps and advertising, including two pages devoted to the *Day Book*. A sampling of more recent historical works suggests that the paper is still forgotten.

12. The most extensive treatment of *PM* appears in a book by Paul Milkman, *PM: A New Deal in Journalism: 1940-1948* (New Brunswick, NJ: Rutgers University Press, 1997). As an example of textbook attention, *PM* is featured in *Voices of a Nation: A History of Mass Media in the United States* by Jean Folkerts and Dwight L. Teeter Jr., 4th ed. (Boston: Allyn and Bacon, 2002); the *Day Book,* on the other hand, goes unmentioned. A more recent illustration can be found in "Across the Great Divide: Class," by Brent Cunningham in *Columbia Journalism Review,* May/June 2004. In offering examples of connections between the press and the working class, he cites *PM* (and its motto: "*PM* is against people who push other people around"), but not the *Day Book* (33).

13. Sinclair, Upton. *The Brass Check: A Study of American Journalism*. Reprint. New York: Arno and the *New York Times*, 1970, 222–24. In 1919, Sinclair self-published his fierce critique of press performance. The University of Illinois Press reissued *The Brass Check* in 2003, with a 25-page introduction by Robert W. McChesney and Ben Scott.

14. Lee, *Daily Newspaper*, 748–49.

15. William E. Huntzicker, *The Popular Press, 1833-1865* (Westport, Conn.: Greenwood Press, 1999), 8.

16. John C. Nerone, "The Mythology of the Penny Press," *Critical Studies in Mass Communication* 4 (1987): 376–404.

17. Ibid., 378.

18. See, for example, Bagdikian, *Media Monopoly;* C. Edwin Baker, *Advertising and a Democratic Press* (Princeton, NJ: Princeton University Press, 1994); Sinclair, *The Brass Check;* and James D. Squires, *Read All About It: The Corporate Takeover of America's Newspaper* (New York: Times Books, 1993).

19. Max Frankel, "The Wall, Vindicated," *New York Times Magazine*, 9 January 2000, 24.

20. The Times Mirror Company merged with the Tribune Company in 2000, creating a combined company that retained the Tribune name and owned 11 daily newspapers, 22 television stations, and 4 radio stations.

21. Charles Rappleye, "Cracking the Church-State Wall," *Columbia Journalism Review* 36 (January/February 1998): 20–23.

22. Ibid., 23.

23. James Risser, "Lessons from L.A.: The Wall is Heading Back," *Columbia Journalism Review* 38 (January/February 2000).

24. Frankel, "The Wall," 25.

25. Jacques Steinberg, "After the Peaks of Journalism, Budget Realities," *New York Times*, 14 June 2004. The paper ended up cutting about 160 jobs at the newspaper, about 60 of which were held by reporters and others in the editorial operations. "Los Angeles Times Cuts About 160 Jobs," *Los Angeles Times*, 22 June 2004.

26. Tom Wicker, *On The Record: An Insider's Guide to Journalism* (Boston: Bedford/St. Martin's, 2002), 150.

27. Sharyn Vane, "Taking Care of Business," *American Journalism Review* (March 2002), 60.

28. Ibid. See also Doug Underwood, "It's Not Just in L.A.," *Columbia Journalism Review* 36 (January/February 1998), 24–26.

29. Ben H. Bagdikian, *The New Media Monopoly* (Boston: Beacon Press, 2004), 248.

30. Ibid., 235.

31. David Mindich, *Just the Facts: How "Objectivity" Came to Define American Journalism* (New York: New York University Press, 1998), 1.

32. Ibid., 137.

33. Brent Cunningham, "Re-thinking Objectivity," *Columbia Journalism Review* 42 (July/August 2003), 26.

34. Brian Keefer, "Tsunami," *Columbia Journalism Review* 43 (July/August 2004), 23.

35. "Two Women and the Hearst Papers," *Day Book*, 6 November 1915.

Chapter 1: A Time for Dissent and Reform

1. Nelson Lichtenstein, Susan Strasser, and Roy Rosenzweig, *Who Built America? Working People and the Nation's Economy, Politics, Culture, and Society*. Vol. 2 (New York: Worth Publishers, 2000), 167.

2. Ibid.

3. Ibid.

4. Samuel P. Hays, *The Response to Industrialism: 1885-1914*. 2nd ed. (Chicago: University of Chicago Press, 1995), 3.

5. Lichtenstein, *Who Built America?*, 169.

6. Alan Trachtenberg, *The Incorporation of America: Culture and Society in the Gilded Age* (New York: Hill and Wang, 1982), 87.

7. Sean Dennis Cashman, *America in the Gilded Age: From the Death of Lincoln to the Rise of Theodore Roosevelt* (New York: New York University Press, 1984), 12.

8. Trachtenberg, *Incorporation*, 4.

9. Nell Irvin Painter, *Standing at Armageddon: The United States, 1877-1919* (New York: W.W. Norton, 1987), 177.

10. Trachtenberg, *Incorporation*, 87.

11. Lichtenstein, *Who Built America?*, 175.

12. Ibid., 176.

13. Steven J. Diner, *A Very Different Age: Americans of the Progressive Era* (New York: Hill and Wang, 1998), 51.

14. Ibid., 61.

15. Howard Zinn, *A People's History of the United States* (New York: HarperPerennial, 1980), 323.

16. Trachtenberg, *Incorporation*, 212.

17. Jon Bekken, "The Working-Class Press at the Turn of the Century," *Ruthless Criticism: New Perspectives in U.S. Communication History* (Minneapolis: University of Minnesota Press, 1993), 159.

18. Robert D. Putnam, *Bowling Alone: The Collapse and Revival of American Community* (New York: Simon & Schuster, 2000), 384–85. This investment in social capital was not lost on the *Day Book*. An unsigned author—perhaps Negley Cochran, the editor—wrote, "In France, Germany, England, Spain—every spot on the earth's surface—MEN ARE GETTING TOGETHER IN SOME FORM OF BROTHERHOOD. It may be in clubs, societies, granges, fraternal organizations, labor unions. But they are getting together—the great 95 per cent. Whenever they get together, they find that IN UNION THERE IS STRENGTH," in "The World Is Progressive," *Day Book*, 2 October 1911.

19. Putnam, *Bowling Alone*, 383.

20. Hays, *Response to Industrialism*, 47.

21. Cashman, *America in the Gilded Age*, 87.

22. Carl S. Smith, *Chicago and the American Literary Imagination, 1880-1920* (Chicago: University of Chicago Press, 1984), x.

23. The Chicago Daily News Company, *Chicago Daily News Almanac and Year-Book for 1912*, (Chicago: Daily News, 1911).

24. Bekken, 154.

25. Lichtenstein, *Who Built America?*, 207

26. Ibid., 208.

27. Hofstadter, Richard, Daniel Aaron and William Miller. *The United States: The History of a Republic* (Englewood Cliffs, NJ: Prentice Hall, 1957), 575.

28. Cashman, *America in the Gilded Age,* 50.

29. David Paul Nord, *Newspapers and New Politics: Midwestern Municipal Reform, 1890-1900* (Ann Arbor, Mich.: UMI Research Press, 1981), 11.

30. Ibid., 11–12.

31. Louis Filler, *The Muckrakers* (Stanford, CA: Stanford University Press, 1968), 9.

32. Ibid., 10

33. Ibid., 9.

34. Robert W. McChesney and Ben Scott point out that while *The Jungle* remains "a staple of American literature," a later book by Sinclair, *The Brass Check,* which constitutes a vigorous critique of the press, likening journalists to prostitutes dependent on monied elites, "has been all but forgotten." For a fuller discussion of Sinclair, see their article "Upton Sinclair and the Contradictions of Capitalist Journalism," *Monthly Review* 54 (May 2002) and their introduction to a reissue of *The Brass Check: A Study of American Journalism* (Urbana: University of Illinois Press, 2003).

35. Ibid., viii.

36. Baldasty, *E. W. Scripps,* 86.

37. David Nasaw, *Children of the City: At Work and At Play* (Garden City, NY: Anchor Press, 1985), 63.

38. Hard, William, "De Kid Wot Works at Night," *Everybody's Magazine* (January 1908), reprinted in *The Muckrakers* by Arthur and Lila Weinberg (New York: Capricorn Books, 1961), 371.

39. Nasaw, *Children of the City,* 75.

40. Negley D. Cochran to E. W. Scripps, 10 November 1912, E. W. Scripps Papers, subseries 1.1, box 31, folder 5.

41. Nasaw, *Children of the City,* 65.

42. *Day Book,* 2 June 1913.

43. Marion Tuttle Marzolf, *Civilizing Voices: American Press Criticism 1880-1950* (New York: Longman, 1991), 34.

44. [A New York Editor], "Is an Honest Newspaper Possible?" *Atlantic Monthly.* Vol. CII (Cambridge: The Riverside Press, 1908), 441–47.

45. Will Irwin, "All the News That's Fit to Print," *The American Newspaper: A Series First Appearing in Collier's, January-July 1911* (Ames: Iowa State University Press, 1969).

46. Ibid., IX, "The Advertising Influence."

47. Ibid., XI, "Our Kind of People."

48. Edward Alsworth Ross, "The Suppression of Important News," *Atlantic Monthly,* March 1910, 311.

49. Ibid.

50. Marzolf, *Civilizing Voices,* 17.

51. "An Endowed Newspaper: A Hint to Philanthropists," *Dial,* 14 (16 January 1893), 35.

52. Ibid., 36.

Chapter 2: Chain-Builder for the Common People

1. Oliver Knight, *I Protest: Selected Disquisitions of E. W. Scripps* (Madison: University of Wisconsin, 1966), 219–30.

2. E. W. Scripps to Paul C. Edwards, 20 May 1911, Scripps Papers, subseries 1.2, box 17, folder 10.

3. Ibid.

4. Ibid.

5. Ibid.

6. Ibid.

7. "Life and Death of Edward W. Scripps—Pioneer Genius of Free Press," *Editor and Publisher*, 20 March 1926, 6.

8. Knight, *I Protest*, 230.

9. Trimble, *Astonishing Mr. Scripps*, 164.

10. Kenneth Steward and John Tebbel, *Makers of Modern Journalism* (New York: Prentice-Hall, 1952), 267.

11. Knight, *I Protest*, 230.

12. Ibid., 3.

13. E. W. Scripps to H. N. Rickey and W. B. Colver, 2 March 1910, Scripps Papers, subseries 1.2, box 16, folder 8.

14. Gerald J. Baldasty, *E. W. Scripps and the Business of Newspapers* (Urbana: University of Illinois Press, 1999), 104.

15. Ibid., 149.

16. Gilson Gardner, *Lusty Scripps* (New York: Vanguard Press, 1932), 45.

17. Ibid., 10.

18. E. W. Scripps to William E. Ritter, Scripps Papers, series 4, box 2, book 4. Scripps was not alone in displaying a superior, disdainful view of the people his papers were intended to serve. At various times, others in the Scripps organization would use similar phrasing, as with B.H. Canfield referring to "the common herd" and Dana Sleeth to "mutts." B. H. Canfield to E. W. Scripps, 15 July 1913, Scripps Papers, subseries 1.1., box 32, folder 10.

19. Knight, *I Protest*, 33.

20. Baldasty, *E. W. Scripps*, 2.

21. Ibid.

22. Lee, *The Daily Newspaper*, 214–15

23. Baldasty, *E. W. Scripps*, 33.

24. Ibid., 33.

25. Ibid., 40.

26. Ibid., 41.

27. Ibid., 47.

28. Negley D. Cochran, *E. W. Scripps* (New York: Harcourt, Brace and Co., 1933), 82.

29. Knight, *I Protest*, 300.

30. Scripps's disquisitions can be found in the Scripps Papers, series 4. Indexes for the disquisitions provide both alphabetical and date order. A published collec-

tion is also available in Oliver Knight, *I Protest: Selected Disquisitions of E. W. Scripps* (Madison: University of Wisconsin, 1966).

31. D. W. Hollis, *The ABC-CLIO Companion to Media in America* (Santa Barbara, CA: ABC-CLIO, 1995). Lee, in *The Daily Newspaper*, 214–15, notes that there were eight smaller chains established before 1900.

32. Baldasty, *E. W. Scripps*, 69.

33. E. W. Scripps to Negley D. Cochran, 14 January 1911, Scripps Papers, sub-series 1.2, box 17, folder 6.

34. Baldasty, *E. W. Scripps*, 70.

35. Gerald J. Baldasty and Myron K. Jordan, "Scripps' Competitive Strategy: The Art of Non-Competition," *Journalism Quarterly*, 70 (Summer 1993): 265–75.

36. Edward E. Adams, "Secret Combinations and Collusive Agreements: The Scripps Newspaper Empire and the Early Roots of Joint Operating Agreements," *Journalism Quarterly*, 73 (Spring 1996): 195–205.

37. Ibid., 197.

38. Bagdikian, *The Media Monopoly*, 99–100.

39. Baldasty, *E. W. Scripps*, 91.

40. Knight, *I Protest*, 205.

41. Scripps Papers, Series 1.2, Box 11, Folder 10.

42. Baldasty, *E. W. Scripps*, 93.

43. Ibid.

44. Ibid.

45. Ibid., 94–95. Baldasty describes the preeminence of editors through mana-gerial decree; newsrooms were not necessarily physically "walled off" from busi-ness offices.

46. Knight, *I Protest*, 206.

47. E. W. Scripps to Robert F. Paine, 19 January 1900, Scripps Papers, series 2, box 4, book 5.

48. Knight, *I Protest*, 206.

49. Ibid.

50. Cochran, *E. W. Scripps*, 124.

51. E. W. Scripps to H. N. Rickey and W.B. Colver, 2 March 1910, Scripps Papers, subseries 1.2, box 16, folder 8.

Chapter 3: The Secret Plan Takes Shape

1. E. W. Scripps, Non-Advertising Newspaper Scheme, 2 November 1904, 9.

2. Ibid.

3. Janet E. Steele, *The Sun Shines for All: Journalism and Ideology in the Life of Charles A. Dana* (New York: Syracuse University Press, 1993), 34.

4. Ibid.

5. Ibid., 63. Dana left the *Republican* after 10 months for reasons that, Steele says, are not entirely clear.

6. Willard G. Bleyer, *Main Currents in the History of American Journalism* (Hough-ton Mifflin, 1927; reprint, New York: Da Capo Press, 1973), 299.

7. Ibid.

8. Ibid., 300.

9. Folkerts and Teeter, *Voices of a Nation,* 248.

10. The *War Cry* began publishing in 1879. In 1890, its circulation exceeded 300,000. See Arch Wiggins's *The History of the Salvation Army, Volume Four, 1886-1904* (New York: Salvation Army), 169. See also F. A. Mackenzie's *Booth-Tucker: Sadhu and Saint* (London: Hodder and Stoughton, 1930).

11. Knight, *I Protest,* 208.

12. Scripps, "Non-Advertising Newspaper Scheme," 2 November 1904, 3.

13. Ibid., 5.

14. Ibid., 8.

15. Ibid., 12.

16. Ibid., 12.

17. Ibid., 17.

18. Baldasty, *E. W. Scripps,* 47.

19. Ibid., 74–75.

20. Scripps, "Non-Advertising Newspaper Scheme," 2 November 1904, 12.

21. E. W. Scripps, "Non-Advertising Newspaper Scheme," 23 November 1904, Scripps Papers, subseries 1.2, box 7, folder 5, p. 5.

22. Scripps lists the salaries but not the corresponding positions; elsewhere Scripps and Cochran talk about having an editor, managing editor, and a couple of reporters, and those positions would fit in the salary grid that Scripps laid out.

23. Scripps, "Non-Advertising Newspaper Scheme," 23 November 1904, 4.

24. Issues of the *Press* are apparently no longer extant. The Scripps paper should not be confused with a paper by the same name that was later briefly published in Chicago by Charles R. Crane, a businessman, and that was somewhat merged into the *Day Book* in 1914.

25. Knight, *I Protest,* 207.

26. David Nasaw, *The Chief: The Life of William Randolph Hearst* (Boston: Houghton Mifflin, 2000), 152–153; W. A. Swanberg, *Citizen Hearst* (New York: Bantam Books, 1961), 216.

27. In 1907, Scripps made it clear that he still preferred Chicago as the site for an adless paper, though others in the organization favored New York and Philadelphia. He also had considered others in his cabinet as editors of the enterprise, including W. B. Colver, president and general manager of Newspaper Enterprise Association, as well as his son James. E. W. Scripps to H. B. Clark, 12 January 1907, Scripps Papers, subseries 1.2, box 11, folder 6; E. W. Scripps to L. T. Atwood, 21 January 1907, Scripps Papers, subseries 1.2, box 11, folder 7.

28. John Vandercook to E. W. Scripps, 3 March 1905, Scripps Papers, subseries 1.1, box 24, folder 1.

29. Trimble, *Astonishing Mr. Scripps,* 222.

30. Vandercook added that he may have published "the smallest paper on record" as a schoolboy. Called the *Monthly Croaker,* the paper was three inches by four and a half inches. John Vandercook to E. W. Scripps, 28 March 1906, Scripps Papers, subseries 1.1, box 25, folder 15.

31. "Death Ends Brilliant Career of 'Neg' Cochran," *Memphis Press Scimitar,* 14 April 1941, 13.

32. "Reporters Who Became a Power for Community Good," *Ohio Newspaper,* 16, May 1935.

33. Knight, *I Protest,* 208.

34. Cochran, *E. W. Scripps,* 123.

35. Ibid., 130.

36. Ibid., 126.

37. Trimble, *Astonishing Mr. Scripps,* 21, 42.

38. Harold M. Mayer and Richard C. Wade, *Chicago: Growth of a Metropolis* (Chicago: University of Chicago Press, 1969), 214.

39. Ibid., 214–30.

40. Norma Green, Stephen Lacy, and Jean Folkerts. "Chicago Journalists at the Turn of the Century: Bohemians All?" *Journalism Quarterly* 66 (Winter 1989), 815.

41. Negley D. Cochran to E. W. Scripps, 23 May 1911, Scripps Papers, subseries 1.1, box 30, folder 2.

42. Baldasty, *E. W. Scripps,* 72.

43. Ibid., 75.

44. Negley D. Cochran to E. W. Scripps, 15 September 1911, Scripps Papers, subseries 1.1, box 30, folder 2.

45. Ibid.

46. E. W. Scripps to Negley D. Cochran, 14 January 1911, Scripps Papers, subseries 1.2, box 17, folder 6.

47. Negley D. Cochran to E. W. Scripps, 23 May 1911, Scripps Papers, subseries 1.1, box 30, folder 2.

48. E. W. Scripps to Negley D. Cochran, 10 August 1910, Scripps Papers, subseries 1.2, box 16, folder 13.

49. Ibid.

50. Negley D. Cochran to E. W. Scripps, 15 September 1911, Scripps Papers, subseries 1.1, box 30, folder 2.

51. Ibid.

52. E. W. Scripps to Negley D. Cochran, 10 August 1910, Scripps Papers, subseries 1.2, box 16, folder 13.

53. Cochran, *E. W. Scripps,* 132.

54. E. W. Scripps to Negley D. Cochran, 14 January 1911, Scripps Papers, subseries 1.2, box 17, folder 6.

Chapter 4: The *Day Book's* Debut

1. Trimble, *Astonishing Mr. Scripps,* 305.

2. Ibid.

3. In his disquisition entitled "The Common Crowd, the Herd, the Vulgar Mob," Scripps pointed out that "the word 'vulgar' from its Latin root is indentically synonimous [*sic*] with our word 'common.'" 10 December 1912, Scripps Papers, series 4, box 2, book 4.

4. "Society Life of Riches and Trouble Outdone by Simple Life and Happiness," *Day Book,* 28 September 1911.

5. "John Bertram Thinks of Suicide; But Decides on Marriage Instead," *Day Book,* 29 September 1911.

6. Negley D. Cochran to E. W. Scripps, 14 October 1911, Scripps Papers, subseries 1.1, box 30, folder 2.

7. Negley D. Cochran to E. W. Scripps, 9 October 1911, Scripps Papers, subseries 1.1, box 30, folder 2.

8. E. W. Scripps to Negley D. Cochran, 2 October 1911, Scripps Papers, subseries 1.2, box 18., folder 3. Interestingly, John Vandercook had suggested a quite different name when he was being considered as editor: The United States Daily. John Vandercook to E. W. Scripps, 30 May 1905, subseries 1.1, box 24, folder 1.

9. Ibid.

10. Steele, *The Sun,* 83. The author cites an unpublished paper of the historian William Taylor as describing that pastiche quality as being characteristic of commercial culture in the Gilded Age.

11. "The Way to Help the Girls of Chicago is to Help Them to Organize," *Day Book,* 28 October 1911.

12. Geoffrey Cowan, *The People v. Clarence Darrow: The Bribery Trial of America's Greatest Lawyer* (New York: Times Books, 1993), xix.

13. Cochran noted that the McNamaras used to live near the paper's office and that the mother of another defendant, Ortie McManigal, still lived within a couple of blocks of the office.

14. Negley D. Cochran to Harold M. Cochran, 9 April 1912, Cochran Papers.

15. Negley Cochran to E. W. Scripps, 8 December 1911, 13 December 1911, Scripps Papers, subseries 1.1, box 30, folder 4.

16. Ibid.

17. Ibid.

18. Ibid.

19. Early on, Cochran subscribed to several English magazines, including *Answers, Tip Bits, Horner's Weekly, Pearson's,* and "others not so well known on this side of the water," thinking they might provide a model. Negley D. Cochran to E. W. Scripps, 7 March 1912, Scripps Papers, subseries 1.1, box 31, folder 3.

20. Negley Cochran to E. W. Scripps, 11 October 1911, Scripps Papers, subseries 1.1, box 30, folder 2.

21. Ibid.

22. Negley Cochran to E. W. Scripps, 9 November 1911, Scripps Papers, subseries 1.1, box 30, folder 3.

23. E. W. Scripps to Negley Cochran, 27 October 1911, Scripps Papers, subseries 1.2, box 18, folder 3.

24. Ibid.

25. Negley Cochran to E. W. Scripps, 11 October 1911, Scripps Papers, subseries 1.1, box 30, folder 2.

26. E. W. Scripps to Negley Cochran, 27 October 1911, Scripps Papers, subseries 1.2, box 18, folder 3.

27. Ibid.

28. E. W. Scripps to Negley Cochran, 16 November 1911, Scripps Papers, subseries 1.2, box 18, folder 4.

29. Ibid.

30. The prime circulation nearest the office included what Cochran, in the terminology of his day, described as "several distinct colonies of foreigners which are

not worth anything to us; and yet that is where population is thickest. There are Jews, Italians, Sicilians, Poles, Lithuanians, Hungarians and Niggers. The Jews and niggers are the only ones that are any good to us at all. The Jews are only fair—so many of them are not reading English at all. The niggers will order it, but they are bad pay and make trouble for the carriers." Negley D. Cochran to E. W. Scripps, 1 October 1912, Scripps Papers, subseries 1.1, box 31, folder 5.

31. Negley Cochran to E. W. Scripps, 13 December 1911, Scripps Papers, subseries 1.1, box 30, folder 4.

32. "The Day Book—A New West Side Daily Magazine," *Day Book,* 14 October 1911.

33. "Are Your Eyes Worth a Million Dollars?" *Day Book,* 16 October 1911.

34. *Day Book,* 1 January 1912.

35. *Day Book,* 2 January 1912.

36. "The *Day Book* and the Newspapers," *Day Book,* 29 January, 1912.

37. E. W. Scripps to Negley D. Cochran, 3 January 1912, Scripps Papers, subseries 1.2, box 18, folder 6.

38. E. W. Scripps to Negley D. Cochran, 30 January 1912, Scripps Papers, subseries 1.2, box 18, folder 6.

39. Cochran, *E. W. Scripps,* 9–15.

40. Ibid.

41. "Circus Clown Preaches Sermon in Emergency—Will Join Ministry," *Day Book,* 2 February 1912.

42. "Hoboes Have Passwords—But Reporters Can Get In—They're Undesirable Citizens, Too," *Day Book,* 3 February 1912.

43. E. W. Scripps to Negley D. Cochran, 12 February 1912, Scripps Papers, subseries 1.2, box 18, folder 7.

44. Negley D. Cochran to E. W. Scripps, 3 March 1912, Scripps Papers, subseries 1.1, box 31, folder 3.

45. E. W. Scripps to Negley D. Cochran, 2 April 1912, Scripps Papers, subseries 1.2, box 18, folder 9.

46. Negley D. Cochran to E. W. Scripps, 19 March 1912, Scripps Papers, subseries 1.2, box 31, folder 3.

47. Negley D. Cochran to E. W. Scripps, 16 March 1912, Scripps Papers, subseries 1.1, box 31, 3.

48. Negley D. Cochran to E. W. Scripps, 27 March 1912, Scripps Papers, subseries 1.1, box 31, folder 3.

Chapter 5: Critic of the Hometown Press

1. Negley Cochran to E. W. Scripps, 16 November 1911, Scripps Papers, subseries 1.1, box 30, folder 3. The correspondence between Scripps and Cochran does not indicate whether Scripps relayed the request to Darrow, and, if so, whether Darrow forwarded the names of any lawyers to Cochran.

2. Negley Cochran to E. W. Scripps, 16 November 1911, Scripps Papers, subseries 1.1, box 30, folder 3.

3. Ibid.

4. Ibid.

5. Scripps had actually begun his first adless experiment in Chicago in April 1900, personally directing the start-up of the *Press*. But he abruptly ended the experiment weeks later when Hearst began publishing the *American,* which Scripps knew would tap into the working-class market he was after. See Oliver Knight, *I Protest,* 207.

6. Nasaw, *The Chief,* 31.

7. Ibid., 74–81; Swanberg, *Citizen Hearst,* 47–65.

8. Nasaw, *The Chief,* 80–89.

9. Swanberg, *Citizen Hearst,* 95.

10. Emerys, *The Press and America,* 200–3.

11. Steve Mills, "Vending Violence in a .38–Caliber Circulation Drive," *The Chicago Tribune* via its Web site at chicago.digitalcity.com, posted 8 June 1997.

12. Swanberg, *Citizen Hearst,* 217.

13. Joseph Gies, *The Colonel of Chicago* (New York: E.P. Dutton, 1979), 35.

14. Ibid.

15. Christopher Ogden, *Legacy: A Biography of Moses and Walter Annenberg* (Boston: Little, Brown and Company, 1999), 47.

16. Ibid., 48.

17. Gies, *The Colonel,* 35.

18. Ogden, *Legacy,* 49.

19. Ibid.

20. Lloyd Wendt, *Chicago Tribune: The Rise of a Great American Newspaper* (Chicago: Rand McNally, 1979), 383.

21. Ogden, *Legacy,* 49.

22. Swanberg, *Citizen Hearst,* 322.

23. Gies, *The Colonel,* 36.

24. Ibid.

25. Ibid. 37

26. Mills, "Vending Violence."

27. "Hearst Papers Lock Out Pressmen—All Trust Papers Follow Their Lead and Suspend," *Day Book,* 2 May 1912.

28. Ibid.

29. "Trust Press Tie-up Complete; Newsboys and Wagon Drivers Out in Sympathy Strike," *Day Book,* 3 May 1912.

30. Philip Taft, "The Limits of Labor Unity: The Chicago Newspaper Strike of 1912," *Labor History* 19 (Winter 1978): 102.

31. Ibid., 101.

32. Cochran, *E. W. Scripps,* 138.

33. Jon Bekken ("The Chicago Newspaper Scene: An Ecological Perspective," *Journalism & Mass Communication Quarterly,* Autumn 1997, 498) refers to a short-lived daily that began in the wake of the 1912 newspaper strike "to appeal to the large numbers of union sympathizers who could not in good conscience buy the 'trust papers.'" That paper, the *Press,* published by Charles R. Crane and aimed at the working class, was apparently not listed in any directory; it is reflected in Scripps's correspondence with Crane and others, as well as a few pink clippings

from late 1912 and early 1913 in a scrapbook in the John Fitzpatrick Papers at the Chicago Historical Society. There was consideration of folding the paper into the *Day Book*. Crane invested several thousand dollars in the *Day Book*, but no formal merger of the papers came about. Scripps noted that the *Press*, which ran ads, had a circulation of about 10,600 scattered over five editions; this apparently included 450 carrier deliveries and 1,800 mail deliveries. The *Day Book* declined to pick up this subscriber base or any *Press* employees. E. W. Scripps to Negley D. Cochran, 12 December 1913, Scripps Papers, subseries 1.2, box 19, folder 11.

34. E. W. Scripps to Negley D. Cochran, 3 April 1912, Scripps Papers, subseries 1.2, box 18, folder 9.

35. Bekken, "The Working-Class Press," 165.

36. "Police Charge Citizens and Newsies at Fifth and Madison," *Day Book*, 4 May 1912.

37. Bekken, "The Working-Class Press," 159. On May 6, 1912, for example, the *Chicago Daily Socialist* reported that "sluggers employed by the trust newspapers this morning beat up into unconsciousness Alexander Hickey," a news driver who was delivering the paper ("Tribune Manager Is Charged With Attempted Murder").

38. Ibid., 172.

39. "Freel's Revocation of Stereotypers' Charter Appealed to Convention," *Day Book*, 10 May 1912.

40. "Publishers Won't See Gompers—A.F. of L. to Back Locked-Out and Striking Unions," *Day Book*, 24 May 1912.

41. Ibid.

42. "Mothers, Wives, Sisters, and Sweethearts of Locked-Out and Striking Men Lend a Hand," *Day Book*, 27 May 1912.

43. "Paddy Lavin Says Maybe The American Will Give Murderer Up to the Police," *Day Book*, 9 August 1912.

44. Ibid.

45. Ibid.

46. "Disarm Those Hired Thugs!" *Day Book*, 14 August 1912.

47. "Call for Investigation of Trust Papers' Thugs," *Day Book*, 19 August 1912.

48. Swanberg, *Citizen Hearst*, 325.

49. Ibid., 326.

50. Taft, "The Limits of Labor Unity," 111.

51. Ibid.

52. Ibid., 112.

53. Swanberg, *Citizen Hearst*, 326.

54. "Disarm Those Hired Thugs!" *Day Book*, 14 August 1912.

55. Ibid.

56. Ibid.

57. "Chicago Newspaper Trust Conspires to Suppress the Daily Day Book," *Day Book*, 26 March 1913. Jacob C. Harper, a legal counsel and member of Scripps's inner cabinet, also noted that the fight had been precipitated by the introduction of newsstands that had room for only four papers to be displayed. The *Day Book* and the *Press* were to go on a shelf down below, out of sight. Jacob C. Harper to E. W. Scripps, 27 March 1913, Scripps Papers, box 32, folder 12.

58. Ibid.

59. There was no report on the newsstand banning in the *Chicago American, Chicago Daily News, Chicago Evening Post,* or *Chicago Tribune.*

60. "Police Obey Orders and Stop Sale of The *Day Book* on Stands of Chicago," *Day Book,* 27 March 1913.

61. "The *Day Book* Wins Its First Battle for Free Speech and a Free Press," *Day Book,* 28 March 1913.

62. "Features of The *Day Book*," *Day Book,* 24 January 1912.

Chapter 6: Sandburg and Company

1. Fred Fedler, *Lessons From the Past: Journalists' Lives and Work, 1850-1950* (Prospect Heights, IL: Waveland Press, 2000), 5.

2. Ibid., 1. For a description of low wages, erratic dismissals, and minimal prestige in Chicago, see Green, Lacy, and Folkerts, "Chicago Journalists," 816.

3. A. A. Dornfeld, *Behind the Front Page* (Chicago: Academy Chicago/Publishers,1983), 132–33.

4. Theodore Dreiser, *Sister Carrie* (New York: Holt, Rinehart and Winston, 1957), 15.

5. Fedler, *Lessons From the Past,* 17.

6. Marianne Salcetti, "The Emergence of the Reporter: Mechanization and the Devaluation of Editorial Workers," *Newsworkers: Toward a History of the Rank and File* (Minneapolis: University of Minnesota Press, 1995), 55.

7. E. W. Scripps to Ben Lindsey, Jan. 25, 1910, Scripps Papers, subseries 1.2, box 16, folder 6.

8. Baldasty, *E. W. Scripps,* 109.

9. Hugh Dalziel Duncan, *The Rise of Chicago as a Literary Center from 1885 to 1920* (Totowa, N.J.: Bedminster Press, 1964), 164.

10. Ted Curtis Smythe, "The Reporter, 1880–1900: Working Conditions and Their Influence on the News," *Journalism History* 7 (Spring 1980): 1–10.

11. Fedler, *Lessons From the Past,* 63.

12. Ibid.

13. Mott, *American Journalism,* 603.

14. William S. Solomon, "The Site of Newsroom Labor," *Newsworkers: Toward a History of the Rank and File* (Minneapolis: University of Minnesota Press, 1995), 126.

15. Smythe, "The Reporter," 158.

16. Fedler, *Lessons From the Past,* 61.

17. Smythe, "The Reporter," 2. Mott noted that the salaries of New York reporters ranged from less than $20 a week to $60, and that in smaller cities reporters received $5 to $20 a week at the turn of the century (*American Journalism,* 603).

18. *Historical Statistics of the United States: Colonial Times to 1970,* Part 1, 168.

19. Fedler, *Lessons From the Past,* 59.

20. Duncan, *The Rise of Chicago,* 114.

21. Green, Lacy, and Folkerts, "Chicago Journalists," 818–19.

22. Ibid., 820.

23. Salcetti, "The Emergence of the Reporter," 73.

24. Jon Bekken, "The Working-Class Press at the Turn of the Century," in *Ruthless Criticism: New Perspectives in U.S. Communication History.* Ed. William S. Solomon and Robert W. McChesney (Minneapolis: University of Minnesota Press, 1993), 165.

25. Whether under the name *Chicago Daily Socialist* or *Chicago Evening World,* the paper attracted advertisers who wanted to reach "the workers." For example, one display ad read "Union Made Funeral Equipment" (16 September 1912) and "A Socialist Watch at an Anti-Trust Price" (12 January 1912).

26. Penelope Niven, *Carl Sandburg: A Biography* (New York: Charles Scribner's Sons, 1991), 90.

27. Ibid., 136.

28. Ibid., 211.

29. Ibid.

30. Philip R. Yannella, *The Other Carl Sandburg* (Jackson: University Press of Mississippi, 1996), 22.

31. Niven, *Carl Sandburg,* 211.

32. Carl Sandburg, *Chicago Poems* (New York: Henry Holt, 1916).

33. Ibid., 230.

34. Harry Golden, *Carl Sandburg* (Cleveland: The World Publishing Company, 1961). The book carries a photograph of the *Day Book* newsroom, with Sandburg seated before a typewriter, dressed in a suit and tie.

35. *Day Book,* issues of March 1913.

36. "Showing How a City Ordinance Is Snubbed," *Day Book,* 17 January 1913.

37. A review of the *Chicago American, Chicago Daily News,* and *Chicago Daily Tribune* confirmed the *Day's Book's* claim.

38. At least one competing paper, the *Chicago Daily Tribune,* readily noted the name of the store in a dramatic recounting of the accident. The story began: "Mary Dors stopped into the shaft of an elevator on the fifth floor of Hillman's department store yesterday and dropped, screaming, to her death. 'Stop! stop! Take me up!' she shouted to the negro operator of the elevator, Albert Borton, as he was closing the door to the elevator. The boy did not appear to heed her command" ("Excited Woman Meets Death in Hillman's Department Store," 14 January 1913).

39. In 1912, Cochran noted that his son Harold was serving as managing editor; MacGregor was writing the major news stories and supervising two cub reporters on the street; a third cub reporter was writing news briefs. Negley D. Cochran to E. W. Scripps, 7 September 1912, Scripps Papers, subseries 1.1, box 31, folder 4.

40. Another son, Frank, assisted with circulation canvassing and office finances.

41. Negley D. Cochran to E. W. Scripps, 9 October 1911, Scripps Papers, subseries 1.1, box 30, folder 2.

42. Scripps was not alone in expressing misgivings about the impact of Cochran's absence on the *Day Book.* Hamilton B. Clark, another editor in the Scripps organization, stopped in Chicago for a visit and afterward recommended to Scripps "that Neg handle every line of copy that goes into it. To do the latter he would have to divorce himself entirely from any plans and thoughts of the *News-Bee* and the Ohio papers. Whether this latter would be profitable to the *News-Bee* and Ohio I

don't know but it certainly would be profitable to the *Day Book*." Hamilton B. Clark to E. W. Scripps, 14 April 1912, Scripps Papers, subseries 1.1, box 31, folder 2.

43. Negley D. Cochran to E. W. Scripps, 10 November 1912, Scripps Papers, subseries 1.1, box 31, folder 5.

44. Harold Cochran to Negley D. Cochran, Cochran Papers. There may have been additional letters that were not added to the files.

45. Negley D. Cochran to Harold Cochran, 9 April 1912, Cochran Papers.

46. Negley D. Cochran to John T. Watters, 30 April 1912, Cochran Papers.

47. Negley D. Cochran to John T. Watters, 23 May 1912, Cochran Papers.

48. E. W. Scripps would continue to press for bylines, especially bearing Cochran's name. He wrote, "Sign every article that you write that's good; if it isn't good don't sign it. Sign every article that's written by anyone else that's good, if the person will stand for it; if the person won't, fire him or her." E. W. Scripps to Negley D. Cochran, 17 December 1913, Scripps Papers, subseries 1.2, box 19, folder 11; 10 December 1913, Scripps Papers, subseries 1.2, box 19, folder 11.

49. "The American Kid," *Day Book*, 29 January 1914.

50. "Has Freedom Come?" *Day Book*, 27 February 1914.

51. Fedler, *Lessons From the Past*, 21.

52. Harold Cochran to Negley D. Cochran, 22 October 1913, Cochran Papers.

53. "Young Girl Explains What Waitresses Are Forced to Put Up With," *Day Book*, 5 March 1914. The *Day Book* was not alone in covering the labor struggles at Henrici's, but its sympathetic portrayals stood out. For example, the *Chicago Daily News* presented the protest as little more than posturing—certainly not a serious standoff between labor and capital. Under a subhead "Like a Movie Spectacle," one article referred to "the almost daily performance of the arrest of girl pickets" and went on to say that "clerks and office employes have come to regard the Henrici restaurant troubles as a ready substitute for 'the movies.'" "Mounted Policemen Charge Loop Crowd," *Chicago Daily News*, 27 February 1914.

54. Cochran said that when MacGregor was first hired "he looked forward to Saturday night when he could get drunk and blow in his entire weeks [*sic*] wages; and on Monday he was ready to borrow from me so as to eat the remainder of the week." Negley D. Cochran to E. W. Scripps, 9 June 1912, Scripps Papers, subseries 1.1., box 31, folder 4.

55. Negley D. Cochran to E. W. Scripps, 26 August 1913, Scripps Papers, subseries 1.1, box 32, folder 9.

56. "'Remember Ludlow!' Was the Cry of Miners in Walsenburg Battle," *Day Book*, 5 May 1914.

57. Herbert Mitgang, *Letters of Carl Sandburg* (New York: Harcourt, Brace and World, 1968), 271.

58. George and Willene Hendrick, *Carl Sandburg: Poems for the People* (Chicago: Ivan R. Dee, 1999), 26–27.

59. Mitgang, *Letters*, 271.

60. Carl Sandburg, *Cornhuskers*, (New York: Henry Holt, 1918), 50–51.

61. Hendrick, *Carl Sandburg*, 28.

62. Ibid.

63. A year earlier, C. L. Edson, a fellow socialist, said he understood Sandburg's

concerns about money: "You are dead right in being dissatisfied with $25 a week."
He encouraged Sandburg to build up "an outside market" of other publications
that would pay for free-lance articles. C. L. Edson to Carl Sandburg, 4 January
1912, Sandburg Papers.

64. Niven, *Carl Sandburg,* 231.

65. Ibid., 231.

66. "Willum Is Working A Fine Little Game," *Day Book,* 22 January 1913.

67. Oliver Knight, "Scripps and His Adless Newspaper, The *Day Book,*" *Journalism Quarterly* 41 (Winter 1964): 57.

68. Sandburg to Cochran, 25 January 1921, Cochran Papers.

69. Sandburg won the Pulitzer Prize in 1940 for *Abraham Lincoln: The War Years*
and in 1951 for *Complete Poems.*

70. Sandburg's years as a reporter and movie critic at the *Daily News* are examined in several publications, including James C. Y. Chu's "Carl Sandburg: His Association with Henry Justin Smith," *Journalism Quarterly* 50 (Spring 1973): 43–47,
133; and Arnie Bernstein, ed., *"The Movies Are": Carl Sandburg's Film Reviews and
Essays, 1920-1928* (Chicago: Lake Claremont Press, 2000).

71. N. Frederick Nash and Gwenna Weshinsky, "Carl Sandburg and The *Day
Book," American Book Collector,* November-December 1982, 23–34.

72. The *Day Book* also published without page numbers and often without datelines. The editor, Negley Cochran, cited his interest in saving space in the interest
of printing more news, but given the large run of feature and sports pages in every
issue, critics might argue that it was laziness or a lack of professionalism that led
to such omissions instead.

73. Nash and Weshinsky acknowledged that their list was only partial and could
not have represented Sandburg's output over the course of about four years with
the *Day Book.* In fact, at least two bylined and undated articles in the Sandburg collection at Illinois are not listed by Nash and Weshinsky: "Labor Record of Democratic Congress Never Equaled, Says Owen" and "Newspapers to Publish Wholesale Food Prices? Garner Says Yes." The search for Sandburg's articles is made more
difficult because of gaps in the runs at Northwestern University, The Center for
Research Libraries (Chicago), and the Library of Congress.

74. Niven, *Sandburg,* 249.

75. Nash and Weshinsky, "Carl Sandburg," 26.

76. Chu, "Carl Sandburg," 46.

77. John Woods, "Trippers," *Motorman and Conductor,* June 1940, Sandburg
Papers.

78. "Henry Favill Was One Real Man—Doctor Who Was Everybody's Friend,"
Day Book, 22 February 1916.

79. "Theodore B. Sachs," *Day Book,* 5 April 1916.

80. "Arthur Brisbane and Tedious Liars," *Day Book,* 29 March 1916. Sandburg
did not provide citations for the columns that he had in mind; presumably, one
was headlined "Teach Economy—That Is One of the First and Highest Virtues; It
Begins With Saving Money," attributed to Abraham Lincoln (*Chicago American,*
20 March 1916). The unsigned column urges personal restraint: "Saving or thrift,

preached by Benjamin Franklin, Lincoln and others who understood the people's needs, is the thing most lacking in the United States to-day."

81. "Honest Guesses on Politics Have Lowden Ahead—Something About Him," *Day Book,* 10 August 1916.

82. "Lowden Must a Wanted That Governor's Chair—He Sure Dug For It," *Day Book,* 17 November 1916

83. "Wilson's Speech," *Day Book,* 15 April 1916.

84. "Sandburg Discusses Work Being Done for Jews Abroad and for Those at Home," *Day Book,* 18 May 1916.

85. Niven, *Sandburg,* 249.

86. Ibid.

87. Sandburg, *Complete Poems,* 33.

88. Niven, *Sandburg,* 599.

89. Hendricks, *Carl Sandburg,* 13.

90. Sandburg, *Complete Poems,* 6, 16.

91. "American Poet Sings of 'Hog Butchers of the World,'" *Day Book,* 2 June 1916.

Chapter 7: Watchdog on State Street

1. Wayne Andrews, *Battle for Chicago* (New York: Harcourt, Brace, 1946), 241.

2. Irvin C. Lambert, "Cathedral of all the stores," a poem in "The Store of Service" Marshall Field's brochure, undated.

3. "Marshall Field and Company," official store viewbook, 1913, Chicago; Lloyd Wendt and Herman Kogan, *Give The Lady What She Wants: The Story of Marshall Field & Company* (Chicago: Rand McNally, 1952), 270–72. Some discrepancies are apparent in the descriptions of the store from the official company booklet and from Wendt and Kogan, perhaps due to slight variations in dates. For example, while the store booklet lays claim to 142 wagons and 375 horses, Wendt and Kogan fix the numbers at 400 wagons and 700 horses.

4. "Marshall Field and Company," official store viewbook, 1913, Chicago.

5. Wendt and Kogan, *Give The Lady What She Wants,* 270–72.

6. "Marshall Field and Company," official store viewbook, 1913, Chicago.

7. Emerys, *The Press and America,* 186.

8. Ibid.

9. Folkerts and Teeter, *Voices of a Nation,* 244. See also Stuart Ewen's *Captains of Consciousness: Advertising and the Social Roots of the Consumer Culture* (New York: McGraw-Hill, 1976), in which he describes how advertising "raised the banner of consumable social democracy," 190.

10. Folkerts and Teeter, *Voices of a Nation,* 246.

11. Ibid.

12. Baldasty, *E. W. Scripps,* 90.

13. E. W. Scripps to L. T. Atwood, 4 March 1907, Scripps Papers.

14. Scripps reported in 1915 that a member of the Illinois Manufacturing Association had been sent by someone—presumably the president of Marshall Field's—

to meet with Milton McRae, a Scripps executive, in an effort to learn more about the *Day Book*'s ownership and induce it be "more 'reasonable' in its attitude toward business." E. W. Scripps to Negley D. Cochran, 4 August 1915, Scripps Papers, subseries 1.2, box 21, folder 9.

15. "Marshall Field and Carson, Pirie, Scott Wages Named as Cause of Vice," *Day Book,* 4 November 1912.

16. "Free Girls Forced to Steal Food by Low Wages at the Fair," *Day Book,* 16 June 1916.

17. Wendt and Kogan, *Give The Lady What She Wants,* 181.

18. Ibid., 180–81.

19. *The Value of a Dollar: Prices and Incomes in the United States, 1860-1999* (Lakeville, Conn.: Grey House Publishing, 1999), 98.

20. Ibid., 221.

21. Ibid., 278.

22. By one set of calculations, Marshall Field profits were as follows: 1911, $7.7 million; 1912, $9.7 million; 1913, $10.8 million; 1914, $6.7 million; 1915, $15.5 million; 1916, $19.6 million. Arthur Hawxhurst, "An Abridged Review of the First Bond Issue of Marshall Field & Company," 1927.

23. "Marshall Field Xmas 'Present' to Help Joke of State St.," *Day Book,* 4 January 1917. In an advertisement in the *Chicago Daily Tribune* on January 1, 1917, Marshall Field & Co. said its retail store had "exceeded all records" in 1916, including a record volume of distribution. The store had expanded its manufacturing capacity across the country, including an underwear mill and wide sheeting mill in North Carolina.

24. Montgomery Ward & Co. also paid a bonus of one to five weeks' pay, depending on years of service, "Montgomery Ward & Co. Make 1916 Salary Gifts," *Chicago Daily Tribune,* 4 January 1917.

25. "Marshall Field Xmas," *Day Book,* 4 January 1917. The tone and thrust of the note appear typical of the store's communications with employees. In 1918, President John Shedd wrote: "Greetings in the spirit of Christmas, good will, cordiality, fellowship. It is a pleasure for us to thank you for your efforts during the past year; a year unusually full of problems and difficulties. With the new year we enter fully upon what is universally acclaimed as a new era in the world's history Our great desire is that this organization shall be foremost in giving practical expression to this newer spirit in terms of business. To this end we invite your best thought and endeavor." John G. Shedd, Christmas card to Marshall Field employees, December 1918, Chicago Historical Society.

26. "What Marshall Field Employes [*sic*] Think of That Xmas 'Present,'" *Day Book,* 5 January 1917.

27. Donald L. Miller, *City of the Century: The Epic of Chicago and the Making of America* (New York: Simon and Schuster, 1996), 260.

28. Though the *Day Book* does not provide revenue figures, Lloyd Wendt and Herman Kogan note the earnings for some years in *Give the Lady What She Wants,* 238. In 1901, the retail gross was $14 million, and net profit $989,000; in 1903, retail sales were $17 million, and profits $1,445,000.

29. "An Open Letter to the Marshall Field Boss," *Day Book,* 6 January 1917.

30. Wendt and Kogan, *Give the Lady What She Wants,* 188.

31. A review of articles in the *Chicago American, Chicago Daily News,* and *Chicago Daily Tribune* showed no coverage of the Marshall Field bonus controversy during the first week of January 1917. But the *Chicago American* did run a special shopping report on Page 1 on January 4: Under the headline "You Will Profit by January Shopping," the report listed "reasons for January opportunities for clothing buyers," and quoted George Lytton, vice president of The Hub, as saying, among other things, "The prices of woolens for next season's wear have advanced far beyond figures of previous years." The *Chicago Daily News* ran a Marshall Field display ad on January 2 on Page 2 under the heading: "Interesting Reading for Men of All Ages: 30th Annual January Sale of Men's Shirts, Pajamas and Nightshirts." And the *Chicago Daily Tribune* published an ad on January 1 in which Marshall Field's promoted its "unswerving zeal to do many things better than they ever were done before" and noted that "our retail store has exceeded all records." As if to show that it would not cede the high ground to the *Day Book,* on January 9, 1917, the *Tribune* ran a "Chicago Advertising Score" on Page 1 that showed how it easily led all dailies in columns of advertising published. For the week ending January 7, the *Tribune* published 1,038.37 columns; the nearest competitor, the *Herald,* published 847.83 columns.

32. J. T. Watters to E. W. Scripps, 6 January 1917, Cochran Papers.

33. Cochran, *E. W. Scripps,* 140.

34. "Young People's Civic League Wants to Know About Department Store Wages," *Day Book,* 13 November 1912.

35. "Activity in the Chicago Girl Market," *Day Book,* 21 November 1912.

36. "Jury Says Low-Wage Girl Is Not Guilty Who Steals From Field's," *Day Book,* 16 March 1914.

37. Ibid. Cochran's article/editorial was picked up by Lincoln Steffens, who quoted from it extensively in an article he wrote for *Harper's Weekly* on April 11, 1914. Steffens called the case "a little piece of big news" on the changing law, and in quoting from Cochran's article, he credited the *Day Book,* "itself a little piece of big news."

38. "Fair Employes [*sic*] Strike Against Slaving on Sunday," *Day Book,* 15 December 1913.

39. "Officials of the Fair Try to Force Employes [*sic*] Into Submission," *Day Book,* 16 December 1913.

40. "Fair Employes [*sic*] Strike Against Slaving on Sunday," *Day Book,* 15 December 1913.

41. "Freight Elevator in Seigel, Cooper & Co.'s Store Falls—Many Customers Hurt," *Day Book,* 23 December 1912.

42. A review of the *Chicago American, Chicago Daily News, Chicago Evening Post,* and *Chicago Tribune* confirmed the *Day Book*'s claim.

43. Likewise, a review of the *Chicago American* (all 15 editions), *Chicago Daily News,* and *Chicago Tribune* confirmed the *Day's Book*'s claim.

44. A review of the *Chicago American, Chicago Daily News,* and *Chicago Tribune* confirmed the *Day's Book*'s claim.

45. "Stories of Witnesses at Inquest on Fatal Accident in Hillman's Don't Jibe," *Day Book,* 15 January 1913.

46. "Things You Must Know for Safety," Public Safety Commission of Chicago and Cook County, 1917.

47. Wendt and Kogan, *Give the Lady What She Wants,* 252–53.

48. "Marshall Field, Jr., Was Killed by Vera 'Leroy' at Everleigh Club," *Day Book,* 24 November 1913.

49. "Killing of Marshall Field, Jr., Still Remains a Big Mystery," *Day Book,* 25 November 1913.

50. "The Field Family Gets Special Privileges in the Newspapers," *Day Book,* 28 November 1913.

51. Andrews, *Battle for Chicago,* 220–21.

52. "How Marshall Field III May Become a Real Man in Spite of Field Millions," *Day Book,* 23 January 1915.

53. Ibid.

Chapter 8: Champion of Labor

1. Baldasty, *E. W. Scripps,* 102–3.

2. Ibid., 103.

3. Ibid., 106.

4. Negley D. Cochran to E. W. Scripps, 13 December 1911, Scripps Papers, subseries 1.1, box 30, folder 4.

5. Negley D. Cochran to E. W. Scripps, 5 November 1911, Scripps Papers, subseries 1.1, box 30, folder 3.

6. Negley D. Cochran to E. W. Scripps, 3 November 1911, Scripps Papers, subseries 1.1, box 30, folder 3.

7. Cochran studiously sought independence from the Socialists, wanting to represent the interests of labor in general. In his view many workers in the city were also put off by the party's propagandistic tone, a warning for the *Day Book.* He wrote, "The Socialists, the Lorimerites and others have felt me out to see if they cant [*sic*] get the Day Book hiteched [*sic*] up with them, but I am standing pat for absolute independence, but am gradually leaning toward the socialistic end of things, without putting a label on." Negley D. Cochran to E. W. Scripps, 17 July 1912, Scripps Papers, subseries 1.1, box 31, folder 4.

8. Negley D. Cochran to E. W. Scripps, 8 December 1911, Scripps Papers, subseries 1.1, box 30, folder 4.

9. Ibid.

10. Negley D. Cochran to E. W. Scripps, 16 November 1911, Scripps Papers, subseries 1.1, box 30, folder 3.

11. Negley D. Cochran to E. W. Scripps, 8 December 1911, Scripps Papers, subseries 1.1, box 30, folder 4.

12. E. W. Scripps to Negley D. Cochran, 3 January 1912, Scripps Papers, subseries 1.2, box 18, folder 6.

13. E. W. Scripps to Negley D. Cochran, 10 August 1910, Scripps Papers, subseries 1.2, box 16, folder 13.

14. Cowan, *The People,* xix.

15. E. W. Scripps to Negley D. Cochran, 25 October 1911, Scripps Papers, subseries 1.2, box 18, folder 3.

16. Cowan, *The People,* 122.

17. John Nerone, *Violence Against the Press: Policing the Public Sphere in U.S. History* (New York: Oxford University Press, 1994), 173.

18. Ibid.

19. Paul Avrich, "Darrow in the Dock," *New York Times,* 9 May 1993, 9 (F).

20. "On Eve of His Trial, J. J. McNamara Sends a Message to Wage Earners," *Day Book,* 10 October 1911.

21. "James McNamara to Be Tried First—Court Room Packed at Formal Opening," *Day Book,* 11 October 1911.

22. Cowan, *The People,* 252.

23. "Editorial in W. J. Bryan's Commoner Asks for Square Deal to Union Labor," *Day Book,* 4 January 1912.

24. William Cahn, *Lawrence 1912: The Bread and Roses Strike* (New York: Pilgrim Press, 1980), 94.

25. Ibid., 95.

26. "Mill Owners Seek Trouble," *Day Book,* 18 January 1912.

27. Ibid.

28. "Cannon, Bayonets and Ball Cartridges to Overawe Women of Lawrence," *Day Book,* 23 January 1912.

29. "What's in the Struggle Between Organized Capital and Organized Labor," *Day Book,* 25 January 1912.

30. Ibid.

31. "A Personal Investigation Into Conditions That Confront Working Women of Chicago," *Day Book,* 27 January 1912.

32. "Children Torn From Mothers' Arms—Mothers Clubbed Into Submission at Lawrence," *Day Book,* 24 February 1912.

33. Ibid.

34. "Unoffending Men, Women and Children Clubbed and Thrown in Jail at Lawrence," *Day Book,* 26 February 1912.

35. Ibid.

36. "Who Owns Those Babies," *Day Book,* 29 February 1912.

37. Cahn, *Lawrence,* 212.

38. "Wool Trust Head Indicted for Conspiracy in Lawrence Dynamite Outrage," *Day Book,* 30 August 1912.

39. "Chicago Millionaires to Be Summoned by Senate White Slave Committee," *Day Book,* 1 March 1913.

40. "Mrs. Augusta Lehmann Says Wages of Department Store Girls Are Too High," *Day Book,* 3 March 1913.

41. "Hopkins Can't Understand How Any Girl Exists on Six Dollars a Week," *Day Book,* 4 March 1913.

42. "Lehmann's Slur on Department Store Girls Shocks Father McNamee," *Day Book,* 5 March 1913.

43. "Lt. Gov. O'Hara Pledges Himself to Probe Low Wages of Chicago Girls to

Bottom," *Day Book,* 6 March 1913. According to Cochran, O'Hara credited the *Day Book* with making the investigation possible: "He said Big Business and the other papers would have smothered that investigation at the very outset but for The *Day Book*." Negley D. Cochran to E. W. Scripps, 1 June 1913, Scripps Papers, subseries 1.1, box 32, folder 9.

44. Lyle Benedict, Ellen O'Brien, and Shah Tiwana. "Chicago in 1900: Family Economics." Chicago Public Library. [http://www.chipublib.org/004chicago/1900/fam.html]

45. "Rosenwald's Philanthropies Called Mask to Hide Starvation Wages," *Day Book,* 7 March 1913.

46. "'Dapper Jimmie' Simpson, Marshall Field Boss, Wilts Under Low Wage Fire," *Day Book,* 8 March 1913.

47. Ibid.

48. "What Makes the Newspapers So Timid in the War Against Low Wages?" *Day Book,* 12 March 1913. The other dailies certainly did not shy away from playing the commission's hearings prominently on Page 1. At times, these articles singled out department stores, much as the *Day Book* did as a matter of course. For example, in a lead story, the *Chicago Daily News* pointed out that Edward Hillman, general manager of Hillman's store, estimated that a woman needed $8 to $9 a week to support herself and yet admitted that he employed 150 who were paid less than that amount. "O'Hara Defends Self at the Vice Inquiry," 8 March 1913.

Chapter 9: Struggling in the Shadow of War

1. E. W. Scripps to Negley D. Cochran, 2 April 1914, Scripps Papers, subseries 1.2, box 20, folder 2.

2. E. W. Scripps to Negley D. Cochran, 27 February 1913, Scripps Papers, subseries 1.2, box 19, folder 2.

3. Negley D. Cochran memo, N. D. Cochran Papers.

4. Ibid.

5. Ibid.

6. Negley D. Cochran to E. W. Scripps, 8 November 1915, Scripps Papers, subseries 1.1, box 34, folder 6.

7. Ibid. While Scripps corresponded with several members of the *Day Book* staff aside from Cochran, including Tom Sharp, his nephew, this inserted note from Sandburg to Scripps is the only direct communication between the two that could be found. In retrospect, it seems odd that Scripps would have developed close relationships with some of the nation's most influential progressive voices (e.g., Clarence Darrow) but never reached out to one of his employees who had already achieved prominence in the socialist party and was becoming a national literary figure.

8. Memorandum on the *Day Book,* 22 November 1916, Cochran Papers.

9. Carl Sandburg to Alfred Harcourt, 11 November 1916, Sandburg Papers.

10. Carl Sandburg to Louis Untermyer, 11 November 1915, Sandburg Papers.

11. Carl Sandburg to Alice Corbin Henderson, December 1915 [circa], Sandburg Papers.

12. E. W. Scripps to Negley D. Cochran, 30 April 1914, Scripps Papers, subseries 1.2, box 20, folder 3. And a few months later, Scripps told Cochran that "I can never have too much information" on the *Day Book*. E. W. Scripps to Negley D. Cochran, 12 August 1914, Scripps Papers, subseries 1.2, box 20, folder 8.

13. E. W. Scripps to Negley D. Cochran, 28 March 1915, Scripps Papers, subseries 1.2, box 21, folder 4.

14. E. W. Scripps to Negley D. Cochran, 11 November 1915, Scripps Papers, subseries 1.2, box 22, folder 1.

15. E. W. Scripps to Negley D. Cochran, 6 February 1915, Scripps Papers, subseries 1.2, box 21, folder 2.

16. E. W. Scripps to Negley D. Cochran, 5 July 1914, Scripps Papers, subseries 1.2, box 20, folder 7.

17. E. W. Scripps to Negley D. Cochran, 21 July 1916, Cochran Papers.

18. Cochran, *E. W. Scripps*, 142.

19. E. W. Scripps to Negley D. Cochran, Western Union Telegram, 9 October 1916, Cochran Papers.

20. "Paper Prices Rise While Costs Decline," *New York Times*, 4 November 1916.

21. Ibid. In November 1916, the Federal Trade Commission reported that even as newsprint paper prices soared that year, the average cost of producing the paper was less than the average cost for the three prior years. The commission said that it would hold public hearings before issuing a final report.

22. James G. Scripps to E. W. Scripps and M. A. McRae, 13 November 1916, Scripps Papers.

23. Cochran, *E. W. Scripps*, 140.

24. Ibid., 142.

25. Other papers responded in kind to the escalating newsprint costs. For example, the *Tribune* raised its price to two cents a copy on May 14, 1917. A front-page article announcing the hike said that the price per ton of newsprint had virtually doubled and that "for a long time" the price received for each copy of the paper has been "considerably less than the actual cost of the white paper alone." "The Price of the Daily Tribune Will be 2 Cents a Copy," 10 May 1917, *Chicago Daily Tribune*.

26. Harold M. Cochran to Negley D. Cochran, 28 June 1917, Cochran Papers.

27. Cochran, *E. W. Scripps*, 139.

28. John T. Watters to James G. Scripps, 9 July 1917, Cochran Papers.

29. Cochran, *E. W. Scripps*, 144.

30. Ibid. Cochran does not mention Jane Whitaker in his discussion of former staff members.

31. Carl Sandburg to Negley Cochran, 24 July 1932, Sandburg Papers.

Conclusion

1. "Good Night Edition," *Day Book*, 6 July 1917.

2. "'Adless' Newspaper Dies," *New York Times*, 7 July 1917, 9.

3. Cochran, *E. W. Scripps*, 141–42. At the time of the paper's closing, Cochran

also suggested that his small tabloid was at a physical disadvantage during the war: "I see no immediate prospect of improvement in the local situation because of general interest in big war headlines in other dailies." Negley D. Cochran to E. W. Scripps, 28 June 1917, Scripps Papers, subseries 1.2, box 23, folder 8.

4. "New Print Paper Price Is Fixed," *New York Times,* 5 March 1917.

5. "'Adless' Newspaper," 9.

6. Cochran, *E. W. Scripps,* 124.

7. Ibid., 142.

8. E. W. Scripps to James G. Scripps, 30 June 1917, Scripps Papers, subseries 1.2, box 23, folder 8.

9. E. W. Scripps to James Scripps, 30 June 1917, Scripps Papers, subseries 1.2, box 23, folder 8.

10. Knight, *I Protest,* 209.

11. Ibid.

12. Trimble, *Astonishing Mr. Scripps,* 307. Trimble is apparently referring to Cochran's self-disclosure in a letter to Scripps. Negley D. Cochran to E. W. Scripps, 18 November 1911, Scripps Papers, subseries 1.1., box 30, folder 3.

13. Ibid., 306.

14. E. W. Scripps to Dana Sleeth, 5 August 1913, Scripps Papers, subseries 1.2, box 19, folder 7.

15. Knight, *I Protest,* 78.

16. Carl Sandburg to Negley D. Cochran, 18 May 1926, Cochran Papers.

17. Bekken, "The Chicago Newspaper Scene," 490.

18. Elizabeth Dewey Johns, "Chicago's Newspapers and The News: A Study of Public Communication in a Metropolis." (Ph.D. diss., University of Chicago, 1942).

19. N. W. Ayer and Sons, *American Newspaper Annual and Directory, 1911* (Philadelphia: N. W. Ayer, 1911)

20. See Appendix 3.

21. Folkerts and Teeter, *Voices of a Nation,* 313.

22. Nerone, *Violence Against the Press,* 181.

23. Ibid.

24. Steele, *The Sun Shines for All,* 158.

25. Ibid.

26. Doug Underwood, *When MBAs Rule the Newsroom* (New York: Columbia University Press, 1993), 135, 227–28; Baker, *Advertising and a Democratic Press;* and Squires, *Read All About It.*

27. A. J. Liebling, *The Press* (New York: Ballantine Books, 1961), 23.

28. When Microsoft announced that it might sell Slate, the online magazine was said to have achieved marginal profitability in one quarter in 2003 and was now "a breakeven proposition" with annual revenue of about $6 million. David Carr, "Microsoft May Sell Slate, a Pioneer in Web Magazines," *New York Times,* 24 July 2004.

29. David Carr, "Washington Post Company Buys Slate Magazine," *New York Times,* 22 December 2004.

30. Salon Premium's "Find Out More," 27 July 2004, https://sub.salon.com /registration.

31. "The State of the News Media 2004," Project for Excellence in Journalism, http//www.journalism.org.

32. Mindich, David T. Z. *Tuned Out: Why Americans Under 40 Don't Follow the News.* New York: Oxford University Press, 2005.

33. Ibid., 71.

34. Robert W. McChesney, "The Internet and U.S. Communication Policy-Making in Historical and Critical Perspective," *Journal of Communication* 46 (Winter 1996), 98–124.

35. E. W. Scripps to Thomas Sharp, 12 December 1916, Scripps Papers, subseries 1.2, box 22, folder 14.

36. Ibid.

37. E. W. Scripps to H. N. Rickey and W. B. Colver, 2 March 1910, Scripps Papers, subseries 1.2, box 16, folder 8.

Epilogue

1. Though *PM* represented the last major daily newspaper experiment in adless publishing to date, the efforts of several specialized magazines to survive without ads should be noted. One of the best-known magazine experiments in adless journalism has been *Ms.,* which was founded in 1972 as an opinion leader for the women's movement and in 1990 adopted a no-advertising policy, relying solely on newsstand sales and subscriptions for its revenue. Other contemporary examples of specialized ad-free publications include *Consumer Reports* and *Cook's Illustrated.*

2. Paul Milkman, *PM: A New Deal in Journalism: 1940-1948* (New Brunswick, NJ: Rutgers University Press, 1997), 39.

3. Marshall Field III, *Freedom Is More Than a Word* (Chicago: University of Chicago Press, 1945).

4. M. A. Weston, "Marshall Field III," in *Dictionary of Literary Biography.* Ed. P. J. Ashley (Detroit: Gale Research, 1993), 81–85.

5. Milkman, *PM,* 39.

6. Ibid, 38.

7. R. Hoopes, *Ralph Ingersoll: A Biography* (New York: Atheneum, 1985), 213.

8. Milkman, *PM.*

9. Paul Milkman, *"PM:* A New Deal in Journalism: 1940-1948" (Ph.D. diss., Rutgers University, 1994), 222.

10. Hoopes, *Ralph Ingersoll,* 404.

11. Ibid., 407.

12. Milkman, *PM.*

13. A. Patner, *I. F. Stone: A Portrait* (New York: Pantheon Books, 1988), 75.

14. Weston, "Marshall Field III."

15. Hoopes, *Ralph Ingersoll,* 221.

16. Ibid., 233.

17. John Tebbel, *The Marshall Fields: A Study in Wealth* (New York: E. P. Dutton, 1947), 186.

18. Milkman, *PM.*

19. Ibid., 1.

20. Hoopes, *Ralph Ingersoll.*

21. Milkman, *PM,* 210.

22. Ibid., 212.

Bibliography

Manuscript Collections

Alden Library, Ohio University, Athens (E. W. Scripps Papers, Manuscript Collection #117)
Center for Research Libraries, Chicago
Chicago Historical Society
Newberry Library, Chicago
Toledo-Lucas County Public Library, Ohio (N. D. Cochran Papers)
Rare Book and Special Collections Library, University of Illinois at Urbana-Champaign (Carl Sandburg Papers)

Newspapers

The Chicago American
The Chicago Daily News
The Chicago Evening Post
The Chicago Examiner
The Chicago Herald
The Chicago Tribune
The Chicago Evening World
The Day Book
The Dial
The Memphis Press Scimitar
The New York Times
The Ohio Newspaper
The Record-Herald

Trade Publications

American Newspaper Annual and Directory (N. W. Ayer & Son's)
Chicago Daily News Almanac and Year-Book
Editor and Publisher

Books, Articles, and Dissertations

Adams, Edward E. "Secret Combinations and Collusive Agreements: The Scripps Newspaper Empire and the Early Roots of Joint Operating Agreements." *Journalism & Mass Communication Quarterly*, 73 (Spring 1996): 195–205.

"'Adless' Newspaper Dies." *New York Times*, 7 July 1917, 9.

Andrews, Wayne. *Battle for Chicago*. New York: Harcourt, Brace, 1946.

Avrich, Paul. "Darrow in the Dock." *New York Times*, 9 May 1993, 9 (F).

Bagdikian, Ben H. *The Media Monopoly*. 6th ed. Boston: Beacon Press, 2000.

———. *The New Media Monopoly*. Boston: Beacon Press, 2004.

Baker, C. Edwin. *Advertising and a Democratic Press*. Princeton, NJ: Princeton University Press, 1994.

Baker, Russ. "The Squeeze." *Columbia Journalism Review* 36 (September/October 1997): 30–36.

Baldasty, Gerald J. and Myron K. Jordan. "Scripps' Competitive Strategy: The Art of Non-Competition." *Journalism Quarterly*, 70 (Summer 1993): 265–75.

———. *E. W. Scripps and the Business of Newspapers*. Urbana: University of Illinois Press, 1999.

Bekken, Jon. "Working-Class Newspapers, Community and Consciousness in Chicago, 1880–1930." Ph.D. diss., University of Illinois at Urbana-Champaign, 1992.

———. "The Working-Class Press at the Turn of the Century." *Ruthless Criticism: New Perspectives in U.S. Communication History*. Minneapolis: University of Minnesota Press, 1993

———. "The Chicago Newspaper Scene: An Ecological Perspective." *Journalism & Mass Communication Quarterly* 74 (Autumn 1997): 490–500.

Benedict, Lyle, Ellen O'Brien, and Shah Tiwana. "Chicago in 1900: Family Economics." Chicago Public Library. [http://www.chipublib.org/004chicago/1900/fam.html].

Bleyer, Willard G. *Main Currents in the History of American Journalism*. Houghton Mifflin Co., 1927; reprint, New York: Da Capo Press, 1973.

Cahn, William. *Lawrence 1912: the Bread and Roses Strike*. New York: Pilgrim Press, 1980.

Carr, David. "Microsoft May Sell Slate, a Pioneer in Web Magazines." *New York Times*, 24 July 2004, 1 (D).

———. "Washington Post Company Buys Slate Magazine," *New York Times*, 22 December 2004.

Cashman, Sean Dennis. *America in the Gilded Age: From the Death of Lincoln to the Rise of Theodore Roosevelt*. New York: New York University Press, 1984.

Cochran, Negley D. *E. W. Scripps*. New York: Harcourt, Brace and Co., 1933.

Cowan, Geoffrey. *The People v. Clarence Darrow: The Bribery Trial of America's Greatest Lawyer*. New York: Times Books, 1993.

Cunningham, Brent. "Re-thinking Objectivity." *Columbia Journalism Review* 42 (July/August 2003).

———. "Across the Great Divide." *Columbia Journalism Review* 43 (May/June 2004): 31–38.

Diner, Steven J. *A Very Different Age: Americans of the Progressive Era*. New York: Hill and Wang, 1998.

Dornfeld, A. A. *Behind the Front Page*. Chicago: Academy Chicago/Publishers, 1983.

Dreiser, Theodore. *Sister Carrie*. New York: Holt, Rinehart and Winston, 1957.

Duncan, Hugh Dalziel. *The Rise of Chicago as a Literary Center from 1885 to 1920.* Totowa, NJ: Bedminster Press, 1964.

Emery, Michael and Edwin. *The Press and America: An Interpretive History of the Mass Media.* 8th ed. Boston: Allyn and Bacon, 1966.

Ewen, Stuart. *Captains of Consciousness: Advertising and the Social Roots of the Consumer Culture.* New York: McGraw-Hill, 1976

Fedler, Fred. *Lessons From the Past: Journalists' Lives and Work, 1850-1950.* Prospect Heights, IL: Waveland Press, 2000.

Field, Marshall III. *Freedom Is More Than a Word.* Chicago: University of Chicago Press, 1945.

Filler, Louis. *The Muckrakers.* Stanford, CA: Stanford University Press, 1968.

Folkerts, Jean, and Dwight L. Teeter. *Voices of a Nation: A History of the Media in the United States.* New York: Macmillan, 1989.

Frankel, Max. "The Wall, Vindicated." *New York Times Magazine,* 9 January 2000, 24.

Gardner, Gilson. *Lusty Scripps.* New York: Vanguard Press, 1932.

Gies, Joseph. *The Colonel of Chicago.* New York: E. P. Dutton, 1979.

Glaberson, William. "The Press: Bought and Sold and Gray All Over." *New York Times,* 30 July 1995, D1 and D4.

Golden, Harry. *Carl Sandburg.* Cleveland: The World Publishing Company, 1961.

Green, Norma, Stephen Lacy, and Jean Folkerts. "Chicago Journalists at the Turn of the Century: Bohemians All?" *Journalism Quarterly* 66 (Winter 1989): 813–21.

Greider, William. *Who Will Tell The People? The Betrayal of American Democracy.* New York: Touchstone, 1992.

Habermas, Jurgen. *The Structural Transformation of the Public Sphere: An Inquiry Into a Category of Bourgeois Society.* Translated by Thomas Burger with the assistance of Frederick Lawrence, 1962. Cambridge: MIT Press, 1989.

Hard, William. "De Kid Wot Works at Night." *Everybody's Magazine* (January 1908), reprinted in *The Muckrakers* by Arthur and Lila Weinberg (New York: Capricorn Books, 1961).

Hays, Samuel P. *The Response to Industrialism: 1885-1914.* 2nd ed. Chicago: University of Chicago Press, 1995.

Herman, Edward S., and Robert W. McChesney. *The Global Media: The New Missionaries of Corporate Capitalism.* London: Cassell, 1997.

Heuvel, J. Vanden. *Untapped Sources: America's Newspaper Archives and Histories.* New York: Gannett Foundation Media Center, 1991.

Hofstadter, Richard, Daniel Aaron, and William Miller. *The United States: The History of a Republic.* Englewood Cliffs, NJ: Prentice Hall, 1957.

Hollis, D. W. *The ABC-CLIO Companion to Media in America.* Santa Barbara, CA: ABC-CLIO, 1995.

Hoopes, R. *Ralph Ingersoll: A Biography.* New York: Atheneum, 1985.

"Is an Honest Newspaper Possible?" *Atlantic Monthly* vol. CII (Cambridge: The Riverside Press, 1908).

Huntzicker, William E. *The Popular Press, 1833-1865.* Westport, Conn.: Greenwood Press, 1999.

Irwin, Will. "All the News That's Fit to Print." *The American Newspaper: A Series*

First Appearing in Collier's, January-July 1911. Ames: Iowa State University Press, 1969.

Johns, Elizabeth Dewey. "Chicago's Newspapers and The News: A Study of Public Communication in a Metropolis." Ph.D. diss., University of Chicago, 1942.

Keefer, Brian. "Tsunami." *Columbia Journalism Review* 43 (July/August 2004), 18–23.

Knight, Oliver. *I Protest: Selected Disquisitions of E. W. Scripps*. Madison: University of Wisconsin Press, 1966.

Lee, Alfred M. *The Daily Newspaper in America: The Evolution of a Social Instrument*. New York: The Macmillan Company, 1947.

Lichtenstein, Nelson, Susan Strasser, and Roy Rosenzweig. *Who Built America? Working People and the Nation's Economy, Politics, Culture, and Society*. Vol. 2. New York: Worth Publishers, 2000.

Liebling, A. J. *The Press*. New York: Ballantine Books, 1961.

Mackenzie, F. A. *Booth-Tucker: Sadhu and Saint*. London: Hodder and Stoughton, 1930.

Marzolf, Marion Tuttle. *Civilizing Voices: American Press Criticism 1880-1950*. New York: Longman, 1991.

Mayer, Harold M., and Richard C. Wade. *Chicago: Growth of a Metropolis*. Chicago: University of Chicago Press, 1969.

McChesney, Robert W. "The Internet and U.S. Communication Policy-Making in Historical and Critical Perspective." *Journal of Communication* 46 (Winter 1996): 98–124.

McChesney, Robert W., and Ben Scott. "Upton Sinclair and the Contradictions of Capitalist Journalism." *Monthly Review* 54 (May 2002): 1–14.

Milkman, Paul. "*PM*: A New Deal in Journalism: 1940–1948." Ph.D. diss., Rutgers University, 1994.

———. *PM: A New Deal in Journalism: 1940-1948*. New Brunswick, NJ: Rutgers University Press, 1997.

Miller, Donald L. *City of the Century: The Epic of Chicago and the Making of America*. New York: Simon and Schuster, 1996.

Mindich, David T. Z. *Just the Facts: How "Objectivity" Came to Define American Journalism*. New York: New York University Press, 1998.

———. *Tuned Out: Why Americans Under 40 Don't Follow the News*. New York: Oxford University Press, 2005

Mitgang, Herbert. *Letters of Carl Sandburg*. New York: Harcourt, Brace and World, 1968.

Mott, Frank Luther. *American Journalism: A History of Newspapers in the United States Through 250 Years: 1690 to 1940*. New York: Macmillan Co., 1947.

Nasaw, David. *Children of the City: At Work and At Play*. Garden City, NY: Anchor Press, 1985.

———. *The Chief: The Life of William Randolph Hearst*. Boston: Houghton Mifflin, 2000.

Nerone, John C. "The Mythology of the Penny Press." *Critical Studies in Mass Communication* 4 (1987): 376–404.

———. *Violence Against the Press: Policing the Public Sphere in U.S. History*. New York: Oxford University Press, 1994.

Niven, Penelope. *Carl Sandburg: A Biography.* New York: Charles Scribner's Sons, 1991.

Nord, David Paul. *Newspapers and New Politics: Midwestern Municipal Reform, 1890-1900.* Ann Arbor, Mich.: UMI Research Press, 1981.

Ogden, Christopher. *Legacy: A Biography of Moses and Walter Annenberg.* Boston: Little, Brown and Company, 1999.

Painter, Nell Irvin. *Standing at Armageddon: The United States, 1877-1919.* New York: W. W. Norton, 1987.

Park, Robert E. "The Natural History of the Newspaper," in *The City,* by Park, E. W. Burgess and R. D. McKenzie Chicago: University of Chicago Press, 1925.

Patner, A. *I. F. Stone: A Portrait.* New York: Pantheon Books, 1988.

Pew, M. E. "Shop Talk at Thirty." *Editor & Publisher,* 20 August 1932.

Pogrebin, Robin. "Magazine Publishers Circling Wagons Against Advertisers." *New York Times,* 29 September 1997, D1 and D6.

Putnam, Robert D. *Bowling Alone: The Collapse and Revival of American Community.* New York: Simon & Schuster, 2000.

Rappleye, Charles. "Cracking the Church-State Wall." *Columbia Journalism Review* 36 (January/February 1998): 20–23.

Risser, James. "Lessons from L.A.: The Wall is Heading Back." *Columbia Journalism Review* 38 (January/February 2000).

Ross, Edward Alsworth. "The Suppression of Important News." *Atlantic Monthly,* March 1910, 303–11.

Salcetti, Marianne. "The Emergence of the Reporter: Mechanization and the Devaluation of Editorial Workers." In *Newsworkers: Toward a History of the Rank and File.* Minneapolis: University of Minnesota Press, 1995.

Sandburg, Carl. *Chicago Poems.* New York: Henry Holt & Co., 1916.

———. *Cornhuskers.* New York: Henry Holt & Co., 1918.

Schudson, Michael. *Discovering the News: A Social History of American Newspapers.* New York: Basic Books, 1978.

Sinclair, Upton. *The Brass Check: A Study of American Journalism,* reprint. New York: Arno and *New York Times,* 1970.

———. *The Brass Check: A Study of American Journalism.* Urbana: University of Illinois Press, 2003.

Smith, Carl S. *Chicago and the American Literary Imagination, 1880-1920.* Chicago: University of Chicago Press, 1984.

Smythe, Ted Curtis. "The Reporter, 1880–1900: Working Conditions and Their Influence on the News." *Journalism History* 7 (Spring 1980): 1–10.

Solomon, William S., and Robert W. McChesney, eds. *Ruthless Criticism: New Perspectives in U.S. Communication History.* Minneapolis: University of Minnesota Press, 1993.

Solomon, William S. "The Site of Newsroom Labor." *Newsworkers: Toward a History of the Rank and File.* Minneapolis: University of Minnesota Press, 1995.

Squires, James D. *Read All About It: The Corporate Takeover of America's Newspaper.* New York: Times Books, 1993.

"The State of the News Media 2004," Project for Excellence in Journalism, http://www.journalism.org.

Steele, Janet E. *The Sun Shines for All: Journalism and Ideology in the Life of Charles A. Dana.* New York: Syracuse University Press, 1993.

Steffens, Lincoln. *Harper's Weekly,* 11 April 1914.

Steward, Kenneth, and John Tebbel. *Makers of Modern Journalism.* New York: Prentice-Hall, 1952.

Swanberg, W. A. *Citizen Hearst.* New York: Bantam Books, 1961.

Taft, Philip. "The Limits of Labor Unity: The Chicago Newspaper Strike of 1912." *Labor History* 19 (Winter 1978): 102

Tebbel, John. *The Marshall Fields: A Study in Wealth.* New York: E. P. Dutton, 1947.

Trachtenberg, Alan. *The Incorporation of America: Culture and Society in the Gilded Age.* New York: Hill and Wang, 1982.

Trimble, Vance H. *The Astonishing Mr. Scripps.* Ames: Iowa State University Press, 1992.

Underwood, Doug. *When MBAs Rule the Newsroom.* New York: Columbia University Press, 1993.

———. "It's Not Just in L.A." *Columbia Journalism Review* 36 (January/February 1998): 24–26.

The Value of a Dollar: Prices and Incomes in the United States, 1860-1999. Lakeville, Conn.: Grey House Publishing, 1999.

Vane, Sharyn. "Taking Care of Business," *American Journalism Review* (March 2002), 60–65.

Wendt, Lloyd, and Herman Kogan. *Give The Lady What She Wants: The Story of Marshall Field & Company.* Chicago: Rand McNally, 1952.

Wendt, Lloyd. *Chicago Tribune: The Rise of a Great American Newspaper.* Chicago: Rand McNally, 1979.

Weston, M. A. "Marshall Field III." *Dictionary of Literary Biography.* Ed. P.J. Ashley. (Detroit: Gale Research, 1993) 81–85.

Wicker, Tom. *On The Record: An Insider's Guide to Journalism.* Boston: Bedford/St. Martin's, 2002.

Wiggins, Arch. *The History of the Salvation Army, Volume Four, 1886-1904.* New York: Salvation Army.

Yannella, Philip R. *The Other Carl Sandburg.* Jackson: University Press of Mississippi, 1996.

Zinn, Howard. *A People's History of the United States.* New York: HarperPerennial, 1980.

Index

advertising: cost of, 5–6, 19–20, 29, 33; department stores, 99; "dirty" ads, 37; during Chicago circulation wars, 74; relations with newsroom, 6–7, 43; Scripps's distrust of, 22–23, 26, 35–37; supplanting circulation as source of revenue, 1; types of, 6
American Federation of Labor, 13, 112
Annenberg brothers, Max and Moe: circulation managers, 69–71
Associated Press: as Scripps rival, 29, 33
Atwood, Lemuel: as treasurer for Scripps organization, 36

Bagdikian, Ben H.: critic of advertising, 6, 8; on E. W. Scripps's adless experiments, ix, 4
Bertram, John: character in the *Day Book,* 54–55
Booth-Tucker, Frederick: on Salvation Army's adless paper, 42
Brisbane, Arthur: as target of the *Day Book,* 68

Chicago Daily Socialist (also *Chicago Evening World*): during labor dispute, 71, 73; and propaganda, 114
Chicago Federation of Labor, 58
Chicago Sun, 143
Chicago Tribune: on comparison with *Day Book,* 55
Cincinnati Post: Scripps experience at, 43
circulation wars: among Chicago newspapers, 66–67, 69–71, 73–76
City News Bureau, 79

Cochran, Harold: as editor of the *Day Book,* 125–28, 131; son of Negley D. Cochran, 86–88
Cochran, Negley D.: early life, 46; and Marshall Field's department store, 103–4; qualifications as editor, 136–37; as Scripps editor, 3, 31, 37, 49–50, 58, 60–61, 86–87, 113–14, 125–28; and the Toledo *News-Bee,* 47, 127
comics, 126
crime: as a result of low wages, 100, 104–5
Cronin, A. J.: security chief at Carson Pirie Scott department store, 107–8

Dana, Charles A.: efforts to reduce advertising, 2, 41–42, 139
Darrow, Clarence: as ally of *Day Book,* 66; as lawyer representing the McNamara brothers case, 116–17
The *Day Book* (Chicago): as adless newspaper, 1–4, 42, 60–61, 135; as advocate of workplace safety, 107–9; ally of the working class, 5, 63, 98–106, 112–13; circulation, 59–62, 73, 76, 115, 126; content, 55–59, 63–64, 78, 138–39; costs, 3–4, 51, 130–31; debut, 52–54; decline of, 129–32, 134; failures, 136–38; inception, 47–48; naming, 49; as newspaper or magazine, 50–51, 64–65, 76–78; quality of writing, 92; redefining news, 138–39; Scripps's interest in success of, 60; transportation links, 48; use of humor, 63–64
department stores: safety, 107–9; wages, 86, 104–6

DUANE C. S. STOLTZFUS is an associate professor of communication at Goshen College. He has worked as an editor at the *New York Times*, and as a reporter at several newspapers.

The History of Communication

Selling Free Enterprise: The Business Assault on Labor and Liberalism, 1945–60   *Elizabeth A. Fones-Wolf*

Last Rights: Revisiting *Four Theories of the Press*   *Edited by John C. Nerone*

"We Called Each Other Comrade": Charles H. Kerr & Company, Radical Publishers   *Allen Ruff*

WCFL, Chicago's Voice of Labor, 1926–78   *Nathan Godfried*

Taking the Risk Out of Democracy: Corporate Propaganda versus Freedom and Liberty   *Alex Carey; edited by Andrew Lohrey*

Media, Market, and Democracy in China: Between the Party Line and the Bottom Line   *Yuezhi Zhao*

Print Culture in a Diverse America   *Edited by James P. Danky and Wayne A. Wiegand*

The Newspaper Indian: Native American Identity in the Press, 1820–90   *John M. Coward*

E.W. Scripps and the Business of Newspapers   *Gerald J. Baldasty*

Picturing the Past: Media, History, and Photography   *Edited by Bonnie Brennen and Hanno Hardt*

Rich Media, Poor Democracy: Communication Politics in Dubious Times   *Robert W. McChesney*

Silencing the Opposition: Antinuclear Movements and the Media in the Cold War   *Andrew Rojecki*

Citizen Critics: Literary Public Spheres   *Rosa A. Eberly*

Communities of Journalism: A History of American Newspapers and Their Readers   *David Paul Nord*

From Yahweh to Yahoo!: The Religious Roots of the Secular Press   *Doug Underwood*

The Struggle for Control of Global Communication: The Formative Century   *Jill Hills*

Fanatics and Fire-eaters: Newspapers and the Coming of the Civil War   *Lorman A. Ratner and Dwight L. Teeter Jr.*

Media Power in Central America   *Rick Rockwell and Noreene Janus*

The Consumer Trap: Big Business Marketing in American Life   *Michael Dawson*

How Free Can the Press Be?   *Randall P. Bezanson*

Cultural Politics and the Mass Media: Alaska Native Voices   *Patrick J. Daley and Beverly A. James*

Journalism in the Movies   *Matthew C. Ehrlich*

Democracy, Inc.: The Press and Law in the Corporate Rationalization of the Public Sphere   *David S. Allen*

Investigated Reporting: Television Muckraking and Regulation   *Chad Raphael*

The University of Illinois Press
is a founding member of the
Association of American University Presses.

———————————————

Composed in 9/13 ITC Stone Serif
with ITC Stone Sans display
by Type One, LLC
for the University of Illinois Press
Designed by Paula Newcomb
Manufactured by Thomson-Shore, Inc.

University of Illinois Press
1325 South Oak Street
Champaign, IL 61820-6903
www.press.uillinois.edu